Talking
with
Female
Serial Killers

Born in Winchester, Hampshire, in 1948, **Christopher Berry-Dee** is a direct descendant of Dr John Dee, Court Astrologer to Queen Elizabeth I. A former Royal Marine Commando, he is the founder and former Director of The Criminology Research Institute (CRI), and the former publisher and Editor-in-Chief of *The Criminologist* – the world's oldest and most respected journal on matters concerning law enforcement, penology, forensic psychiatry/psychology, penal reform, the judiciary, and all criminology subjects.

Christopher has interviewed and interrogated more than thirty of the world's most notorious serial killers and mass murderers. He has appeared on TV as a consultant on serial homicide, and was co-producer/interviewer for the acclaimed twelve-part documentary series *The Serial Killers*, as well as consulting on the cases of Fred and Rose West, Ian Brady and Myra Hindley, and Dr Harold Shipman in the TwoFour-produced TV series *Born to Kill*.

Notable book successes include: *Monster* – the book that formed the basis for the movie of the same name, starring Charlize Theron, about the US serial killer Aileen 'Lee' Carol Wuornos; *Dad Help Me Please* – concerning the tragic case of Derek Bentley who was hanged for a murder he did not commit, and was subsequently detailed in the film *Let Him Have It*, starring Christopher Ecclestone; and *Talking with Serial Killers 1*, his 2003 bestselling true-crime book, with more than 100,000 copies sold. His most recent book, *Talking With Psychopaths and Savages*, was the UK's bestselling true-crime title in 2017.

Christopher Berry-Dee

Talking
with
Female
Serial Killers

A chilling study of the most
evil women in the world

JOHN BLAKE

Published by John Blake Publishing,
2.25, The Plaza,
535 Kings Road,
Chelsea Harbour
London, SW10 0SZ

www.johnblakebooks.com

www.facebook.com/johnblakebooks ⬛
twitter.com/jblakebooks ⬛

First published in paperback in 2018

ISBN: 978-1-78606-900-9

British Library Cataloguing-in-Publication Data:

A catalogue record for this book is available from the British Library.

Design by www.envydesign.co.uk

Printed and bound in Great Britain by Clays Ltd, Elcograf S.p.A.

5 7 9 10 8 6 4

Papers used by John Blake Publishing are natural, recyclable products made from
wood grown in sustainable forests. The manufacturing processes conform to the
environmental regulations of the country of origin.

Every attempt has been made to contact the relevant copyright-holders,
but some were unobtainable. We would be grateful if the appropriate people
could contact us.

John Blake Publishing is an imprint of Bonnier Books UK
www.bonnierbooks.co.uk

For Maui

Contents

Acknowledgements

Many thanks to: John Blake, Toby Buchan, all the team at John Blake Publishing, Tony Brown, Lizzy, Rod, Clive Sturdy, Ann Sidney, Fi Smyth, Vilija, Ed, Frazer Ashford, Umutetsi, Boris, Jennie, Hollie, Karl, Gary Roberts, Marina Koroleva, Liam Greaney, Laura-Dee Cooper – Sherri, Chris Richardson, Shany, Nicholas Quartermaine, Steve, Ray Pedretti, Brook, Claire, Bree, Willi B. Wilhelmson, Malcolm Powell and Simon Carr.

Foreword: Sablino Prison for Women

Throughout my decades of studying serial killers, indeed murderers of all types, I've visited many prisons dedicated to the incarceration of female offenders and one, in particular, stands out amongst the rest: Sablino Prison for Women. As such it deserves a mention from the outset of this book for reasons that will become patently apparent later.

Forty-five kilometres south of St Petersburg, Sablino, houses some 1,800 offenders. It squats in the middle of a flat-as-the-eye can see 'nowhere land'.

There is one road in, the same road out.

In winter the surrounding landscape is as white and hard as a plaster cast.

Temperatures plunge to minus thirty-five degrees. Your breath freezes in this place. My beard was as snowy as Santa's...farm tracts need months of thaw to make deep mud, even longer where the snow has drifted on shorter, colder days.

At night, even an incidental flash of a passing car's headlights will illuminate the sparse variety of surfaces – a mix of dormant grass, hard-packed snow, a frozen creek the colour of tannin – precisely the same toxic-polluted colour as the water that comes out of the taps of local residents living hundreds of square miles around – there's even a fallen utility pole, or a plank now serving as a makeshift bridge, layered in fog.

There is no railway station at Sablino. It is not even the end of the line, for no trains carrying the green-uniformed, stern-faced provodniks, or their steaming hot samovars, need to come here. When the mood takes him, a bus driver might venture out to Sablino, but only when a cash bonus allows him to buy his favourite drink – vodka. He will probably be stoned out of his mind when he gets behind the wheel but traffic police never pull over a bus, or a licensed taxi, unless they, themselves, need to impose some form of minor 'invented' fine so that they can buy drink.

When I visited Sablino Prison for Women it was fifteen degrees below, the temperature still plummeting. There was a blizzard, the knee-deep snow perimeter patrolled by female guards accompanied by vicious dogs straining at their leashes. No glinting razor wire entanglements here at Sablino. No flowerbeds to greet visitors – to get the picture, think of the Nazi concentration camp, Auschwitz, in winter – but for my visit, the 'girls' were out chipping away at the ice with shovels and sweeping it away.

They all knew that I was arriving. The St Petersburg State Police had seen to that, for a bonus, of course. They had known ever since I had arrived in Buzuluk, in the Orenburgskaya Oblast. My host, I shall call him 'Igor', a fictitious name for legal reasons, formerly a helicopter pilot with Spetznaz (Russian special forces), had made the introductions. My train to Samara, then my flight to St Petersburg, were first-class and gratis, thank you very much!

No hitches, no worries about getting a first-class hotel suite – this was all organised by the cops, for an extra bonus, quite naturally. Taxis? No! The cops provided cars. Blue lights flashing straight-lining to an already overbooked restaurant where a flash of a warrant card guaranteed a table at the expense of paying diners already eating their meal, where the drink flowed till chemical imbalance took over, with everyone pledging to become friends till the end of time.

Most of the broken-windowed dormitories at Sablino are filled with over one hundred women; hot bunking, crammed together like sardines in a can, most of them with a pet cat. The stench of condensed, incarcerated humanity, feline faeces and urine was gaggingly awful. No privacy. No radio. Censored TV. No heating. Food for the inmates was so unappetising that you wouldn't feed it to a dog in the UK.

And, there they were. Huddled together in small, grey, stooped groups. Shivering women – old and young – wearing thin clothes and cheap, plastic shoes, out in the cold.

Yet, Sablino inmates get by the best way they can. Under the care of an almost Mother Teresa-like governor, Anna personally teaches each prisoner to read and write if they are illiterate. With scant financial support from the state, inmates were making plastic music cassette cases in a wind-blown, snow-blown barn, just to earn enough to feed themselves.

The chief cook labouring away in the steamy kitchen had been incarcerated for hacking up her abusive husband. Then, after careful culinary preparation, she treated her unwitting friends and neighbours to a meal. You will meet Marinka later in this book.

I still write to her, even today.

There are one or two female serial killers at Sablino – all of them gangster and Mafia associated molls with not one of them being convicted of sex crimes (in fact there was not a single sex offender in the entire facility). I was also given unprecedented access to where they are housed, the rust-caged, most secure part of the prison. Here, while handing out packs of Marlboro Red cigarettes, I interviewed these killers who had participated in multiple-shooting death robberies or gangland executions. They thought the world of their governor. They were respectful to me.

No Rose West or Myra Hindley to be found here, in Sablino.

No luxuries are to be had at Sablino either. They do have a kinda-cute hairdressing salon; a small room, all decorated in 'girly-pink' with photos of international showbiz stars carefully snipped from Western magazines then pasted onto the damp walls. Yes, they tried to tease me into having a haircut. It was an offer I politely refused.

There is a well-appointed library, and a small chapel that one of the inmates took me to. Here she prayed to be reunited with her children soon. Then I saw a large community hall, where I was treated to a sizzling concert at the expense of the inmates, whose meagre earnings were docked to give me the chance to mingle and for the women to say a 'Big Thank You' to me for just being there. I was the first Westerner to have ever visited a Russian women's prison, let alone film as much as I wanted.

As far as I know, no one from the West has ever readmitted since.

There is no mega-splash-out of around £180,000 of the taxpayers' money for alleged rehabilitation at Sablino, as has recently occurred at HMP & YOI Bronzefield, where the British love-of-blood serial killer, Joanna Dennehy, enjoys a better life than she ought to.

In Sablino the show was all about national costumes, national music and Mother Russia. No such thing as happens at HMP Bronzefield, with women prancing around in stockings and undies to titillate voyeuristic, £40-per-head-paying ticket holders in the name of 'rehabilitation'. There was nothing like this at Sablino, or, for that matter, any of the other prisons I have visited throughout the world during the past four decades.

Saying goodbye to Sablino's governor – all captured on videotape – was heartbreaking. Sitting at her desk, this woman wanted me to meet four of *her* girls, now waiting patiently in the corridor outside her office. They spoke broken English. Before they came to Sablino they were all but illiterate, in their own tongue. Now educated, giggling and ever-so-pleased, they were soon to be released back into society.

Ninety-six percent of female Russian offenders never reoffend, and you can understand why.

My trip to Sablino had been organised by September Films (London), and the St Petersburg State Police in return for a few 'bonuses': Scotch whisky, shortbread for the officers' wives, and a wad of crisp new US dollars to be exchanged on the black market for roubles.

And, here is something else for us to consider. The governor absolutely refused to take a single dollar from me in return for her cooperation:

'Please tell everyone in England how hard my staff work

here to look after my girls,' she begged. Then she broke down and cried.

I left Sablino to climb into a battered Skoda police car with the obligatory cracked windscreen, to be driven, blue lights flashing, to a four-star St Petersburg hotel, my two senior police officer escorts now well lubricated with vodka.

Later, the governor would find the $1,000 in crisp new notes I'd secreted under a book on her desk. When she did, she telephoned me to say: '*Spasibo, spasibo*. You will now be known in Russia as "Christopski". God bless you!'

For two weeks I enjoyed the hospitality that the Russians can give only to the English. It is like 'respect', for they are less keen on the Americans, with their loud mouths and equally loud shirts. So, the governor at Sablino is rightly proud of her prison. Over the decades I have been given unfettered access to correctional facilities around the world – from the US, all over the EU, India and throughout the Far East. And, as God is my witness, I have never before heard of any prison putting on a £180,000 theatre production involving inmates wearing their undies and ostrich feathers as was the case at HMP Bronzefield, as I mentioned before. But, I guess there is always a first time for such a performance, and to my mind it is downright outrageous! To quote an inmate: 'The conditions in here [Bronzefield] are crap. A fuckin' disgrace. It is "do this, do that every minute".' (Joanna Dennehy, letter to the author, 2014.)

So, I will never forget Sablino, or the genuine hospitality of the Russian police and people. Therefore, I will not have any truck with the likes of Joanna Dennehy, who complains that the conditions at Bronzefield are not to her liking, so much so that she plotted to escape, but was rumbled after notes detailing the scheme were found in her room, leaving the Prison Service to issue the following statement: 'In September 2013, searches by staff uncovered intelligence which could have been interpreted as an escape plan. The matter was dealt with swiftly with no security breaches and a prisoner [Dennehy] was relocated to the segregation unit.'

To my way of thinking, and after considering the facilities offered at Sablino, Bronzefield, with its state-of-the-art correctional care – with its central heating, air-con, fine food, 24/7 heath care, counselling and other in-house recreational facilities, is a place female offenders would wish to break *into*, not break out of!

Joanna Dennehy, and those of her disgusting ilk, should consider themselves very lucky women indeed!

Russia? I love it. I have done so ever since, as a youngster, I watched the 1965 movie *Dr Zhivago*, starring Omar Sharif and Julie Christie. I went there first on a school education cruise aboard the MS *Dunera*, since when I have revisited many times.

Yes, the Mafia and the police work hand-in-hand. Yes, corruption is rife. Period!

Having got that off of my chest, I will now get down to the matters in hand: to *Talking with Female Serial Killers* – and the age-old question of whether the female of the species is more deadly than the male.

CHRISTOPHER BERRY-DEE
SOUTHSEA

Introduction

'I myself have cut the throats of six women,' I whispered to a victim, who was called Hanen, as she died.
(Serial killer Sakina Aly-Hamman executed alongside her sister, Raya, Alexandria, Egypt, Monday, 16 May 1921)

My first and last request is that you please read this Introduction and not leap straight into the first chapter in search of blood-battered corpses; knives and hammers covered in 'claret', or hastily dug moonlit shallow graves with their sides falling in. I ask this of you for two reasons:

Firstly I have written this Introduction for your benefit.

Secondly, you have paid for this book, therefore hopefully you should profit from every word...

...so thank you because, for want of something better to do like cultivating roses, over many decades I have been interviewing male serial killers, quite obviously because there are so many to choose from. Indeed, if you were to dropkick a football over any American penitentiary wall into the inmate-packed yard, the odds are high that a homicidal sexual psychopathic serial murderer would pick it up.

In this context, however, female serial killers working alone are as rare as hen's teeth – there are around fifty in the US, past and present, with many less born and bred to kill in the UK; all of which somewhat gives the lie to Joseph Rudyard Kipling's 1911 poem, *The Female of the Species*. Here, he repeats six times, 'That the Female of Her Species is more deadly than the Male'; a somewhat sweeping generalisation that bears little truth to the facts, although he may have garnered some support from the ghost of Greek playwright, Euripides, who wrote: 'There is no worse evil than a bad woman; and nothing has ever been produced better than a good one.' However, as Euripides grew older, so did his state of mind. At one time he got himself quite worked up – probably over divorce proceedings or some other female sleight – when he chiseled into stone for the benefit of generations to come: 'Terrible is the force of the waves of the sea, terrible is the rush of the river and blasts of hot fire, and terrible are a thousand [unspecified] things; but none is such a terrible evil as woman.' Bless him!

We might also consider the somewhat misogynistic, most unfair quote from Jean Giraudoux (1882–1944), a French novelist, essayist, playwright and diplomat who undiplomatically penned: 'All women are born evil. Some just realise their potential later in life than others.' What his wife Suzanne Boland made of this, alas, was not recorded, but if this is what Jean generally thought about women his spouse must have regarded their marriage as an arrangement by which the two of them had started by getting the best out of each other and ended by getting the worst!

For the benefit of our younger generations I would be remiss in excluding Elvis Presley (1935-1977), with his song lyrics: 'You look like an angel, walk like an angel, talk like an angel. But I got wise, you're the devil in disguise.'

Alice Cooper (1963-) who penned: 'Satan sent her from the bowels of hell, I should have recognised old Jezebel.'

Billy Joel (1949-) also referred to women thus: 'She'll carelessly cut you and laugh while you are bleeding.'

However, perhaps we should not believe, even for a moment, that the female of *our* species is more deadly than the male, and here is a notable fact possibly confirming why at any one time there are more male serial killers incarcerated within the Texas Department of Corrections than the sum of all of the female killers, serial murderers or otherwise, past or present in the black annals of US and UK history. Not to put a finer point on it, this probably also applies to global history.

At the time of writing, in the US there are about fifty-two female killers, some of them on death row. They come and go – if you catch my drift? This comprises only 2 per cent of the total (death row) population, which is a very small fraction. Many are mothers and, until they committed first-degree homicide, their whole lives lay ahead of them. Now they haven't any kind of future.

According to the US Bureau of Justice Statistics (BJS) at any one time there are around 2,220,300 male adults incarcerated in US federal and state prisons while circa 111,300 adult women are behind bars. The UK government confirm that at any one time there are at least 82,000 men in prison and

3,919 women, making men twenty-two times more likely as women to be imprisoned – all which somewhat discredits any claim that the female of our species is more deadly, dangerous or evil or indeed more criminally inclined than the male.

The FBI claims there are as many fifty male serial killers at large throughout the US at any one time. There are not even 'guesswork statistics' for female serial offenders but this is not to say there are none out there. Trust me, because of the ever-increasing drug addiction problems and the mind-warping effects of crystal meth, female serial killers will continue to pop up for ever and a day.

As a brief breakdown, current records list twelve female English serial killers past and present, some acting alone, others with a male accomplice: nurse Beverly Allitt; bleach-blonde Myra Hindley; Mary Ann Britland; Mary Ann Cotton; Joanna Dennehy; baby farmer Amelia Dyer; Catherine Flannigan; Margaret Higgins; Rosemary West; Margaret Waters; Catherine Wilson and Mary Elizabeth Wilson.

There are no recorded female serial killers emanating from Scotland or Wales. In comparison there are just six known female serial killers from Australia: Catherine Birnie; Kathleen Folbigg; Caroline Grills; Sarah Makin; Martha Needle and Martha Rendell.

Austria has Elfriede Blauensteiner. Then there are the 'Lainz Angels of Death': Maria Gruber; Irene Leidolf; Stephanija Mayer and Waltraud Wagner, who were responsible for the murder of forty-nine patients between 1983 and 1989. The Czech Republic boasts just one: Marie Fiká ková, who was hanged in 1961 for murdering ten babies. Canada records only Elizabeth Wettlaufer, while the Danish woman Dagmar Johanne Amalie Overby killed between nine and twenty-five children between 1913 and 1920, including one of her own.

Female serial killers in The Peoples Republic of China, if not thin on the ground appear not to exist; the same applies to Colombia, Croatia, Equador, Indonesia, Iraq, Iran, Israel, Italy, Jamaica, Japan, Kazakhstan, Latvia, Philippines, China, Macedonia, New Zealand, Pakistan, Poland and Portugal.

Raya and Sakina were Egypt's most infamous female serial murderers. They were executed along with their husbands in 1921. Finland has Aino Nykopp-Koski – the country's only known female serial murderer who has committed five known kills and five attempted kills.

What France makes up for in its dearth of female serial killers is the number of murders committed by aristocratic Marie-Madeleine-Marguérite d'Aubray (three kills); Hélène Jégardo (twenty-three kills); Christine Malèvre (thirty kills); and Jeanne Weber, who committed six murders – adding up to a grand homicidal total of sixty-two, all of them committed by small, delicately proportioned women who could have easily passed themselves off as sour faced doctors' receptionists or, at a push, traffic wardens wearing the obligatory 'sucked-lemon' expression.

Considering the size of the country, somewhat surprisingly Germany has a mere twenty-six serial killers listed, of which five are female. Marianne Nölle, a Cologne nurse, killed seven hospital patients while being suspected of dispatching a further seventeen. Sophie Charlotte Elisabeth Ursinus did in her aunt, boyfriend and a husband. Between 1902 and 1903, Elisabeth Wiese, aka, 'The Angel Maker of St Paul' poisoned a grandchild and four others with morphine, then burned the bodies in a stove. Anna Maria Zwanziger poisoned four people and was hanged in 1811.

Hungary comes in topping the charts with Countess Erzebet Bathory, aka, 'The Blood Countess' – certainly a female Vlad the Impaler – who killed and butchered servant girls. There is credible surviving witness evidence suggesting she was responsible for approximately 600 kills. Born in 1560 then dying while confined in 1614, she racked up an average of eleven murders for every year of her life which, to my mind, makes her the most notoriously bloodthirsty woman that ever walked the face of the earth.

As far as I can tell, India is all but bereft of female serial killers. At the time of writing Seema Gavit and Renuke Shinde face execution by hanging with all appeals exhausted – the first women to be executed in India for seventy-two years. I interviewed both of them, and a more detailed account of this follows later in this book.

Mexico certainly has its fair share of women who kill multiple times. Sara Aldrete; former professional wrestler Juana Barraza (who murdered between forty-two and forty-eight elderly women); sisters Delfina and Maria de Jesús González; Anna Villeda; Silvia Meraz; Felícitas Sánchez Aguillón, aka, 'The Ogress of Colonia Roma' and Magdalena Solís, all putting the Netherlands in the shade with just Maria Swanenburg, who, in the 1880s, used poison to knock off between twenty-seven and ninety people.

So, we are already seeing some sort of pattern here. As we work deeper into the minds and motives of female serial killers we see that when women are working alone, they most often use poison and their victimology is inclined towards the elderly, the infirm, little children and babies.

Amongst other common motives appears to be the opportunity to get rid of an obnoxious rival, the chance for financial gain or else just pure sadistic pleasure, as was the case with Darya Nikolayevna Saltykova, a noblewoman from Moscow, Russia, who, in the eighteenth century, tortured and killed thirty-eight serfs on her estate.

Irina Gaidamachuk, aka, 'Satan in a Skirt', killed seventeen elderly women in Sverdlovsk Oblast between 2002 and 2010. She got off lightly, being sentenced to just twenty years in prison. Of course there are plenty more one-off female killers held in Russian prisons and I have met many of them, but for now let's move on to Slovakia, Slovenia, South Africa and South Korea, where there have been no women who kill multiple times at all.

Spain shows a total of twelve serial killers, only two of whom are women: Francisca Ballesteros, aka, *La Viuda Negra* (The Black Widow) poisoned her husband and two of her three children between 1990 and 2004. She could be described as a lightweight compared to Enriqueta Martí, a self-proclaimed witch. This monster flying on a broomstick was certainly off-the-wall if we can believe every word written about her. There is no doubt that in the early twentieth century she kidnapped/procured, prostituted and murdered some small children in Barcelona, and made potions from their remains. Indeed, she herself was murdered in prison while awaiting trial. However, there is evidence emerging that the boiled bones recovered from her home, and her cauldron if she had one, were mostly those of animals.

And, that's about it as far as I can determine. Obviously, for practical reasons I cannot list every one of the 195 countries in the world and I am sure the dedicated reader will find another female serial killer locked up in some far flung place be it east, west, north or south. So, with that said and done, at this point I am now asking myself why I'm writing a book about female serial killers and women murderers in general.

As usual, this wasn't my idea, far from it. During the decades of my criminological research, throughout countless interviews with homicidal maniacs and people from law enforcement, I can tell you that sometimes one cannot tell the difference between a murderous redneck cop (Frederick Allan Gore or Gerard John Schaefer for example) or a deranged life-insurance salesman like Michael Bruce Ross), clearing up the occasional cold case, visiting crime scenes, writing over thirty books and spending more than a healthy amount of time trying to get into prisons which are built with the sole purpose of preventing people from getting out, the very thought of writing about the alleged fairer sex who have strayed into Godforsaken depravity never crossed my mind. Honestly, the whole thought suddenly popped into the head of my publisher, John Blake, who was very likely prompted by the greatest editor-in-chief any writer could wish for, namely one Toby Buchan, in what can only be called a 'homicidal light bulb moment', just at the point when I was about to take up the cultivation of roses, maybe even 'going extremis' and taking on an allotment to grow organic vegetables.

Nevertheless, it was shortly after the proposal for this book arrived by email that I had a sort of light bulb moment of my own. It didn't come as a flash of blinding light, more of a dim flicker as I slumbered abed – my second hobby as I inexorably age towards senility and the time when my underpants will need to be changed by a night carer. 'Hey! Christopher,' I thought to myself, 'why didn't you think of this idea before, as in thirty years ago? Silly you!' Then all dimmed as several obstacles crept into my semi-conscious state.

Without wishing to stray into even the merest misogynistic territory once inhabited, if only momentarily, by the aforementioned Jean Giraudoux, it occurred to me that I find most women can be difficult to understand at the best of times, most of all the matronly-type souls who go around chopping people up – even eating them when they feel the need to shallow fry in butter the body part men value the most and from whence most often their mental processing system springs forth.

And, I met a Russian killer who did precisely that; going further to package everything up into small, neatly string-tied brown paper parcels and sell the 'meat' to her neighbours. Notwithstanding this, while making a TV documentary I met this woman of extremely substantial proportions at the Sablino Prison for women where she was the *zaklyuchennyye shef-povar* (prisoner's chef). Actually, I could, and still can, sympathise with her motive for killing her brutal husband and I think that you will too: her vodka-soaked husband ill-treated her – beat her black and blue. When she complained he locked her out of their apartment in minus twenty degrees and let her freeze. When she hammered on the window he opened it and squirted lighter fluid over her then set her alight – to 'warm her up'. But, this wasn't the end of it. He was also raping his two young children – one of whom was a three-year-old boy. At her wits end, she took an axe from a woodpile and bludgeoned him to death. Well done, you!

The second hurdle I would have to vault while considering this book is the undeniable fact that women multi-task while it has been argued – with little scientific evidence to support it – that men, most especially me, experience extreme difficulty in doing very much at all. However I would add the proviso that getting 'inside the head' of male serial killers comes easily to me because they are men, with whom I can empathise more easily. We blokes have one-track minds, and are only just about able to focus, think or do one thing at a time, so for me comprehending the mentality of these self-alleged Alpha Males is almost as simple as shelling peas. Women are wired up differently, and as such are altogether dissimilar.

Nevertheless, I was able to rekindle the flame of enthusiasm for this book in the knowledge that I have worked with, corresponded – often at length – and interviewed quite a few female serial murderers and one-off killers in my time.

For example there is Aileen 'Lee' Carol Wuornos, who was executed by the Florida Department of Corrections on Wednesday, 9 October 2002. My book, *Monster*, extensively covered the life and the crimes of Aileen and it accompanied the 2003-released motion picture of the same name, starring Charlize Theron.

Another female serial killer I have spent time communicating with is bisexual British-born Joanna Dennehy. Jo suffers from paraphilia sadomasochism accompanied by a love of blood. She is now serving a natural life prison tariff at HMP Bronzefield, Ashford, Kent. And, just to spice things up a bit, if you were getting friendly with her and decided to share her bed, you'd count your blessings if you actually woke up the next morning. Indeed, if you were a woman – and Jo has already tried to kill two female inmates including Rose West – you'd be in the same boat as the sexually interested man. And this brings me neatly back to one trying to understand what goes on inside a woman's head; so imagine that you are entering the mind of someone like Dennehy who, before she started snuffing out lives, had been Sectioned under the Mental Health Act – twice!

Generally speaking, a serial killer is defined by the fact that he, or she, has killed three times or more with a cooling off period between the 'events', whereas a mass-murderer is a person who kills numerous people in a *single event*, such as shooting to death as many as possible at one location because of some unspecified grievance, or simply because he was having a bad hair day. On the other hand, a spree killer is a homicidal offender who wanders around a neighbourhood randomly shooting anyone who falls into the sights of his firearm with this *event* lasting minutes or even hours until police apprehend him or shoot him dead. Also, for the purposes of this book we are not concerning ourselves with female terrorists, even less so with the barbaric atrocities committed by women war criminals, for they are of a different sort entirely.

Much of this book focuses on women serial murderers defined by the fact they have killed three times or more with a cooling off period in between the 'events', and it is fair to say that a number of them would never have committed murder had they not been working alongside a partner-in-crime; most often a male who is more often than not the more dominant of the pair. For example, Myra Hindley could never have become a serial killer by her own volition had it not been for her lover Ian Brady's manipulative influence that led her down 'Murder Road' to committing the vilest of crimes – which does not imply any mitigation for Hindley at all.

I also suggest that the same criteria apply to Rosemary and

Frederick 'Fred' Walter Stephen West, with Fred being the dominant of the deadly duo, while it certainly *does not* with Joanna Dennehy. In her case the ball was on the other foot with this 'She Devil' being the manipulative personality in 'Team Jo Dennehy and Gary Stretch, aka, "The Undertaker"'.

Of course, the above relates to male serial killers too. However, while reading this book please bear in mind that one might regard the weaker of the two accomplices as mere 'tools' in the homicidal box of the more domineering of the deadly duos. Fred West often used his wife as bait – a 'tool' if you prefer – to lure unsuspecting women into his murderous web. Likewise, Brady used Hindley to entice children into their trap. Dennehy utilised Gary Stretch as a multi-purpose utensil, enabling her to commit blood-drenched murder. The same applies to Cathy May Wood who could not have killed five elderly nursing home patients without her entirely stupid lesbian lover, Gwendolyn Graham, around to assist her.

It would fair to say that females *ought* to be instinctively nurturing and maternal. Most reasonable people simply cannot imagine why a woman, being the mother figure, could harbour such evil desires, the overwhelming, sickening need, or indeed perverse inclination to destroy human life, especially in abhorrent cases such as multiple child torturing kills – the case in point exhibited by Myra Hindley, or others of her ilk referred to later in this book.

As Deborah Denno, Professor of Law, Fordham Law School, puts it in the 2017 *Women on Death Row* Discovery TV documentary: 'Women are typically viewed as nurturers but when they commit violent crimes this takes away that identity or public perception, so they may look more terrible and monstrous then men.'

It does not bear thinking that an English woman could con vulnerable babies away from their parents, strangle them to death, wrap their pathetic little bodies in newspaper then dump the corpses like so much trash. What was the motive behind all of this?

In Mumbai, India, Seema Gavit and Renuke Shinde went even further. Not only did they steal children from the filthy impoverished streets and alleyways, they beat them, they broke arms, they smashed legs, fractured jawbones, scalded their faces and bodies with acid then forced them into begging and child prostitution. Once the kids had passed their 'sell-by-date' they were garroted. I was given exclusive access to these heinous killers on Mumbai's Arthurs Road Jail death row. What follows later in this book will shock you. What was the motive behind it all? Well I'll put money on it that you have guessed the answer already…this time you could be right…maybe you could be wrong because the whodunits, whatdunits and whydunits have become the stock-in-trade fascination of every true crime buff, aspiring Sherlock Holmes, or one of those *very rare* individuals who has watched a particular *Columbo* movie just the once.

It is also generally bandied about that *all* serial murderers are psychopaths. I don't buy into this because the label 'Psychopath' or 'Sociopath' is an all too convenient label to hang around a multiple killer's neck when quite often the opposite can apply. You may react in shocked horror then, to find that I totally disagree that Aileen Wuornos was psychopathic, as hard as this may be to swallow for the professionals, who will argue to the end of their days saying otherwise.

But, so as not to disappoint, there is the flip side of the homicidal coin.

When, on the rare occasions I have witnessed 'alleged' remorse from a serial killer I look at the body language and deep into their eyes. There may be a few crocodile tears but I can smell bullshit a mile away. Their regret is never for the victims of their crimes or the mental anguish these heinous people have caused to next-of-kin, relations or family friends. The tears are only for themselves and the mess these disgusting people have now found themselves in. To quote the Bible: 'I will punish you as your deeds deserve declares the LORD. I will kindle a fire in your forests that will consume everything about you. (Jeremiah 21:14 *NIV.*)

I am not a 'Bible Thumper' by any means, but Jeremiah 21:14 seems quite appropriate as I digress for a few moments to take a look at Judias 'Judy' Buenoano who spent just over a decade on Florida's death row before she was executed in the electric chair at Florida's Starke State Prison, at 7:01 a.m., on Monday, 30 March 1998. I only briefly met this stone-cold killer once while visiting with serial killer Aileen 'Lee' Carol Wuornos, although I did spend a few years on-and-off corresponding with Judy. If ever there was the perfect example of a female serial killer dressed up in a wolf's clothing, it has to be her.

In a nutshell, Judy was born Judias Welty, Sunday, 4 April 1943, at Quanah, a small city (population circa 2000) and the county seat of Hardeman County, Texas. I have travelled far and wide across the 'Lone Star State'. I love Texas but what can I tell you about Quanah other than it was founded in around 1884 as a stopping-off point for the Fort Worth and Denver Railway? It is named after Quanah Parker, the last principle Comanche chief, who as the name 'Quanah/Kwana' means 'smell odour' – thus implying rather lot about Chief Parker's attention to personal hygiene to be sure. Even more worthy of note was the fact that this old warhorse had no less than seven wives, although not all at once, or so I am led to believe.

Judy is listed on the city's website as being a former Quanah resident. Other than this, Quanah has little to offer unless you are interested by the riveting facts that amongst the notable folk born here is William 'Bill' Lawrence Evans, awarded a Bronze and Silver Stars for bravery in WWII, and a professional baseball player to boot. There is a certain Welborn Barton Griffith, Jr, an American officer who also served in WWII. A Mr John Sandford Gilliand, Jr, a radio broadcaster. There is Edward 'Ed' Givens, astronaut. Fred Chase Koch, chemical engineer and founder of Koch Industries, then Texas Ranger William 'Bill' Jesse McDonald, aka, 'Captain Bill McDonald'.

For the benefit of my American readers I can't leave Quanah just yet because as a footnote I am obliged to add that Ed Givens didn't actually get himself rocketed into space at all. Sadly, he was killed in a car accident before even being assigned to a prime, even less a backup space flight – therefore, he got to meet his Maker via a different route.

Bill Evans was a six-foot two-inch relief pitcher who played for the Chicago White Sox, later the Boston Red Sox. He's revered to have thrown right-handed. Nice one, Bill!

For his part, Welborn stands out as being exceptional if the reader cares to look him up on the web – so exceptional is he that his city of birth has signally failed to erect a statue commemorating his outstanding world-applauded achievements, all of which brings me to Fred Koch. There is no statue of him either.

Fred was a very successful international businessman who

suffered health problems throughout his life and he finally suffered a fatal heart attack while on a bird-hunting trip. According to his son, David: 'He was having heart palpitations and wasn't shooting that well. Finally a lone bird came over. He took the shot and hit it square. The duck falls from the air. He turns to the loader and says, "Boy that was a magnificent shot", then he keels over stone dead.'

Then, finally we have someone really worth noting and having looked him up on the Internet, as I suggest you do too, Texas Ranger Bill McDonald is the bee's knees in my book with the opposite side of the law enforcement coin being of course Judy Buenoano, aka, 'The Black Widow'.

Buenoano was convicted of killing her former husband James Goodyear by arsenic poisoning, then dispatching a live-in partner, Bobby Joe Morris, by the same means. Thereafter, she poisoned her own paraplegic son, Michael, then rolled him (still alive) out of a canoe. He drowned, weighed down by his arm and leg braces. Her motive was financial gain through life insurance fraud. Nevertheless, let me try and paint a word picture of how this woman came across to all who ever met her, including me.

Plausible to a fault, slight, even fragile in build; imagine if you will a Sunday church fete; the ladies, some elderly, some not, all bustling round with Christian charity painted over their faces using a trowel, and charitable in their dress sense too. Think doctor's surgery receptionist, spinster of your parish, schoolteacher perhaps; community do-gooder and you have pictured Judy Buenoano to a tee. But let's read her own chilling poem called *Masks* that was somewhat nervously penned just before she was executed. It says everything that one can say from a fully-emerged psychopath who denied all guilt, right up to her inevitable death in the electric chair, saying: 'Don't be fooled by me. Don't be fooled by the face that I wear for I wear a thousand masks; masks that I'm afraid to take off and none of them are me. Pretending is an art that is second nature to me but do not be fooled. For God's sake don't be fooled.'

I have visited the courthouse where Buenoano was sentenced to death. Above the judge's bench is this quote from Deuteronomy 16:20: 'Justice and only Justice you will pursue'. Judy became the first and last woman to be executed in Florida's electric chair. Fred A. Leucher, JR, consultant and designer of electric chairs for three states, testified at her appeal that electrocution is a cruel and inhumane punishment, adding grimly that: 'This woman [Appellate DC # 160663] Buenoano will be burned alive.' He would not be at the top of my party list.

Just to digress for a moment, to liven things up a bit, if I may, upon examining Florida's 'Old Sparky' Leucher had determined that it was faulty, and in need of an upgrade costing $US 3,425 which the State of Florida considered 'too expensive'. Goodness me…a mere £2,500 to fix an allegedly humane death machine? You can't buy a decent Aga for that sort of money!

Electric chair consultant Leucher went on to justify the cost, explaining that: 'Of course, this quote *does* include a leg stock, including two leg electrodes, and a replacement helmet along with the shipping costs,' adding, 'The old army leg boot and copper strip designed ad hoc by Mr Robin Adair [representative of the Florida Dept. Corrections] who is not competent to design electric chairs is inadequate for a competent execution.' He concluded with: 'This woman will be tortured and will suffer great pain.' And wouldn't you too?

The night before Buenoano's execution she met her two children, a cousin and a priest for Communion. According to the Death House log, she then dozed off from 1 a.m. until 4 a.m., when she received her last meal of steamed vegetables, fresh strawberries and hot tea.

One retired American executioner (I prefer my own invented term 'Electrocutioner') told me: '...this is really about comfort food for them. It serves no nutritional purpose. Other than during autopsy examination when the stomach contents are examined what they eat has no value at all. Next question, please?'

I liked that bald statement very much indeed, even more so because he took me out to dinner and showed me precisely how a well-done slab of steak should be served – as in crispy on the outside, still pink inside and allowed to cool a little before tucking in, with ranch fries and gravy on the side, as you do!

When Buenoano entered the death chamber shortly after 7 a.m., she held tightly to the hands of two male officers who helped her walk. She was pale and terrified and on the verge of collapse, then at once seemingly determined to face her death with some sort of stoic dignity.

After the 'strap down team' had completed their work (all volunteers, I must add), she was asked if she had any last words, replying in a barely audible voice with: 'No sir.'

Moments later the switch was thrown. The current flowed, her fists clenched. She seemed almost dwarfed in the seventy-five-year-old well-used and badly functioning oak chair. Smoke poured from the top of her head, from beneath the death mask and from the makeshift copper electrode attached to her right leg. As engineer Leucher had rightly predicted, Buenoano was tortured to death – burned alive – in much the same way as happened to the character Eduard 'Del' Delacroix played by actor Michael Jeter in the 1999 Stephen King movie *The Green Mile*.

So there you have it. Considering the terrible crimes Buenoano was convicted of many will argue that she warranted her gruesome death sentence. Others say otherwise. What I will say is that the ultimate sanction acts as no deterrent, whatsoever, for it certainly did not in her case.

During a prison interview with serial killer Joanna Dennehy at HMP Bronzefield, she said this to me: 'Christopher, killing you would be good for me.'

Rose West wanted to marry me, with my response being unprintable in this book on my publisher's lawyer's legal advice, for it would certainly upset any lady reader with an undisturbed delicate highbrow disposition.

I am pleased to say that serial killer Aileen Wuornos made no intimate advances towards me at all, while the petite, in real life drop-dead gorgeous, magazine-cover-glossy, classy-act turned into one-off killer, Melanie 'Mel' McGuire, aka, 'The Scarlet Woman', aka, 'The Ice Queen', out of New Jersey, appreciated the Chanel 'Egoist' cologne I liberally sprinkled on my stationery.

This well-read, high-class, upscale brunette femme fatale who drugged, then shot, then Stihl power-sawed up her husband, Bill, then dumped his body parts into the Chesapeake Bay, wrote to me saying: 'My dearest Christopher. We would make perfect partners. My favorite food is Asian (be it Japanese, Chinese). French (no, you cant get decent foi gras in prison). Seafood (hey, I'm from the shore). I fail to cite Italian, as that is my "ordinary food".'

Veronica 'VerLyn' Wallace Compton? I interviewed her in the Western Washington Correctional Centre for Women ((WWCCW) Gig Harbor, for my 12-part TV series *The Serial Killers* way back in early 2000.

In the waning days of 1979–80, traffic-stopping Veronica was partying every night, heavily dependent on cocaine highs that fuelled her fantasies and fed her enormous bisexual appetite for whipping the flesh of LA's movers and shakers, and judges too. You will find some of her story, written in her own words, in the chapter on serial killer Kenneth Alessio Bianchi, whom she fell in love with, then unsuccessfully tried to kill a woman called Kim Breed at his behest. (See: *Talking with Serial Killers 2*.)

As a matter of the public record, during approximately the late seventies, VerLyn was indeed a statuesque beauty with sultry, raven hair. She had a figure that made most men, and many women, drool and, as one woman observed: 'VerLyn has a figure most women would die for.' Indeed, even after serving fifteen years in prison she was still drop-dead gorgeous – bubbly, highly intelligent when she suggested to me off-camera that we could enjoy the most extreme and erotic relationship ever. What she failed to reveal from her already well-documented criminal CV was that while planning to marry Ken Bianchi – who was then, and still is, serving the rest of his worthless life in the Washington State Penitentiary, Walla Wall – she was also corresponding with Douglas Clark, aka, 'The Sunset Slayer'. She wanted to open up a morgue with Doug to have sex with the corpses. VerLyn has long since been released from prison from whence she escaped at one time.

CHRISTOPHER BERRY-DEE

In 1989, whilst Veronica was serving her sentence she married Professor James Wallace of Eastern Washington University. In an interview with *The Spokesman-Review*, Wallace is reported as saying that Compton kicked her drug habit, got an Associate's Degree and began worshipping God. In 1993, she gave birth to the couple's daughter.

Women commit murder for many reasons, as do men, but, as this book will document – cold blooded women serial killers and the fairer sex takers of life *are* as different from their male counterparts as is teachers' chalk and a hefty chunk of kickass 'Stinking Bishop' cheese.

Enjoy. No nightmares, please!

Getting to Being Dead –
Judging Evil

What immediately follows the grammatically incorrect header to this very brief chapter will seem banal in extremis, however, the one thing; the only *single* thing that *all* murderers have in common, is that all of their victims end up being dead. But the yardstick we can use in judging evil is precisely how, and by what means, the victims arrive at their end.

So, let's consider this for a moment. Some people die easily while others die the hard way. A homicidal female nurse, for example, might inject her trusting patients with overdoses of insulin while they slumber in their beds, thus being completely and painlessly unaware of their impending doom. The flip side of the coin might be a Crystal Meth-crazed teenager, who in need of cash to feed her habit, beats, tortures, cuts and stabs her victims for hours at a time, maybe setting them on fire until death supervenes.

Cases abound where women have quietly suffocated children to death while gut-wrenchingly there are others who have thrown numerous babies into red-hot furnaces to burn them alive. There are women who, in need to get rid of a spouse or a lover, simply expedite the matter by popping a bullet into the back of the man's head. He would not have suspected a thing, nor felt any pain and he would be dead before he hit the floor. The fact that the body is power-sawed up after death means little to the victim, but it most certainly will no doubt have an impact on any right-minded jury and a judge at trial, I'll wager on that as evidenced by the beautiful convicted one-off killer, Jodi Ann Arias who is now serving a life sentence without the possibility of parole for the horrendous multiple stabbing/shooting to death of 'All-American Hunk' Travis Victor Alexander, aged 30, at his home in Mesa, Arizona, on Wednesday, 4 June 2008.

Conversely, there are the females of our species who systematically torture their weaker husbands for days on end; subjecting them to pain and suffering on an unimaginable scale with whipping, beating, cutting, slicing, starving them, forcing them to drink caustic fluids, submerging them in scalding bath water and scrubbing their injuries with wire bushes until they mercifully pass away. You are to meet one of these female monstrosities later in this book.

When a jealous woman makes the decision to kill a rival, it is often the case that a shooting, or a blitz knife attack will quickly do the job. But there are others who will lure their prey to some isolated spot, torture, bludgeon, carve Pentagrams into breasts and buttocks, or even cave in the dying person's cranium, turning their brain matter into mush – as in the case of Christa Gail Pike featured within these pages. She used part of her victim's skull as a spoon while eating her breakfast.

There are thousands of us who unwittingly start on a trip along what I call 'Murder Road'. This is a route that will bring the less fortunate to a terminus called 'Murder Crossroads', a spot where two lives meet; one life will end in some fashion or another, the other whose life is changed forever – in many legal jurisdictions across the world, to forfeit their very own existence at the end of a rope, in the electric chair, or strapped to the lethal injection gurney, when their whining appeals for mercy expire. You'll meet some of these evil women too.

So, I am hoping now that you can understand that the act of murder comes accompanied by many degrees of human suffering: from the almost sublime to atrocities that no sane person can imagine. Yes, it is true to say that all of these victims end up dead, however, as I mentioned earlier the yardstick for judging their degree of evil depends on the question of how they got to be dead. As a starter for ten, let's begin with two nurses' aides from Grand Rapids, Michigan, both of whom I have interviewed. Look into the face of Cathy May Wood and you will see pure evil staring straight back at you.

Catherine 'Cathy' May Wood and Gwendolyn 'Gwen' Gail Graham – The Deadly Nurses

Method of killing: 'burking'
This term is often ascribed to a method of murder that involves simultaneous smothering by placing a hand over the mouth, squeezing the nostrils shut and mechanically compressing the torso, thus limiting expansion of the lungs – hence interfering with breathing.
Victims
Marguerite Chambers (sixty), Myrtle Luce (ninety-five), Edith Cole (eighty-nine), Mae Mason (seventy-nine) and Belle Burkhard (seventy-nine)

In the opinion of Lt Tom Freeman of Walker County PD: 'Together, Cathy Wood and Gwendolyn Graham were basically a lethal weapon. They are like parasites and they needed each other.'

And when I interviewed Cathy May Wood at the

Federal Correctional Institute, Dublin, California, she said: 'Gwen told me she killed those people to relieve the tension. Sometimes I'd like to say that I made it all up. That would make everyone happy, I guess. If I would have gone to the police after the first murder I would have hoped it would have stopped. I'm eligible for parole in 1995.'

Whereas Gwen Graham told me: 'Cathy has a sick mind. She'd say anything. I hate her, I hate her. She's violated my whole life and the lives of other people with her stupid ass games. I'm sentenced to six life terms – the rest of my life. I'm innocent. I can no more prove I'm innocent than they can ever prove that I was guilty.' (Interviewed at Women's Huron Valley Correctional Facility, Ypsilanti, Michigan, 1995.)

Ken Kolker, reporter at *Grand Rapids Press*, said to me during an interview in March 1995: 'Grand Rapids is quite a conservative community and when news of five murders came out the city was shocked.'

This was a multiple murder case that gripped west Michigan. Twenty-four-year-old Wood and twenty-three-year-old Graham had met while working at the Grand Rapids Alpine Manor Nursing Home in 1986. The two became lovers. One year later they started killing, their victims being smothered so that it appeared they had died of natural causes and police now believe that as many as eight elderly people died.

As far as it can be determined, the killings became a game because the two murderers specifically picked their victims so that their initials would spell out the word 'MURDER'. In fact they even told colleagues what they were doing but were dismissed as sick jokers. Then the couple broke up and the murders stopped as quickly as they had started. A year later Wood's ex-husband, Ken, went to police. Investigators started exhuming bodies, autopsies were performed and both women were charged with five killings. During the trial, Wood testified against her former lover and Graham was sent to prison for the remainder of her natural life. Wood got a lesser sentence – today she may be eligible for parole but this does not imply she'll get it.

Before we dig into the heinous offences committed by these two women, please understand that I'm not going to pull any punches here for I have met a great many duplicitous serial killers and one-off murderers during my career as an investigative criminologist – some have been psychopaths, others savages, all have been evil. However, along with Joanna Dennehy, Cathy May Wood takes the biscuit and this is really saying something about the twisted wickedness inside her head. This overweight lump of disgusting humanity made a plea bargain with the prosecution and became a key witness at Graham's trial.

Cathy Wood was overheard sniggering to another inmate following this author's interview with her in prison, saying: 'Do you think that asshole believed all I told him?'

In his book *Forever and Five Days*, author Lowell Cauffiel is firmly of the view that Wood was the dominant partner. Cauffiel is at odds with the conclusions of the US criminal justice system who accepted Wood's story, hook, line and sinker.

I am pleased with the dedication Lowell wrote with his signature when he gave me a copy: 'For Chris. One of the good guys – Lowell Cauffiel'.

During my research into both women's lives and into the crimes they'd committed, I had the pleasure to meet and film Lowell Cauffiel for a TV documentary at his Ann Arbor home on Thursday, 16 March 1995.

Author of *Forever and Five Days – An Account of Obsessive Love and Murder that Rocked Grand Rapids, Michigan*, Lowell had already formed the same opinion I'd arrived at after interviewing both killers, so we were very much in sync. As such, I'd also like to recommend my readers to his *Eye of the Beholder: The Almost Perfect Murder of Anchorwoman Diane Newton King*. As bestselling author Jack Olsen says: 'Lowell Cauffiel is the future of true crime.'

Well done, Lowell!

However, my interest in Wood and Graham lay solely in the fact that I was making a twelve-part documentary series called *The Serial Killers*. I had already lined up for interviews Theodore 'Ted' Bundy, Kenneth Alessio Bianchi aka 'The Hillside Strangler', Arthur John Shawcross aka 'The Monster of the Rivers', Harvey 'The Hammer' Carignan, James Paul, Douglas Daniel Clark aka 'The Sunset Killer', Kenneth Allen McDuff aka 'The Broomstick Killer', William Heirens, Michael Bruce Ross 'The Roadside Strangler', Henry Lee Lucas and Ronald 'Butch' DeFeo aka 'The Amityville Horror'. While at once noting that these were all men, in short order my producer Frazer Ashford needed a couple of women to make up the numbers, so I quickly wrote to Wood and Graham. We would tag the documentary devoted to them *The Lethal Lovers*. This label has stuck ever since.

Because she is a vain egocentric who revels in the limelight, Cathy Wood took the bait immediately. Frazer and I were almost off the hook so-to-speak. Catching the reluctant Gwen Graham would be a single programme double whammy if we could get to her to talk to me on camera, too, so I used a little guile to reel her in. I wrote to her explaining that I wanted to set the record straight...

that I didn't believe a word Cathy Wood had told me on-camera, least of all believed anything I'd read in the press about her. It worked!

As Lowell Cauffiel explained during our meeting, and I cannot sum it up any better: 'There are two Cathy Woods really. For my part I also found that one half of Wood wore a mask of sanity portraying a relatively quiet and intelligent, articulate individual who at first seems quite likeable and rather passive – not very aggressive at all, but behind that façade is a [complex personality],' and I completely agreed with him about there being two Cathy Woods, while the remainder of those living on Planet Earth still appear not to.

The police investigation into the Alpine Manor Nursing Home had begun with rapidly circulating rumours that deaths ruled as 'natural' in early 1987 might not have been so. The then anonymous caller to the police [Cathy's ex-husband Ken] suggested that foul play was involved. As many as six to eight patients may have been suffocated in their beds he explained, so, after a little dragging of feet, law officers zeroed in on Wood and Graham.

On 29 December, 1989, Cathy Wood said to Lowell Cauffiel: 'I enjoyed taking care of those old people.'

One of four sisters, Catherine May Wood *née* Carpenter was born on Wednesday, 7 March 1962, on a Washington State army base where her father was stationed. Shortly after her sister Barbara was born the family moved to Massachusetts while their father prepared himself emotionally for service in Vietnam.

Sister, Barbara Burns *née* Carpenter, explained to me that,

'…in growing up us four sisters argued. We'd play pranks on each other, we'd laugh, we told secrets, and growing up in a dysfunctional family made us very close.'

For her part, Cathy Wood told me that she didn't socialise with her siblings too much. She stayed by herself. 'I was a real shy kid…' she said, adding, '…and, um, my dad…when my dad came back home [from Vietnam] he had really bad dreams. He was an alcoholic, abusive, mentally and emotionally and it was real hard. Um, and when I was twelve or thirteen years old my dad made me feel quite ugly you know and I was getting interested in boys at the time.'

And, this is also partly endorsed by Barbara, who explained: 'Cathy was a bookworm. She was very smart. She would stay in her bedroom and read. I think she also did that because she was tall and also heavy. The other kids could be very cruel to her because of her size.'

Now before you start reaching for a box of tissues to dry your eyes, let's consider what Wood told me at interview. Was she telling the truth or was it just bullshit?

I was going with a boy called David. He was sixteen. We were working our way back to his house and we saw my mom's car there, and he said, 'Get your mom outa there.' He was real frantic. So we were going towards the house. I looked round and he was gone. So we got to the house and knocked on the door and Mom said she'd had a hard time getting in because they said they didn't have a son named David. But there was a big purple Cadillac…um; a pink Cadillac with a 'Labour' bumper sticker on it and David had driven that car to my mom's house many times. That car was now in David's driveway so my mom knew that was the right place.

So when I went in she said, 'Catherine May, sit down,' so I knew I'd done something wrong but I didn't know what it was at the time. So, David's mother said, 'We don't have a son. We have a daughter called Debbie,' and they showed me a picture. It was David with long hair. So, uh, I couldn't say, 'Well Mom we had sex,' because we didn't talk about sex. You know, that was…that was not allowed. And I was confused at this time and I didn't know if David was a man or a woman. I didn't know and I had to find out.'

I had already seen through the lie. Wood's eyes and body language said it all. Innocent face, fake tears, looking down, avoiding eye contact as she tried to elaborate on the yarn she was making up as she went along. Occasionally she would look into my eyes, a kind of furtive look to see if her story was convincing me of this self-alleged truth. I have witnessed this disingenuous eye-contact behaviour before in so many serial killers who have tried to pull a fast one, so, with Wood, I didn't buy any of it at all.

Now think *Judge Judy*. When our favourite TV judge is quizzing either a plaintiff or a defendant she gets kind of wild when they don't look straight into her eyes. 'Look at ME,' she shouts. 'Don't look down or over there, and STOP MAKING UP A STORY AS YOU GO ALONG!' And, this is precisely what I wanted to say to Cathy Wood, but I kept quiet. And, here is a free tip. If you are quizzing someone about something you are not happy about, watch his or her eyes like Judge Judy does. You'll be able to see precisely what I mean.

Perhaps sensing that her story was not quite up to scratch, Cathy Wood again overstepped the mark and this is why I always allow those I believe to be lying to talk as much as they like without interruption. What followed from her didn't disappoint, as I am sure you will agree bearing in mind that the so-called David's parents had already confirmed that 'David' was indeed a 'Debbie', and the photograph of long-haired Debbie in a white blouse, plaid skirt, white bobby socks and black, patent shoes – obviously indicating to all and sundry that David was a girl – was not good enough confirmation to Cathy Wood for she now added to this already phony tale:

> So, Later I told her 'David' or 'Debbie'…I said, I said, 'I know you are a woman.' I don't know why I said that, Christopher, but I had to find out so I did. So, I…she came with me with this man and took me all the way to Lowell, the city she lived in, and we were in this big old house. So, I slept with her so I could see everything and she was a man.

Confusing, is it not? Nevertheless, it has since been debated amongst the circle of her supporters that this yarn was made up by Wood to keep her mother from knowing that she was a lesbian. I don't buy into this either. To begin with most of the United States of America should know that she was bisexual with a 99.9 per cent leaning towards sex with women. The Grand Rapids' homicides had a strong sexual lesbian love pact element to them, moreover, what Wood had failed to tell me, although she did tell the court during her trial that from the outset of her relationship with 'David' aka 'Debbie' or vice versa, she always wore a strap-on dildo – the make, model, colour and size, however, never being remotely established!

With every killing couple I have ever had dealings with, even the ones I have never met, there is always, without exception, a dominant partner. Take for instance the narcissist Ian Brady and his dreadful partner-in-crime Myra Hindley; the latter would never have resorted to committing serial homicide without the dominance of scum-bucket Brady – long may his ashes be completely dissipated to the wind, and hers too come to that. The same criteria applied to Frederick West and his disgusting wife, Rosemary. In fact, I'd even go so far as to state that the giant of a man Gary Stretch – a character whose brainpower wouldn't be enough to propel an ant's motorcycle around the inside of a piece of Cheerios cereal – would never have become involved in serial killing had it not been for the dominating, beguiling influence of vain egocentric Joanna Dennehy, who we will also meet in this book.

I can say the same for the two notorious 'Hillside Stranglers' – Messrs Kenneth Alessio Bianchi and the stuttering, ferret-faced Angelo Buono; the former whom I spent several years corresponding with before interviewing him at the Washington State Penitentiary (WSP), Walla Walla, Washington State, in September 1966. There will, of course, be scores of people who will argue the toss with me that it was poor Ken who was led along and encouraged to kill by Buono. Once again I don't agree, and here are two solid explanations as to why.

First and foremost, extreme egotist Bianchi is still considered the No. 1 suspect in the triple killings of Rochester, NY, schoolgirls Carmen Colon, Wanda Walkowitz and Michelle Maenza, committed between November 1971 and

November 1973. These murders were dubbed by the media 'The Double Initial Murders' and 'The Alphabet Murders' for the most obvious reasons.

Secondly, after Bianchi and Buono's killing spree in Los Angeles carried out between 17 October 1977 and 16 February 1978 (a total of ten kills), Bianchi split up from Buono and travelled north to the sleepy Washington State town of Bellingham where, on his own, he killed two university students, Karin Manic and Diane Wilder during the late evening of Thursday, 11 January 1979. Bianchi's life and crimes are fully documented in my book, *Talking with Serial Killers 2* – first published in hardback by John Blake, London, 2005.

And, just like Cathy Wood, Bianchi never stops talking. He courts publicity at every turn. He never shuts the fuck up. He hasn't done so since the day he was arrested on 12 January 1979 in sleepy, snow-covered Bellingham, Washington State; he spent all of two years in the witness box at Buono's trial in LA, and he keeps rambling on and on even today. In fact, if you care to write to him even suggesting that he's innocent, better still if you enclose a photo of a beautiful young woman (even if you are a guy) you'll get a reply faster than a mousetrap snaps shut: # 266961 BIANCHI. A Kenneth. Washington Corrections Center. PO Box 900. Shelton. WA 98584. USA.

The point I am trying to make is that when you take into consideration all of Bianchi's back history and compare this with that of Buono's, it becomes an inescapable fact that Kenneth was the most dominant of the duo and, in the absence of Bianchi's perverted desires, the now deceased Buono would have carried on ambling through his own worthless life with the thought of killing multiple times never entering his mind – although it is right to say that both men are as guilty as sin – the same also relates to Wood and Graham.

I have digressed, so let's get back to Cathy and Gwen and why size *does* matter when 'burking' is used to suffocate the life out of some poor soul.

The definition of the verb 'burking' or 'burked', is to carry out murder by suffocation so as to leave few or no marks. It is named after the undersized and thickset William Burke, who was hanged in Edinburgh on 28 January 1829. Along with William Hare, the two men have since become known as 'The Body Snatchers'. They more-or-less invented murder by suffocation by sitting on their snoozing victims, after which they sold the corpses to one of Edinburgh's most sought after anatomy lecturers, Dr Robert Knox FRSE FRCSE MWS, who was a brilliant, yet totally unscrupulous surgeon. By all accounts, Dr Knox was a gnarled little fellow, a package of malice and jealousy. He had only one eye and was nicknamed 'Old Cyclops', but his eccentric brilliance as an anatomist earned him respect in Edinburgh's medical circles. However, his dubious practice of purchasing the fresh corpses supplied by Burke and Hare was to ruin his once glittering career.

Both Burke and Hare were all but cretins. Burke, with his shambling gait, needed to drink heavily before each murder. He was often so drunk he couldn't even recall the details of his killings. Hare had a lighthearted clowning personality. He liked the excitement of his deadly trade and had no understanding of his behaviour and was as unthinking and spontaneous as a small child.

Therefore, Wood and Graham used the same technique.

They killed their elderly victims by sitting on their chests and suffocated them by putting a washcloth over their noses and mouths, while using the other hand to push their victims' jaws upwards. The corpses exhibited only a few visible injuries, which could easily be explained away because elderly patients, especially those suffering dementia, often lash out and have to be restrained so as not to hurt themselves, or their carers, into the bargain.

Although some may disagree, it is said that size doesn't matter but it most certainly did to the patients who lay sedated and sleeping in their beds when Cathy May Wood took it upon herself to sit on their chests, because Wood is a hefty woman, which is an understatement at best. She literally stood head and shoulders over her peers, and was most certainly a lot taller than the diminutive Gwen Graham. A quarter inch shy of six feet and every bit of 330 pounds, Wood was, and still as, strong as an ox – she was the perfect killing machine when everything is weighed up. We will come to Gwen Graham sooner rather than later. But for the moment I would like you to consider the aspect of the pair's relative sizes. This will help us to determine precisely who did the actual hands-on burking, because when we compare the relatively small prison tariff handed down to the heavily built Cathy Wood to the size of the natural life sentence given to the 154-lb Gwen Graham, we find, despite Wood's claim that she merely stood and kept watch outside the patients' rooms while Gwen did the suffocating, that the opposite is patently far more likely to be true.

Ken Wood, Cathy's ex-husband said to me in 1995: 'I would do anything for that girl and she knew that. And, I knew at certain times I was being manipulated but I didn't care because I loved her.' In the same year, Barbara Burns told me: 'He [Ken] wasn't a companion to Cathy. He wanted to keep her in the house. He wanted to control her.'

During my interview with Cathy Wood she explained: 'I met Ken and when you see Ken he is obviously a man. On our first date I said, "Wanna go to your apartment?" He said, "Yeah".' Now, with crocodile tears pouring down her cheeks, she then said that when they got to his place he sat down and started taking his clothes off but she didn't want to have sex with him, she only wanted to look at him. When she had seen everything she told him to get dressed.

When she was either sixteen or seventeen years old (she could not remember exactly) the couple got married and Ken took Cathy away from her family and out of school. 'I still tried to go to school even though I was pregnant and it was my senior year,' she told me. Cathy soon gave birth to a daughter.

Clearly marriage to Ken was not ideal for Cathy Wood. 'I was growing up and Ken and my relationship was getting more physical. You know I didn't like him touching me and I didn't like spending any time with him and there was always fighting. And, it was too much. I never had any peace. He wouldn't leave me alone.'

Then to spitefully stick the knife right into her ex-husband she said: 'Sex...it was...it was nuthin'...nuthin'. Uh, it was something he had to do. It was something you did because your husband wanted it. It wasn't fun. It wasn't interesting. He just did it and went and watched football. You know, it was nuthin'.'

Tearful Wood went on to admit that she was not a good wife to Ken. 'I wouldn't do the things his mom did. I didn't do those things so I left him.' And it was at this point of her life that Cathy Wood started looking for a job. She soon found a position at the Alpine Manor Nursing Home in Grand Rapids.

'When I was a teenager I'd been a "Candy Striper" [a volunteer hospital worker so named for their pink-and-white striped uniforms].' Wood said that she liked the job a lot and she thought this past work, added to some added hands-on experience, would make her a suitable employee, and they hired her.

And in March 1995, Ken Kolker, reporter on *Grand Rapids Press*, confided in me: 'One of the nurses told me that Alpine Manor [which has since changed ownership and its name] was a cubby of lesbians.'

Now separated from Ken, Cathy Wood started to find her own two feet. The money, albeit just $3.35 an hour, was regular and, apart from her nursing shifts, she could come and go as she pleased. After a while she bought a car, began to make her own decisions and started to fall in with some of the girls who worked there.

'So, Christopher, I go to work and there was [this] woman called Jane [name changed by the author to protect her identity],' she told me. 'I'd been working there for six months, maybe a year. I'm not too sure. And that woman was eighteen, and she started giving me attention, and I thought about what had happened when I was a teenager, that maybe I was gay.' She added: 'Gwen worked in the nursing home and I didn't pay her much attention, but one day I was sitting in the break room with Jane. Gwen and Jane were good friends, and Gwen had come up from Texas to be with her girlfriend, Fran. They'd been together for a long time. So, I was sitting in the break room with Jane when Gwen walked in and this was the first time I noticed her [Gwen's] scars, so I started watching her a bit.'

Cathy's sister, Barbara Burns recalled: 'When Cathy first met Gwen it was the first time in her life that she sowed her oats *per se* because she was a stay-at-home person. She got married to Ken, she never left their house, so when she separated from Ken and met Gwen she started going out to movies, playing pool, started living for the first time in her life, but over time she changed.'

Barbara, Cathy's younger sibling, says that her sister became hard. 'Talking over the phone Cathy wasn't herself,' adding, 'and she wasn't fun loving, not her normal easy-going self. She was short and rude. This was out of character.' She went on to tell me: 'Gwen took an interest in Cathy which nobody ever did before. Cathy craved love so badly. She craved attention and when Gwen gave that to her Cathy just followed. Gwen is a bitch!'

This is an interesting, quite vindictive remark made by Barbara for it is one that offers us further insight into how manipulative Cathy Wood is. While we might forgive Barbara for being over-protective of her older sister, all but believing everything she says, we must also remember that Cathy Wood is without a conscience and up until a point these people can be very convincing indeed. Most of the time the mask these killers hide behind is bullshit. Sooner or later we always find out who they truly are.

Enter Gwendolyn Graham – born on Tuesday, 6 August 1963. She briefly described her early years to me during my prison interview with her:

'I grew up mostly in Texas. After my Fifth Grade my

parents moved to Texas and we lived there for most of my teenage years,' she said, looking very crestfallen. 'Most of my childhood memories on upwards are from Texas. We lived on a farm at a place called Gresham, near Tyler City. We worked on the farm. We had pigs, cows, chickens, everything and as far back as I can remember I've always been attracted to women.'

According to Lowell Cauffiel, Graham is a very mixed-up woman who came out of childhood suffering a certain amount of abuse. 'She's a very dependent individual,' he explained to me, adding, '...a person eager to please the partner she is with. Something of a tragic figure actually. She self-mutilated herself with razor blades and cigarettes and this is a greater kind of pathology that is very typical of a borderline personality disorder.' This observation from Lowell is an important one for he says Graham showed behaviour shared by those of a 'borderline personality disorder' as distinct from a fully emerged one. I would add to this by suggesting that Cathy Wood has no conscience, but that Gwen is not psychopathic and did not exhibit any signs of psychopathy when I interviewed her in prison.

When I interviewed Gwen Graham I asked her to show me her scars. She rolled up both sleeves of her blue prison fatigues and said: '...these are cigarette burns. I have cuts, a few. They were done when I was sixteen. Um, I never [knew] why I really did it, I just knew that I was angry. I was abused so I did it to make myself look ugly so that it would never happen again.' This statement wasn't quite true because the prison doctor told me that she was still self-harming, quite often too. Taking a closer look, I saw thirty-one in all – nineteen circular scars on her left arm, twelve on her right.

There were also more than twenty less apparent marks – tiny lines of scar tissue at odd angles and all razor thin.

Aged twenty, Graham had travelled from Texas to Michigan. Her girlfriend had previously moved up there to be with her parents who lived and worked in Grand Rapids. Shortly after arriving Gwen started working at the Alpine Manor Nursing Home. 'We bathed the patients. We did everything for them…the ones that needed it,' says Graham. 'There were ones that were total care and needed everything to the ones who could do things on their own and needed a little assistance.'

Describing how she met Wood, Graham told me: 'I met Catherine May Wood at the nursing home. She was on the midnight shift and I was working that midnight shift, too. We moved into a small house together approximately three weeks after I met her.'

Initially they moved in together as roommates to share the rent. Within a few days they became lovers. 'She [Gwen] made me feel pretty,' says Wood. 'She made me feel special. She'd do things that I wanted to do. She was caring. She was nice to me,' somewhat over-egging it a bit with, 'she didn't yell at me. She didn't say any bad things at all. We did things together. We made decisions together. Everything was fifty-fifty. Equal. If I was doing the cleaning or cooking she'd be doing the laundry or at the laundromat. It seemed to me as if I was equal.'

Both women were very heavy drinkers during their time off work and according to Wood she and Gwen talked about everything and anything with Gwen explaining that she had spent time in a 'mental place'. 'At one time Gwen told me about killing a dog; that she'd shot it in the head, and then it went from there,' with the two discussing how one could kill somebody. 'Would you sneak into their house and what would you wear?' asked Wood of Graham.

Ever keen to bring sex into her account of this alleged idyllic life of domestic bliss, Wood told me: 'She taught me more. She taught me about myself. That sex is a fun thing. That…sex…it's nice, and we would do things I'd never done before and experiment with things.' Countering this, Graham said, 'Cathy was the most dominant in the bedroom situation and out of it.'

Describing the relationship between the two women, Lowell Cauffiel explained that, 'The nature of the association between Gwen Graham and Cathy Wood was, on the surface, a sexual relationship with a lot more going on there with Gwen, for a period of time showing Cathy a great amount of care and love. She got her into more fashionable clothes, doted over her and Cathy is right up for it. Cathy is the more mother figure; more domineering figure who took care of the bills in the house and determined what they were going to do, obviously pulling the strings in the relationship.'

Cathy Wood went even further, telling me, '…at this time Gwen was getting more physical and violent and sex was getting rough. We would fight all the time. She never struck me or hit me. Just in the context of sex.'

Now in full swing and playing the 'Miss Innocent', Wood explained, 'I let her tie me because she promised she'd never hurt me, and I believed her and I trusted her because I believed and she took a rifle and put it in my vagina and she told me she was going to shoot me.'

For her part, Graham said, '…she tied me up and put a gun between my legs…my rifle in between my legs, and I was begging because I thought she would shoot me. And, then she stood there for a minute with it in me and then she took it out then looked at me all strange then she left the room.'

Both women told stories that they were tied up by the other during the sex act. That a firearm was held to the private parts by the other person in an attempt to intimidate, is, of course, one person's word against the other, However what you have to remember is that almost everything thing that is said in this case comes from the garrulous Cathy Wood and all the things she asserts are a determined effort to portray Gwendolyn Graham as being the monster, but why? The answer is spite, brought about by jealousy.

Despite Wood going to great pains to portray herself as the vulnerable and abused partner in the relationship the opposite is true, for she was certainly the dominant member of the couple and what follows applies to the scope of domestic violence among lesbian relationships displaying the pattern of intimidation, coercion, terrorism, or violence that achieves enhanced power and control for the perpetrator over her partner. The forms of domestic violence in lesbian relationships include physical abuse, such as hitting, choking, using weapons, or restraining, often referred to as 'battering'; emotional abuse, such as lying, neglecting, and degrading; intimidation threats, such as threats to harm the victim, their family, or their pets; sexual abuse, such as forcing sex or refusing safe sex; destruction of property, such as vandalising the home and damaging furniture, clothing, or personal objects; economic, such as controlling the victim's money and forcing financial dependence. In addition, psychological abuse has been found to be common among lesbian victims.

Findings from studies have shown that slapping was most the commonly reported form of abuse, while beatings and assaults with weapons were less frequent. Sexual violence, often as the result of jealousy or fear of losing a partner within lesbian relationships, was found to be as high as 55 per cent. The most frequent type included forced kissing, breast and genital fondling, and oral, anal, or vaginal penetration abuse, which I believed Wood dished out in spades.

And perhaps Cathy Wood had every reason to be defensive about Gwendolyn, for Carol (name changed by the author to protect her identity), formerly a close friend, was still on the scene, as Wood spitefully recalled:

'Gwen wanted to stay friends with that bitch Carol almost from the beginning of our relationship. She [Carol] would come over and we'd party together. We'd go to the Carousel Bar. We'd go and have a good time. When we drank we drank, and uh, I just thought we were just good friends. Then I discovered that Gwen was having an affair with Carol. I felt that the love of my life was leaving me. I thought that I'd never be happy again. I thought, "that's it!" I thought I was going to die…I thought I was going to die. I cried all the time. I couldn't talk…I didn't eat…I didn't do anything. I just stayed at home.'

Then came the punch line: 'If I couldn't have Gwen *no one* would!'

This eventually led to Wood giving evidence against Graham. Primarily as a result of Wood's evidence Graham was found guilty of five counts of murder and one count of conspiracy to commit murder, and received five natural life sentences..

Ken Wood told me during an interview: 'There were

certain things Cathy said in January and February 87. It was, uh, "You'd never believe about some of the things we are doing at the nursing home." I knew things were out of control and I talked to one of their neighbours and I knew about the yelling, wild parties and the screaming in their house. I know how volatile Cathy is and the fights with Gwen and stuff and I thought "what's going on?"'

MARGUERITE CHAMBERS

On the evening of Sunday, 18 January 1987, Grand Rapids was covered in a three-inch white blanket of snow. A light wind made the snaps on the Alpine Manor flagpole ring in hollow tones. Inside the warmth of the home the sound of *The Blue Danube* played softly as licensed nurses bustled from room to room, passing out evening medication just before one of their patients was about to be murdered.

Earlier, a nurse checked and found the sixty-seven-year-old's pulse running a little over a beat per second, meaning that her blood pressure was within the normal limits for a woman of her age. All through Alpine's third shift, Marguerite had been very restless. She had run a fever of 101 the night before, but now, almost asleep in Room 614 on Dover Ward, she could not speak and would obviously be unable to relate anything to anybody if she had survived what followed.

Marguerite may have noted a presence by her bedside, or perhaps the attack came suddenly and she was jolted from her slumbers. The curtain traverse rod hissed as a hand pulled the divider back. There may have been sounds of a polyester uniform rubbing against itself. Two hands positioned her head, resting it squarely back. Maybe this was sudden. Or, maybe it was gentle. We will never know.

Suddenly there was no air. There was absolutely none. The damp terry cloth was rolled. One hand covered her nostril the other hand was under Marguerite Chambers's chin – one squeezed, the other thrust her chin up violently, pushing her toothless gums together. She began to thrash. Her groans were guttural, deep within her belly.

As the need to breathe became more urgent her cheeks began to puff and collapse. Her lungs were sucking for the pathetically few cubic inches of oxygen that were left before her mouth was slammed shut.

In a great effort, Marguerite twisted her head. But nothing could have prepared her for this. Her last moments were spasmodic.

In the end, in her final seconds of consciousness, her eyes couldn't help but look at the face above her.

Michelangelo might have painted it on a Sistine Chapel cherub, but the face swimming out of focus belonged to an angel of death.

Wood would later tell me: 'When I looked into the room, Gwen was on the far side of the bed. She had a terry washcloth and she was suffocating Marguerite. Afterwards, when other nurses came into the room I kept expecting her to move. I honestly wanted her to move. I just wanted her to move. Gwen was in the corner with her back against the wall just looking at me.'

One by one other nurses entered the room to satisfy themselves that Marguerite was dead. A Registered Nurse, Linda Dapore, made the final entry on the deceased's chart at 8.30 p.m. She was not able to get blood pressure or a pulse.

The patient had been dead for some time. Her colour was 'yellow-gray', she wrote, and her skin was 'mottled'. Her arms and hands were cold. Coroner Dr Piskin would sign the death certificate the following day. He never examined dead bodies on a Sunday.

In her interview with me, Gwen Graham simply said, 'I was not present at any time of these people's deaths. I can't say where I was in the building. I was in the building. That's all I know.' Cathy Wood maintained that she was merely the lookout while Gwen went into the room and suffocated the helpless woman.

MYRTLE LUCE

During my interview with her, Cathy May Wood said: 'Myrtle Luce was a patient on Abbey Lane Ward and Gwen told me that she was going to "do her". That's how we said it so no one would overhear, and if they did overhear I was supposed to say it was a joke. I wasn't supposed to say anything about it. So her name was Myrtle and she, um, um, I don't remember where I was when Gwen killed her. I don't remember where I was.'

Born on 20 February 1891, ninety-five-year-old, black-haired, blue-eyed, five-foot two-inch Myrtle Luce needed plenty of care. Her son, Ted, knew that she had spent her life giving care to others, having worked as a sales assistant in her early years, but she had the 'heart of a missionary', he explained to Lowell Cauffiel. She had taken in a troubled teenage boy to bring up as family. She nursed her husband's two ailing sisters as well as two very sick aunts. She had also done a lot of voluntary work in the community. Recently a series of small strokes had all but overwhelmed her. She was diagnosed with an organic brain disease by her doctor, which car mechanic Ted reckoned was similar to Alzheimer's Disease, 'but her heart was too strong for her own good,' he recalled, adding, 'She had hypertension and arteriosclerosis, but her heart kept pumping, despite all the damage to her brain.'

Myrtle could have lived for five days or five months or five years. There was no way anyone could tell, reasoned her doctor. But lately, feeding her had become difficult. She was losing weight. Nursing staff put her into a geriatric chair to feed her puréed dinner with a large syringe. They stroked her neck, urging her to swallow. According to Ted Luce, the staff at the Grand Rapids home were doing all they could for the dear old soul. They even played her favourite music – *The Blue Danube*. Then, on 3 February, a registered nurse spotted a trickle of blood from Myrtle's right nostril during the second shift. She applied a cold washcloth to stop the flow, but with all the tubes, tired capillaries and cases of high blood pressure around, nurses didn't consider a nosebleed a curious event. Winter, and the increased heating temperatures sometimes made the atmosphere in Alpine Manor exceptionally arid. This dried up the mucous membranes and made patients more vulnerable, especially when the air was so dry it crackled.

What the staff didn't know was that only twenty minutes beforehand Wood and Graham had attempted to 'burke' Myrtle. 'I am going to do Myrtle.' (Cathy Wood to Gwen Graham, evening of 9 February 1987.)

At precisely 2.20 a.m., 10 February 1987, a nurses' aide, Sally Johnson, reported a death in Room 206 Abbey Lane

Ward. Night shift supervisor Martha Slocum found Myrtle Luce lifeless. Cathy Wood helped clean up the body before it was sent to the funeral home. She combed her hair and Wood says she found a damp washcloth on the bed. Martha Slocum says this was untrue. 'Wood never attended to the body at all,' she later said. 'She never saw the body, even when it was moved.'

And, it is here that Cathy Wood says too much again. She told me during interview: '…when I went into the room, I looked at Myrtle and her nose was…smooshed. She had a lot of mucous and things in her nose all of the time, and it was like it had been held there. No one noticed it but me.'

MAE 'MAISY' MASON

It had been Mae Mason's seventy-ninth birthday on Monday 2 February. She had recently been transferred from Camelot Ward to Abbey Lane and she enjoyed a visit from her daughter, Linda and granddaughter Stephanie. They helped Maisy out of bed and walked her to the day room, each holding an arm. Since breaking her leg, the once incessant walker had become afraid to walk alone. She cried when they left. Something told her that she would never see them again, then several days later her end almost came.

Nurses' Aide Shawn Dougherty came to Room 2017-1. Maisy was her responsibility for the shift and, when she tried to open the sliding door it appeared to be jammed. Finally, she levered the door open with no resistance. Cathy Wood and Gwen Graham were standing inside. They giggled, then scurried past her with Wood saying: 'Hah, ha. The joke's on you.'

Dougherty had only been working at the care home not even a month, but she knew that the two women had no business with one of her patients, plus all doors were supposed to remain open on the third shift. She complained to a Registered Nurse but never heard any more about it.

Nothing more of substance occurred until Shawn Dougherty made her 2 a.m. check of Room 207-1 on Monday 16 February. She found Maisy very much awake and active but she lay in her own excrement. Faeces covered her hands and were embedded in her fingernails, all of which made Maisy more active as she was cleaned up with a washcloth and a towel. She seemed terrified at the sight of the washcloth and hung onto it tightly as if she were afraid to let it go.

After changing Maisy, Shawn tucked her up in bed, laid her on her back and fluffed up the pillows then continued with her rounds. When she returned at 4 a.m. she was immediately struck by the colour of Maisy's face – a greyish colour. The old lady was still lying on her back, her hands by her sides, her palms open. Her eyes were closed and her mouth was agape, the jaw open and pushed down on one side. Wood and Graham had killed again.

BELLE BURKHARD

Cathy Wood was quoted as saying: 'I didn't really like Belle. She was so hard to take care of.'

While there is no evidence to suggest that Wood and Graham had attempted to murder other patients at the Grand Rapids nursing home, it has since been established that their last known victim was seventy-nine-year-old Belle Burkhard.

She had been a patient in nursing homes for eleven years, eight of them Alpine Manor. She was senile, deaf and blind. Still, she talked a lot and took food in her wheelchair, and was altogether a non-complaining old lady indeed.

Wednesday, 25 February was Graham's scheduled day off. But for the third shift during the early morning hours of Thursday she had arrived at Alpine Manor for yet more overtime. She was working another shift with Cathy Wood. Gwen was assigned to the 600 and 700 halls on Dover Ward, just a short walk from 100 hall where Wood was stationed on Abbey Lane and where Belle Burkhard was a patient – her bed was next to the window.

Of some interest, for the first two weeks of February, Belle's primary carer during the third shift had been Cathy Wood and, according to her she found the elderly lady 'frustrating'. It also seems that Belle was troublesome when Cathy was around and attempted to turn the old lady in her bed. Belle would often grab the bed rails with an iron grip and refuse to budge. Often she did this and laughed. For her part, Gwen got on very well with Belle. And, an entry made on Belle's chart on Sunday, 15 February was even more noteworthy. That morning an aide had found Belle with reddish bruises around her nose, right cheek and temples. In itself one might expect that this would have raised a red flag, nevertheless, considering her history of seizures and of her often hitting her head against the stainless steel bed rails, the incident was dismissed with no further investigation by the management.

Quite why Cathy Wood was taken off caring for Belle Burkhard and replaced by aide Pat Ritter for the last eleven consecutive days of her life has never been established. What is known is that forty-one-year-old Pat Ritter didn't like Wood at all and she was always criticising the woman. Ritter suspected both Graham and Wood of pouring cold water into patients' beds. They were not changing their own patients and she had reported all of this to her supervisor. However, during the 3 a.m. break on Thursday 26 February, when many staffers took their break, the Abbey Lane station was left to the care of Cathy Wood. She was often seen chewing on her lip and gazing at her nails while she sat alone.

Soon Graham was spotted approaching Wood from the Dover Ward. While Graham took Wood's place at the station and watching the hall, Cathy headed into Burkhard's room 112. During my interview with Wood in prison, she was adamant that it was Graham who had gone into room 112, telling me: 'I heard groans and the rustle of sheets over the intercom linked to the station. I heard gurgling out loud, like dry-heave noises. I did hear that for a while.' Then, changing her story, she claimed: 'Minutes later an intruder walked out of room 112 and turned away into the hall. A washcloth hung out of her back pocket as she strolled down Abbey Lane.'

Ritter was not far into her 4 a.m. rounds on 26 February when she stopped outside the door of room 112. She planned to turn Belle in her bed, as she had done at midnight and at 2 a.m. Moments later, she came screaming out of the room. Belle was her first dead patient. The first person she saw was Cathy Wood standing smirking by the station counter.

Belle Burkhard was pronounced dead at 4.25 a.m. Two aides were tasked to clean up the body. Cathy Wood was selected, and despite her protests she was ordered to do the job.

THE TAG TEAM OF KILLING

The lives and crimes committed by Wood and Graham are all too complex to detail within the confines of this book on female serial killers. However, what we can see here is that there are two killers working as a 'Tag Team', with Wood being the controlling influence over Graham. I doubt very much that Gwen had ever harboured homicidal thoughts until she fell in with Wood, and I'd go further to say that this would have been the last thing on her mind.

Having looked in depth into Gwen's psychopathology and while not mitigating anything she has done, there is again no doubt to my way of thinking that she was happy to please Wood. Although not exactly a professional opinion dressed up in fancy words and phrases, my conclusion about Wood is that she is a homicidal freak of nature without a conscience who has never exhibited any remorse for her awful deeds at all. God help us if this woman should ever be released back into society, for we would all be the worse for it.

The victimology in this case of serial murder will be of interest to the reader too. We can never know how many innocent babies, young children or the elderly and vulnerable have been one-off murdered by nurses and nursing aides working alone, but we can draw some insight from the numbers killed by female serial killers, although what follows can be said as incomplete.

Victims of health-providers-turned-serial-killers are often the most defenseless, including infants, people with developmental delays and adults with dementia, said Beatrice Crofts Yorker, co-author of a 2006 study on doctors, nurses and nurses' aides who kill. And once these caregivers realise how easy it is, 'They sort of get emboldened.'

The study, published in the *Journal of Forensic Sciences*, found ninety worldwide prosecutions of health providers for serial murders since 1970. Fully 86 per cent of them were nurses. Of the fifty-four who were convicted at the time the study was published, all but three were charged for killings in Europe and the U.S. The convicted were found guilty of killing 317 patients and suspected in the deaths of 2,113 others.

Most killings occurred in hospitals; thirteen of the convicted murdered in nursing homes. Injections of non-narcotic medications, including insulin, were the preferred methods.

'The attractive thing about insulin is that it can take a long time to kill someone,' Yorker said in an interview. 'Insulin has a lot of variability. You can be completely done with your shift, gone home, not even on the unit when a patient dies.'

More Carers Who Kill

Having now looked at the burking technique carried out by Wood and Graham, of specific interest will be the method uniquely designed by Vienna nurses Maria Gruber, Irene Leidolf, Stephanija Maya and Waltraud Wagner – almost 'burking by water', if you will. Dubbed 'The Angels of Death', between 1983 and 1989 they murdered forty-nine patients at the Geriatriezentrum Am Wienerwald, in Lainz, by using morphine overdoses or by forcing water into their patients' lungs, causing pulmonary oedema.

In much the same way as Wood and Graham killed, they would hold the victim's head and pinch the nose while another accomplice would pour water into their mouths until they drowned in their bed. Although the patients were feeble but few terminally ill, the motive behind the murders remains unknown. Indeed, this method of killing, much like burking, is almost impossible to prove since elderly patients often have fluid in their lungs. In fact, the murders might have continued had a doctor not overheard a boastful comment, after which the four nurses were arrested.

At the time of writing I have just finished filming a for a TV documentary called *Voice of a Serial Killer* now broadcast by CBS Reality. One of the programmes concerns Canadian Registered Nurse, Elizabeth Mae Wettlaufer, who, between 2007 and 2016 murdered eight elderly patients using morphine, and attempted to kill another six in Southwestern Ontario before she handed herself in to police, making a full confession, showing little remorse if any at all.

Attractive young Czechoslovak neonatal nurse, Marie Fiká ková, was hanged on 13 April 1961 at Pankrac prison for the brutal killings of ten babies. She cracked open their skulls, broke their hands and caused such pain on these newborn that their suffering cannot be imaged. Suspicions had been raised about her involvement, however no responsible physician or administrator was charged, demoted, or even reprimanded, and the entire business was kept secret from the public for decades. Her only mitigation was that she suffered from depression during her menstrual cycles and had killed the babies because they were crying.

Dagmar Johanne Amalie Overby was a Danish professional child carer who murdered between nine and twenty-five children between 1913 and 1920. Quite how she went undetected for some seven years is beyond my comprehension because she strangled or drowned the kiddies, or burned them alive in a hot water heater, to cremate the remains, then buried or hid them in the loft of her house. She was sentenced to death on 3 March 1921. Her sentenced was commuted to life and she died in prison aged forty-two.

So far, we have looked at the number of deaths caused by

CHRISTOPHER BERRY-DEE

Wood, Graham, Wettlaufer, Fikácková, Overby, and the four 'Angels of Death'. Here are nine serial killers in total with an approximate body count of eighty-three; not an insubstantial number you may think. However, we have not even started quite yet as we move on to Aino Nykopp-Koski.

A Finnish nurses' aide, who worked in hospitals, care homes and her patients' homes, Nykopp-Koski killed five people between the ages of seventy-one and ninety-one years, using sedatives and opiates. But the killings were just the high point of her richly-embroidered criminal CV: five attempted murders, three aggravated assaults, four counts of theft, and two counts of drug possession, the latter seems hardly worth a mention. Her mitigation, being subject to an anti personality disorder, didn't wash with the court, even less so her 'Not Guilty' plea, arguing that her patients had overdosed themselves.

Serial murder certainly went to the head of German child carer Elizabeth Wiese, aka 'The Angel Maker of St Paul', and she lost her head when she was guillotined, in Hamburg, on 2 February 1905. Born 1 July 1853, she was an illegal abortionist who served time in prison, and she later murdered at least five children using morphine and other toxic substances, then burned the bodies in her household stove. Marianne Nolle, another German serial killer, ended up serving a life sentence for the murders of seven children in her care between 1984 and 1992. Born in 1938, she is suspected of a further eighteen attempted killings. Nolle used large doses of the antipsychotic drug Chlorprothixene (Truxal) to cause death.

Born in Mexico in 1890, like Elizabeth Wiese, Felícitas Sánchez Aguillón aka Sánchez Neyra also had a criminal history for carrying out illegal abortions before she took up work as a nurse, midwife and baby farmer (that is a person who takes unwanted children from their parents' hands and sells them on – another form of child-trafficking, if you will). Those she couldn't sell them she either poisoned or strangled, dismembered the bodies and burned them in a stove at her home in Salamanca Street, Colonia Roma, Mexico City, or else threw them in a sewer. On 16 June 1941, the 'Human Crusher of Little Angels' also dubbed by the media 'The Ogress of Colonia Roma' and 'The Female Ripper of Colonia Roma', committed suicide while awaiting trial.

Pausing to take a breath for a moment, it is worth remembering that this section of the book is solely concerned with female serial killers (not one-off killers) whose motives, for whatever reasons, murder only the vulnerable such as the elderly, young kiddies, even babies placed into their care. And, this is why I chose Wood and Graham as the prime example. And, yet another issue is starting to emerge as I write because it appears that very few male serial killers charged with nursing the elderly or caring for little children commit the same sort of crimes. Solely in this respect, it appears that women are certainly more deadly than the male, with, perhaps this exception being Norwegian nursing home manager, Arnfinn Nesset. Born on 25 October 1936, he killed twenty-two residents at the Orkdal Alders- og Sjukheim Institution before he was arrested in 1983. Considering the enormity of his crimes one might have expected that the authorities would have locked him up and thrown the key away. Fat chance of that in Norway it seems to me. Sentenced to twenty-one years, Arnfinn served a mere twelve years and eleven months behind bars before being paroled. He is now living somewhere under an assumed name – perhaps right next door to *you!*

Born on 9 September 1839, Maria Catherina Swanenburg was a Dutch serial killer whose many crimes also fit in with this chapter's victimology, although it would be fair to say that almost anybody was fair game to her. The record states that she certainly put twenty-seven people into their graves but was suspected of murdering almost one hundred. Ironically, her nickname was 'Goeie Mie' also spelt as 'Goede Mie', which translates as 'Good Mee', which she certainly wasn't! 'Good Mee' earned the name for the most 'charitable work' that she did, which was caring for the elderly and sick and little children in the poor neighbourhood of Leiden. Arsenic was her choice of poison. Her motive was often that of cashing in on a victim's life insurance or inheritance, and she was a very busy bee. All of her murders and attempted murders were carried out over a period of just three years – between 1880 and 1883. She died in prison in 1915, aged seventy-six.

But why did she use arsenic?

As we have seen, poisoning has traditionally been the preserve of women. Some statistics have revealed that housewives, housekeepers, nurses or domestic servants have committed over 60 per cent of poisonings in the USA. The piece Dan Keating published for *The Washington Post*, 7 May 2105, makes for a fascinating read on the types of weapons women use to kill, however, in the kitchen or in the sickroom, women had and still have the opportunity to use their favourite murder weapon – poison. This may seem obvious when you consider the physical differences between the sexes because as a form of murder, poisoning requires the least strength.

The 'trick' to this method of slow poisoning is to introduce small amounts of poison over a period of time. As the toxic substance accumulates in the body it provides symptoms that will make you wish you had never been born while these very same symptoms could, in earlier times, be easily mistaken for the onset of a natural disease. If luck was with the killer, the crime often went unsolved.

In England, the Victorian times were the golden age of poisoners; the most *popular* 'slow poisons' were metals such as antimony and arsenic. Both produce symptoms akin to gastroenteritis. Moreover, arsenic and antimony have the effect of worsening any existing disease, thereby making its presence even more difficult to pin down. Thallium and 'delayed action' poisons such as phosphorous have also been used, however the application of poisons is limited only by the ingenuity of the murderer. For example, in 1855 a wealthy Yorkshire woman died of repeated arsenic enemas delivered via an enamel pot and rubber tube by an 'unknown hand' and, it is at this point, I would advise the reader that what follows may sound a bit unsavoury.

The sound nineteenth century advice to mothers and governesses regarding the administering of enemas was that women should be trained to have one or two bowel movements a day. This was not an unusual practice and most members of the family had at least one enema weekly; it was a conventional health practice, but can you imagine being subjected to colonic irrigation every seven days let alone twice a day – morning and evening? No way, Jose! And it also eliminated complications that arose from doing a 'Number 2' while wearing a corset and an elaborate set of undies, especially before toilet paper was invented, although I am led to believe that the better off used sponges.

There's another reason why many Victorian women considered enemas a 'good' habit. There were few public facilities. There were no toilets on trains or stagecoaches. Such facilities as there were, were pretty awful – filthy outhouses, mainly. They were cold in winter and stank to high heaven in summer. And sitting on a dirty, partially full public chamber pot in a theatre's restroom for instance, was not a prospect women relished.

But I have digressed. Returning to the 'unknown hand' that poisoned the wealthy Yorkshire woman, I am sure that Sherlock Holmes could have figured out that the person who gave the woman her enemas was not the husband, butler, a footman nor the gardener. It had to be someone intimately trusted with the tampering of her employer's bottom, who would, therefore, be very much closer to hand.

Casting aside motive for a page or so before we enter the mind of other female serial killers, the preponderance of female poisoners was probably due more to social conventions. Until recently, for example, a woman's place was in the kitchen – ideal for a would-be poisoner. One cook who used her position to its fullest advantage was mass-murderer and serial killer Hélène Jégado, who was guillotined in 1852 for poisoning twenty-three diners at one sitting and is believed to have murdered many more.

The sickroom also provided opportunities to kill by poisoning, and it is another place where women have always been active. The sickroom is a poisoner's paradise, never more so than in Victorian times when the mixing of medicines – many of which contained toxic substances – was conducted in the home rather than by the chemist; the apothecary's shop was a place where poisons, to include arsenic and strychnine, were freely available over the counter and not kept in a separate, locked cabinet. Laws governing the sale of poisons would not emerge for almost a decade, in 1868.

The use of cosmetics provided another link between women and poisons. Preparations containing poisons such as belladonna (for the eyes) and arsenic (for the complexion) were common during the early nineteenth century. Even after 1851, when all arsenic sold over the counter had to be coloured with either soot or indigo, that did not prevent Glaswegian socialite and actress Madeleine Hamilton Smith (1835-1928) from claiming, in 1857, that she had bought the substance for a cosmetic purpose rather than for killing her French lover, one Pierre Emile L'Angelier, an apprentice nurseryman who originally came from the Channel Islands. The post-mortem found approximately eighty-eight grains of arsenic in the stomach of the victim, a hitherto unheard of amount, whilst L'Angelier's diary alluded to him feeling ill after being served coffee by Smith, and I bet he did. Smith was found not guilty.

Second only to the butler, the role of housekeeper presented many poisoning possibilities because she supervised the purchase of food and everyday necessities – wait for it…weedkiller and strychnine-based rat poison, the latter being broadly used as a form of pest control in the larger cities. Never mind what strychnine does to *Rattus norvegicus*, it certainly doesn't go down well with humans. It causes frothing at the mouth and muscle spasms, which increase in intensity until the victim dies from asphyxiation due to paralysis of the neural pathways.

And if so inclined, the housekeeper could easily get her hands on cyanide. It was everywhere, in everything from paints to daguerreotypes (photographic processes) to wallpaper. If you were administered cyanide you certainly knew about it for its effects are unmistakable. Starting off with nausea, followed rapidly by convulsions, chest pains to cardiac arrest and death often in seconds, hydrogen/potassium/sodium cyanide is a means of killing people used in gas chamber executions in the USA. And the effects are certainly recognisable to those who are strapped into a gas chamber chair, for the gas is visible to the condemned who are advised to take several deep breaths to speed unconsciousness. Nonetheless, there are often convulsions and excessive drooling. There may also be urinating, defecating and vomiting for up to eight minutes if one is really unlucky.

Therefore, when a Victorian housekeeper's duties were combined with those of being a companion – often to someone mentally and physically incapacitated – the temptation to kill was increased, for the marriage laws had themselves given women a strong incentive/motive to murder.

Previously, a husband owned his wife's property outright. Only his death could give her some measure of financial freedom. The opprobrium attached to divorce acted as a powerful stimulant. Whereas a man was able to remarry regardless, a woman in these unenlightened times was labelled 'used goods'. Poison provided a convenient route towards a spotless character – the motive being one of 'preserving madam's reputation'.

Despite the popularity of cyanide and strychnine, arsenic was easily the most popular poison in the Victorian era and it was comparatively difficult to detect. It is a tasteless odourless compound, its effects easily written off as food poisoning, making any suspicion of foul play harder to trace. Indeed, so popular was its *popularity* amongst Victorian female killers it led to the Arsenic Act of 1851 (14 & 15 Vict c. 13), which enforced tighter restrictions on its sale and required most arsenic to be coloured indigo to make it harder to disguise.

As I have already mentioned, I love visiting The Russian Federation, I truly do and, during my travels in Russia I have visited many male and female 'correctional facilities' with my jaw always dropping to the floor when I discover the leniency offered to women who commit the most dreadful crimes. Here is a case in point and this takes some swallowing. Trust me on this one, please.

At the time of writing, aged forty-five, and dubbed by the media as 'Satan in a Skirt', Irina Viktorovna Gaidamachuk is serving a mere twenty years in prison for bludgeoning to death seventeen elderly people aged between sixty-one and eighty-nine. You don't need a calculator to work out that she is serving just over one year's imprisonment for every life she took in her hometown of Krasnoufimsk, Sverdlovsk Oblast (province or region) and as far afield as Yekaterinburg, Serov, Achit and Druzhinino. Her murders were committed between 2002 and 2010. She posed as a social worker to gain entry into the homes of her gullible victims, beat them to death using an axe or a hammer, and stole whatever she could find to support her alcoholism. On a good killing day she would net £1,000, on a bad killing day just £20.00, if as much as that. Irina was arrested and charged with attempted murder in June 2012, and thereafter charged with seventeen homicides, and has never exhibited any signs of remorse. Knowing the Russian penal system as well as I do, my guess is that she'll be released on parole as early as 2020.

Much has been written about, even more so heatedly debated about, the culpability of Spanish serial killer, Enriqueta Martí I Rippollés. Born in 1886, she died on 12 May 1913, and was suspected of being a witch amongst other things, and most certainly the human remains of some young children were found in her home following her arrest. However, for the purposes of this chapter, hearsay doesn't come into it so it is best if I leave it at that.

Finally we turn to the United Kingdom and Beverly Gail Allitt. Born on 4 October 1968, dubbed 'The Angel of Death', here we find a State Enrolled Paediatric Nurse who killed four babies in her care using insulin. She attempted to murder another nine babies and was sentenced to serve a life term in 1991. Quite what her true motive was may never be known, however she did claim she suffered from the factitious disorder known as Munchausen Syndrome by Proxy (MBPS).

MBPS is an interesting line of mitigation; although not an unusual one amongst parents or caregivers. It is where the sufferer, or alleged sufferer, causes or fabricates symptoms in a child with the adult deliberately misleading others, particularly medical professionals, and they may go as far as to actually cause symptoms in the child through poisoning, medication, or even suffocation. With this being said, in most cases, at least 85 per cent of them, the mother is responsible for causing the illness and symptoms in the first instance.

In Allitt's case, this appeared to be a craving for attention and gaining sympathy from doctors, nurses and her fellow colleagues. Some experts believe that it is not just the attention that is gained from the 'illness' of the child that drives this behaviour, but also the satisfaction gained in *deceiving individuals whom they consider to be more important, and professionally better qualified than themselves.*

I have used the italics above to make another observation, specifically with regard to Cathy Wood and Gwen Graham. For isn't it clear that the deceiving of individuals whom these two caregivers considered to be more important, professionally better qualified than themselves, is writ large throughout their killing time? Indeed, if we drilled down into some of the other case histories listed in this chapter, might we not see a similar motive behind the cunning manipulations of these murderers of children and babies? I think we might. In other words, these types of female killers also get a kick out of pulling the wool over the eyes of colleagues better qualified as medical professionals than they, themselves, will ever be. Nevertheless, because the likes of Wood, Graham and Allitt appeared to be so caring and attentive, no one suspected them of homicidal wrongdoing, for it goes beyond belief that the caregiver would deliberately hurt a vulnerable person of any age in their care – indeed making the crime all the more despicable.

Presently, Allitt is held at the Rampton Secure Hospital in Nottinghamshire. If she is deemed to be posing no further risk to the public, she could be released in 2022, by which time she will be aged fifty-four.

It would be remiss of me to leave out two other British female serial killers, as historic as they are to us today. I refer, of course, to Amelia Dyer and Margaret Waters. As the former stated: 'You'll know all mine [victims] by the tape around their necks.'

Born in 1837, Amelia Elizabeth Dyer, aka 'The Reading

Baby Farmer', was a one-time member of the Salvation Army and a fifty-seven-year-old serial killer who took children into her home in Bristol. In 1895, she moved to Reading, and as my former co-writer, world-renowned crime historian and true crime author Robin Odell says in his bestselling *The Murderers' Who's Who* (first published in hardback by George Harrap 1979): '...she had been baby farming for 15 years... the total kills amounted to seven.' Maybe yes, maybe not, however her motive for killing is again of interest to us because here, again, we find another trained nurse, a caregiver, whom, as some accounts claim without solid evidence, murdered 400 children or thereabouts – her motive being financial gain.

While in Reading she advertised that she would board and adopt children – for a fee of course. Some of these kiddies were then sold on to couples who could not have a child of their own with the remainder being strangled to death, wrapped in parcels and then dumped in canals or other water-driven locations.

In the March of 1895, a bargeman on the Thames fished out of the water a child's corpse with a tape around its neck, wrapped in a parcel bearing a Reading address – Amelia Dyer's address, no less. But Dyer, who used several aliases, had already moved to another house in Reading. Meanwhile, two more dead infants were found in the river.

Dyer was arrested in April 1896. She tried to commit suicide. By the end of the month bodies of seven children had been found; all had been strangled to death with tape and wrapped in paper parcels.

During Amelia Dyer's May 1896 trial her defence intended to prove that she was insane. It was never established how many babies she actually killed, but as she had admitted to baby farming for fifteen years it was likely that the total was more than the seven known victims, although the 400 mark appears a little over-the-top, it seems to me.

There can be no doubt as to Dyer's motive being one of greed in accumulating fictitious boarding fees for infants in her care and whom she soon disposed of. She was hanged on 10 June 1896 at Newgate. It is said that her phantom haunted the Chief Warder until the end of his days. This is yet another spooky story to be proven, but no ghostly manifestations can be applied after the 11 October 1870 hanging of Margaret Waters by executioner William Calcraft at London's Horsemonger Lane Gaol. Born in 1835, Waters lived in Brixton all of her life; again, like Dyer, she was a baby farmer who drugged and starved to death at least nineteen children, only to meet her own Maker at the premature age of thirty-five.

Analysing the Motives
of Female Killers

So where are we now, and what conclusions can we try to come to when studying female serial killers who murder the most vulnerable in society and whom are placed into their care? For maybe Mr Rudyard Kipling – who was not in any way associated with baking cakes – is correct in this regard: that the female [of this particular homicidal species] is more deadly than the male, although I might sit on the fence here.

Looking into 'motive', which may be described as the mental mainspring of the crime, it is not to be confused with the intentions with which the offence was committed. Quoting Christmas Humphreys MA, LL B (Cantab) of the Inner Temple, Barrister-at-Law, later Commissioner at the Old Bailey then Additional Judge:

'A man's motive may be good but his intention bad. A loaf is stolen. The intention was to steal and the act therefore criminal, although the motive, to save a starving child, was good.' (Christmas Humphreys, in the book *Seven Murderers*, William Heinemann Ltd, 1931.)

Of course, in this book we are not talking about pinching a loaf of Hovis. We are discussing the stealing of human lives. However, generally speaking criminal *motive* and *intention* are so entwined that it is difficult to separate them, but I can, on good authority, describe the commonest forms of motive as: (1) the desire to avenge some real or fancied wrong; (2) of getting rid of a rival or obnoxious connection; (3) of escaping from the pressure of pecuniary or other obligation; (4) of obtaining plunder or other coveted objects; (5) of preserving reputation, or (6) of gratifying some other selfish or malignant passion.

The aforementioned 'good authority' dates back to 1991/92 while I was writing *Ladykiller* concerning the emerging, if not an already fully emerged British serial killer, John David Guise Cannan. While debating Cannan's motive with the late Lord Chief Justice of England Lord Lane, it was agreed without any hesitation that Mr Cannan's motive for committing his offences amounted to nearly a full deck of cards as in (1) through (6) above, with (6) being particularly significant regardless of any sex serial killer atypical motivation. In other words he was wholly consumed with a selfish malignant need to abduct women, rape them and kill them. Indeed, as Christmas Humphreys had concisely summed it up six decades earlier, although being somewhat non-PC today as: 'Money, Hatred, and Women'.

For my part I will add – *and* 'Men'!

Indeed, in all of my dealings with over thirty male, female and somewhat confused sexual gender serial murderers I *thought* that I had found that same pack of motivational cards in all of them, now somewhat belatedly with the exception of the women who kill again and again. This was the 'light bulb' moment that had nocturnally occurred to me and that I referred to in the Introduction of this book and this is why I politely asked you to please read the Introduction in the first instance.

THE DESIRE OF AVENGING SOME REAL
OR FANCIED WRONG

This can be interpreted in so many ways. On a deeply personal level a jealous man may take revenge on a rival and beat him up, or kill him/her. He may make the rival's life a misery by sending malicious emails or posting scandalous lies on the Internet but often this is not the case, for his partner is a totally faithful woman or man. The same applies to women who, when spurned or cheated on, have a habit of slashing up their unfaithful partner's suits or ruining his new Porsche with paint remover. In extreme instances women kill their partners out of sheer spite. Hey, who can blame them if the guy is an out-and-out rat? You will recall that model and nightclub hostess, Ruth Ellis was the last woman to be hanged in the UK for murder on 13 July 1955. At her wit's end, she shot to death her cheating lover, David Blakely, outside the Magdala pub in Hampstead, London, on Easter Sunday, 10 April 1955.

OF GETTING RID OF A RIVAL OR
OBNOXIOUS CONNECTION

Which rather implies the killing of a person or persons as in: 'rubbing out'; 'feeding the fishes'; 'hit' or 'whack'; 'pop' and 'ice' being common Mafia terminology. So getting rid of a rival or obnoxious connection is very easily entwined with the desire of avenging some real or fancied wrong, and getting rid of someone by poisoning or having someone killed by other means is a trait one finds in some female serial killers.

OF ESCAPING FROM THE PRESSURE OF PECUNIARY OR OTHER OBLIGATION

Again, this can be interpreted in many ways. In my experience it applies to anyone who, through any type of criminal act will financially benefit. But as far as murderous women are concerned this motive is usually –with a few exceptions – confined to the single murder of a spouse or long-time partner and profiting from the decedent's life insurance policy, or some other financial legacy.

OF OBTAINING PLUNDER OR OTHER COVETED OBJECTS

This appears almost non-existent as a motive amongst women killers, least of all any type of serial murderer, unless one can draw a parallel between plundering (as in the stealing of items such as valuables from a church) and the stealing, the plundering of human lives, which all serial killers do.

OF PRESERVING REPUTATION

Which is another motive sometimes absent in the crimes committed by female serial killers, so we may rule this out altogether.

CHRISTOPHER BERRY-DEE

OF GRATIFYING SOME OTHER SELFISH OR MALIGNANT PASSION

This is where things, as far as serial killer motives are concerned, start to become interesting. Male serial murderers gratify their overwhelming selfish, sexually driven malevolent cravings, for no other reason other than to cause as much pain and suffering to their victims as they can until it becomes like a drug to them. They can only satisfy these deadly hunger pains by killing three times or more over a period of weeks, months, even years with cooling off periods between the 'events' as the murders are labelled in criminal psychology lingo.

With women, however, with the exception of a few very rare cases, this sexual motive is absent. By this I mean rarely does the female serial killer become sexually aroused during the act of committing murder – which men most certainly do! Even the notorious Joanna Dennehy, who stabbed three men to death and attempted to kill two more in the UK in 2013, didn't commit murder for any other motive except to satisfy her malignant passion – a love of blood! She gained no sexual arousal from her killings. As she explained to me during a prison visit she killed because she wanted to.

Other female serial killers satisfy their malignant passions, which may include a secondary motive – for instance an overwhelming need for money (greed), or by killing children or babies for some other deep-seated perverse reason, while other murderesses commit serial homicide for the most intensely bizarre reasons imaginable – step forward Cathy Wood and Gwendoline Graham!

What I can assure the reader is that some women employed

in the medical professions make the decision to burk, strangle, torture, drown, suffocate, poison, batter to death…cleave to death using axes, burn alive little children and babies and kill, without any remorse, those most vulnerable in our society to include the elderly. Even as I write this book, not a month goes by when we do not hear of physical and psychological abuse being roughly handed out to the elderly by spiteful staff in nursing homes around the world. The lot of them should hang their heads in shame.

Joanna Christine Dennehy –
A Love of Blood

Method of killing: stabbing
Knife wounds are classified either as *incised wounds*, where the edge of the blade makes cutting gashes to the body, often during a struggle and frequently on the hands and arms of a victim trying to protect him/herself (defensive wounds); or *stab wounds*, where the point of the blade goes into the body followed by the length of the blade. Joanna Dennehy used a three-inch lock knife.
Her murdered victims were
Lukasz Slaboszewski (thirty-one), John Chapman (fifty-six) and Kevin Lee (forty-eight).

In a letter to me, dated 24 February 2014, Joanna Dennehy stated: 'Christopher, it is no secret that I do not regret my actions but I have refused to give motive or make excuses [for the crimes]. I have maintained my guilt throughout.' In another letter (8 June 2014) she went on to say: 'The lies being told about me, about things I'm meant to have said and done are too numerous for me to care about…now you are really getting my back up.'

As a result of this correspondence, DCI Martin Brunning, from the Bedfordshire, Cambridgeshire and Hertfordshire Major Crime Unit, sent me an email, judging that: 'Christopher, you are certainly pushing her [Dennehy's] buttons.'

If there ever was a homicidal maniac, it has to be Joanna Christine Dennehy, for here is a woman, a petite, well-educated young English woman who committed crimes of such depravity that they leap beyond the scale of human understanding. Indeed, I will go further by adding that I have interviewed over thirty of the most evil serial killers of both sexes, and a whole bunch of females who murdered just the once, but none of them comes close to the evil entity that makes up 'Jo'.

If you are a man, or a woman, there must surely be few scenarios more terrifying to imagine than to find yourself alone with a person who is gentle and sweet one moment and then turns into a knife-wielding blood-crazed psychopath within a heartbeat. You are in a place with nowhere to run to or hide as this evil monster advances towards you and is oblivious to your pleas for help. This is Stephen King nightmare stuff come true and for three men there was no merciful awakening in the comfort of their own beds. The panic, the pain and numbing fear that gripped these men were the starkest of reality. This Dennehy woman with her glinting knife, they too were real, and there was to be no escape, and the only good thing to emerge from the trial and conviction of Dennehy is that she is now serving a full life sentence and will never be released – well she *will be* eventually let out of prison: in a pine box to be cremated and her ashes scattered God knows where. If she is placed in a grave, there will be many who will want to dig her up and drive wooden stakes through her heart to make sure she really is dead, then bury her again.

There, you can see I don't like this serial killer one bit, and the enormity of her crimes almost puts Rosemary West in the shade because most female serial killers work as part of a tag team – in pairs, threes or fours. Where Dennehy stands head and shoulders above the rest – to include the American serial murderer, Aileen Wuornos, who used a revolver – is because on her own she used a knife: a three-inch lock-knife up close and very personal, to stab and stab and stab again and again. She didn't just kill; she went into frenzied overkill by default, such was her hatred for men. Then she licked the still warm blood from the blade.

'In Great Britain, the majority of its 600 or so homicides every year are committed with knives – victims dying of stab wounds or complications arising from stabs to the body,' writes Brian Lane in his *The Encyclopedia of Forensic Science* (published by Headline in 1992), and these statistics have hardly changed since that book was written.

The Office of National Statistics (ONS) published its 2016 summary with 571 recorded England and Wales homicides (murder, manslaughter and infanticide) ending in March of that year. Women were far more likely than men to be killed by partners or former partners (44 per cent of female victims compared with 7 per cent of male victims) and men were more likely to be killed by friends or acquaintances (35 per cent of male victims compared with 13 per cent of female victims). Well before Victorian times the most common method of killing has always been, and continues to be, by knife, with 213 victims killed in this way throughout 2015/16, accounting for over one in three (37 per cent) of homicides.

The FBI's most recent survey for US homicides for approximately the same period also shows a similar pattern with an ever-changing total of 11,961 known homicides of which just 248 were committed using rifles of any type, including small arms, single-shot long arms and assault rifles. In comparison, 1,567 murders were committed using knives, which rather flies in the face of the myth that most murders carried out in the US are by firearm – although I am sure there will be readers who might disagree.

By their very nature, knives are full 'contact' weapons, and to 'stick' someone the victim and assailant have to be within touching distance and it is almost impossible for the attacker to escape being soiled with the victim's blood, as was so with Dennehy. While incised wounds tend to generate a great deal of blood, there will be little external haemorrhaging from stab wounds, the danger in this being damage to the internal organs, causing internal bleeding from which death will result. With one of her victims, Dennehy plunged her knife in some thirty-five times.

As my close friend Claire Harris said to me in 2016: 'Joanna Dennehy despises weakness but she is completely addicted to weakness and the experiencing of her own power over men.'

Joanna Dennehy has always pointblank refused to reveal her motive for stabbing to death three men and attempting to kill more males – perhaps she does not even understand why she committed serial homicide in the first instance, but I believe Claire Harris is correct. Having spent several years studying this evil young killer and having interviewed her in prison, I can only conclude that she hated all men with a blood-soaked passion.

Born on Sunday 29 August 1982, in St Albans, Hertfordshire, to Kevin and Kathleen Dennehy, she was the elder sister of Maria, a young girl who went on to enjoy an excellent career while Jo turned to petty crime, drugs, alcoholism and murder most foul. And, up until the age of fourteen, Joanna excelled at school, enjoyed playing music on a flute and recorder and participating in sports. Indeed, DCI Martin Brunning told me, she was hot-wired to enter the legal profession in her late teens. She was bubbly, articulate, and as bright as a guardsman's button. Without doubt, Jo enjoyed all the benefits of a middle-class upbringing, of this there can be no doubt. But then the wheels started to fall off her train.

Sometime in her fourteenth year, Joanna started to turn rotten. She fell in with a group of itinerate fairground workers, started drinking and was introduced to drugs including 'skunk' – although she denies all of this, such is her twisted psychopathology, saying to me: 'It's all lies. I never took drugs and I drank very little.' In fact, Joanna was drinking, even hard liquor, at school. She because a nuisance to her teachers, disrupted classes and upset fellow pupils, and she became equally disruptive at home to the degree that her parents could no longer control her. She ran away from home, following an eighteen year-old fairground worker to Milton Keynes before she was located and brought back home back, protesting all of the way.

She absconded again. Aged fifteen, she fell in with twenty-one-year-old unemployed John Treanor. They eloped to the seediest part of Luton where the couple took up lodgings in a rundown area used by drug dealers. 'It was a bad situation,' says Treanor. 'We had no money so we turned to shoplifting to get food.' Then Dennehy fell pregnant and they fell upon the State to bail them out. Allocated a council flat in Milton Keynes and receiving benefits, it became obvious to Treanor that Joanna didn't want the baby – a girl born in 1999. In fact she didn't even want to touch her child, preferring to hit the bottle every day and sleep with a number of other men, one of whom was an ex-con.

My book, *Love of Blood*, published by John Blake 2015, with the cooperation of the police, is the definitive work on the life and crimes committed by Joanna Dennehy, so for a complete account of her downward plunge into serial homicide, it will, I am sure, keep you on the edge of your seat and give you nightmares for some time to come. Nevertheless, with Treanor at his wits end, he took the baby and fled to live with his mother, who was then living in Wisbech, Cambridgeshire.

Now alone, and being used as a sex object by men as they so chose, she started to commit more petty crimes, to include dishonesty, shoplifting, openly carrying a razor blade in public and then she was sectioned under the Mental Health Act for a violent assault on a man. She was diagnosed as having a psychotic disorder and found to be 'emotional, unstable and prone to unpredictable behavioural explosions.' In simple terms Dennehy was now a ticking time bomb – one primed to explode at the drop of a hat.

Dennehy vanished off Treanor's radar for about eighteen

months when the penny finally dropped. She contacted him and pledged her forgiveness; literally begging him to return which he did, to then get the obvious – because a leopard never changes its spots. She fell pregnant again, then exhibited zero love towards either of her little children so Treanor left her again accompanied by not one, but two babies. She would never see him or the children again.

Dennehy surfaced again in late February 2013, turning up at Quicklet Ltd, a property letting company based in Peterborough. She was in the company of a giant of a man called Gary Stretch – a recidivist, an ex-con and a not very accomplished burglar. Standing seven-foot three inches tall and weighing in at a pot-bellied twenty-three stone, Stretch was about as bright as a 5-watt light bulb and besotted with Joanna. Dennehy explained to the proprietor, Kevin Lee, that she was looking for somewhere to rent following a lengthy prison term for killing her father, who'd sexually abused her as a child. None of this was true, as witnessed by none other than Mr Dennehy, who still saw himself in the mirror each morning while having a shave.

Kevin Lee was a successful businessman, although it would be fair to say not averse to a few dishonest dealings here and there. He was married to a beautiful wife, Christina, and had two loving children. Christina doted on him. However, without any doubt 'Flash Kev' had a roaming eye with at least one of them always on pretty girls. With a little 'slap' (make-up) on and her hair all washed shiny clean, and with her slim body, seductive Jo instantly caught his attention. He offered her a place at nearby Rolleston Garth – No. 11 Rolleston Garth, Peterborough, to be precise. For little to no rent she would live there, help redecorate the place and Stretch would join her – with Kevin now enjoying the best of four worlds: a lovely wife and children, a profitable business, a couple to help decorate one of his properties and a quick fuck on the side. Within a very short while all these four worlds would come to a terminal end.

LUKASZ SLABOSZEWSKI

The day before his murder, Lukasz Slaboszewski said to a friend, 'Life is beautiful.'

In a much abridged account of thirty-one-year-old Lukasz's tragic story we know that in 2015 he had moved to the UK from Nowa Slupia, a town on the Oder River in western Poland. He was presently employed in a DHL warehouse and, up until the time of his death he was living at 695 Lincoln Road, Peterborough. He was a happy-go-lucky man who enjoyed cards and music; he was, nevertheless, trying to kick a cocaine habit and had been prescribed methadone as substitute to cure his addiction.

On Monday, 18 March 2013, police established that Lukasz bumped into Dennehy at Peterborough's Queensgate shopping mall. Other than this we know nothing more, but it is safe to assume that she won him over, for that evening he phoned a friend explaining that he had met a very flirty young woman and that 'life was beautiful'. The hazel-eyed chap was last seen leaving his home the following day. He had a date with Dennehy. Unfortunately he also had a date with The Grim Reaper, for the moment he stepped through the door and into the kitchen at 11 Rolleston Garth, Dennehy went at him with her knife in an attack that can only be described as 'frenzied'. The blood splatter patterns found at the crime scene showed that he never stood a chance.

Although police could never establish that Stretch was in the property at the time of this murder, later research by me during a forensic study of correspondence between Stretch and Dennehy after their convictions proves that he was in the house at the time of the murder. He certainly helped Joanna to place the body into a green wheelie bin, where it stayed for a number of days before the corpse was dumped into a remote dyke near the village of Thorney. Police recovered the body on 3 April.

JOHN CHAPMAN

The day before this man was murdered he said to a neighbour: 'She [Dennehy] is a man-woman and she'll get me out of the house by any means. She's a madwoman.'

Almost immediately after the murder of Lukasz Slaboszewski, Dennehy telephoned Kevin Lee to explain that someone had been murdered at 11 Rolleston Garth. She needed a car to drive, in order to carry the corpse to a disposal site. Like a fool, Lee gave her the money and she purchased a green Vauxhall Astra, registration number R660 ECT. Dennehy didn't have a driving licence, so Stretch drove the car – for such a tall man his knees were almost forced up under his chin. Thereafter, he revelled in the name of 'The Undertaker'.

Aged fifty-six, John Chapman had been a Royal Navy veteran; now a widower, his only pleasure in life was fishing for carp and drinking. He became an alcoholic, had fallen on desperately hard times and was then living in a bedsit in a filthy house owned by Kevin Lee at 31 Bifield, Orton Goldhay, a suburb of Peterborough. The building was full of lice and the infestation had spread into the homes of neighbours who'd complained to Lee. Exacerbating the problem was the fact that Chapman was behind with his rent and Lee wanted him out.

Never one who was shy to break the law, rather than go through a lengthy, legal eviction process, Lee moved Dennehy into the property – it was her job, along with the formidable Stretch, to throw Chapman out, or to get rid of him by any means at their disposal.

In the early hours of Good Friday, 29 March 2013, Chapman was fast asleep in his bedsit; probably the neatest and tidiest in the house. He was dead drunk and, literally speaking, he would soon be stone dead too.

At autopsy it was determined by pathologist Dr Carey that Chapman had been stabbed five times in the chest. Two of the stabs penetrated the heart – one inflicted with sufficient force to pass through the breastbone – then Joanna Dennehy stabbed him once in the neck, severing the carotid artery. He died without a struggle, his body soon to be dumped in the dyke alongside that of Lukasz Slaboszewski.

KEVIN LEE

About an hour before his murder, Mr Lee said to his best friend, Dave Church: 'Joanna told me that she wanted to rape me while I am wearing a dress. She is like Uma Thurman from *Kill Bill* and the woman from *Terminator*.'

Christina Lee was not only beautiful, intelligent, a wonderful mother, and totally faithful to Kevin, she was also becoming suspicious of her husband and his change of nocturnal behaviour since meeting up with Joanna Dennehy. In fact, she was becoming more and more sure that Kevin was having an affair with the younger woman as each day passed. Perhaps she had aired her suspicions, we will never know, but what goes around often comes around and it would come around for Kevin Lee in the most godforsaken way. Nevertheless, like so many men drawn to Dennehy (most of them idiots and wastrels it is fair to say) Kevin Lee could not stay away from her because by now he was completely infatuated with her.

Any right-minded man would have gone straight to the police when Dennehy first told him of a man being murdered, but instead of this, as mentioned previously, he loaned her the money to buy an old car so that the body could be disposed of – in reality becoming an accessory to murder, or at the very least laying himself open to the charge of aiding and abetting a murder, all of which could carry a substantial prison term upon conviction. Then, he did something even more stupid, an act that bordered upon witless. On Good Friday, the day that Chapman was lying in a pool of congealing blood at 38 Bifield, 'Handsome Kev' sent Jo an Easter card. Later the same day she phoned him and they arranged to rendezvous at 11 Rolleston Garth, but her intentions were not focused on sex – she had a third murder in mind. And her bait? To lure him there by acceding to his fetishistic desire to dress himself up in a sexy black dress, as a prelude to the sexual intimacy he craved.

Early the following morning sixty-eight-year-old Terry Walker was living up to his name, walking his dog in the rural parish of Newborough when he spotted a body face down in a drainage dyke by the side of Middle Road. The corpse was dressed in a black sequined dress, pulled up to expose the buttocks. An 'object' had been pushed into the anus.

'This was a degrading act of post–death humiliation. The body had been posed,' DCI Martin Brunning explained to me during our interview. In fact, photos of the corpse were so unsettling they were later 'sanitised' before the trial jury could view them.

Police attention soon turned toward Dennehy and Stretch, who went on the run with them eventually turning up in the city of Hereford with another criminal called Mark Lloyd in tow. During the afternoon of Tuesday 2 April 2013, they stopped off in Green Lane, at a shop on a roundabout at Wordsworth Road and Westfaling Street. Here, along with Lloyd, Dennehy bought rolling tobacco and a bottle of whisky. Her image was captured on CCTV. She was, according to the shop assistant behind the counter, 'in high spirits, and in a state of euphoria'.

ROBIN BEREZA

During his evidence at Dennehy's trial, Robin Bereza made the following statement: 'I felt a blow to my right shoulder. I did not immediately realise that I was being attacked. I turned around and saw this lady [Dennehy]. She stared straight through me. I kicked her and made contact...'

At about the 3.35 p.m., former fire-service employee, sixty-three-year-old Robin Bereza was walking Samson, his Labrador, along Westfaling Street, a busy road lined by rows of redbrick semi-detached houses. Just as he reached a junction a car pulled up behind him. What followed he related to a stunned court:

...I kicked and made contact. It had no impact on her, Bereza told police. 'She just came straight toward me and I thought she was just going to mug me. I ran into the road. I put my hand to my jacket and saw all this blood and then it triggered and I thought, 'you just want blood'. She tried to come at me again. I kicked her again, but still she didn't react. I asked her, "What are you doing?" She said, "I'm hurting you. I'm going to fuckin' kill you."

Although Dennehy had only managed to inflict two stabs to Robin Bereza she had exacted potentially fatal injuries on him. The deep wound to his back penetrated the chest wall, causing a haemopneumothorax as well as bruising to the lung and fracturing a rib. Had expert medical treatment not promptly drained the blood and air from his chest, his life would have been endangered. The other stab shattered his shoulder blade and fractured the bone in an upper arm – the humerus. It was only by pure chance that the nerves in the arm were not irreparably damaged, that would have caused inevitable loss of function.

According top Mark Lloyd's account of the attack at Dennehy's trial: 'Dennehy struck Robin Bereza like in the film *Psycho*, thrusting and putting her weight behind it. The blade of the knife was black as the handle with blood. She stank of blood. Afterwards, Gary drove off very, very calmly. It was if they had just stopped for a McDonalds.'

Despite his wounds Robin staggered home and dialled 999. At 3.42 p.m. police took a call from Midlands ambulance control saying that a man had been repeatedly stabbed in Westfaling Street. Robin was initially taken to Hereford

County Hospital before being 'Life Flighted' to the Queen Elizabeth Hospital, in Birmingham.

Immediately after the attempted murder of Robin Bereza, Dennehy said to Stretch: 'You've had your fun, now I want mine. I don't want to kill a woman, especially not one with a child. Find me another man with a dog.'

JOHN ROGERS

This unfortunate man said to the police, 'This is where I am going to die.'

The time was about 3.45 p.m., around nine minutes after Dennehy had attacked Robin Bereza when fifty-six-year-old John Rogers was walking his grey lurcher dog called Archie along a footpath close to the River Wye, and between Golden Post and Belmont Estate, Hunderton, Hereford.

Giving his evidence at the joint trial of Dennehy and Stretch in 2013, a gaunt-looking Rogers told the jury:

> I felt a punch to my back. I assumed it was a friend, or a neighbour just messing around. I turned around. I saw the woman who struck me just standing there. She started stabbing me in the chest. I asked her, 'What's this all about?' She replied, 'You're bleeding. I better do some more.'
>
> I said, 'Just leave me alone, please. Please leave me alone,' but she didn't. She didn't seem to be showing any emotion. She didn't seem to be enjoying herself. She just seemed like she was going about business.
>
> I fell to the ground but the attack continued. I was just waiting for it to stop. There was loads and loads

of blood. As I lay there, I thought, 'This is were I am going to die.'

Dennehy had stabbed John Rogers more than thirty times. There were deep wounds to his chest, abdomen and back; both lungs had collapsed. His bowel was perforated and exposed. So severe was the force of the stabbing that nine ribs were fractured. He also received defensive wounds to his hands and arms that could have caused irreparable nerve damage. Like Robin Bereza, he too was to go on to suffer grievous emotional and psychological harm. John never fully recovered from Dennehy's murderous onslaught. He passed away in November 2014.

Dennehy, Stretch and others were arrested the same day as the Hereford attacks. All those involved in some way in the murders and in the cover-ups were sentenced to terms of imprisonment ranging from natural life (Dennehy) and eighteen years (Stretch). She is presently incarcerated at HMP Bronzefield, Woodthorpe Road, Shepperton, Kent.

MAKING SENSE OF HER MURDERS

Joanna Dennehy is smug enough to believe that in withholding her reasons for committing such atrocious murders she regains some form of warped control – because this is what those without a conscience like to do– but in my opinion she let the cat out of the bag long ago, for clues as to her true motives are writ large throughout her grim life of crime.

To begin with, here we have a bisexual woman with a massive chip on her shoulder, one who patently hated men with a passion. We can see this painted in blood, lots and lots and lots of warm sticky blood from her first kill, that of Lukasz Slaboszewski, through to John Chapman, then Kevin Lee, followed in short order by the broad daylight attempted murders of Robin Bereza and John Rogers, the latter suffering more than thirty stabs (now thought to be as many as forty), as he walked his dog in Hereford.

And, let's look at the way she and Gary Stretch disposed of the bodies of Slaboszewski, Chapman and Lee. The corpses were dumped in ditches like so much garbage – in Lee's case he was wearing a black sequined dress with an object forced into his rectum for the whole world to see. We have also learned that Dennehy didn't just kill her three victims; she went into 'overkill' like Uma Thurman did in the movie *Kill Bill*.

Dennehy has made the point that she would never have hurt a woman – least of all a woman with a child. The utter incredibility of this statement is echoed by the fact that she didn't care a damn about whether her victims had any family. Lukasz had a sister and a mother. She could not have cared less about Kevin Lee's wife, Christina, or his daughter. Did she give a second's thought to whether there was a Mrs Bereza or a Mrs Rogers? I suggest that in killing these men Dennehy was hurting them and her own mother and younger sister, ruining their innocent lives into the bargain, too. As a postscript here: since being locked up in HMP Bronzefield, Dennehy has also threatened to murder a fellow lesbian inmate, who she discovered had a girlfriend on the outside. She has also been placed into segregation for months on end for threatening to kill a female guard.

As for not hurting children, what about her own two children? Why did she have them? Could it be that she had these kiddies merely to gain social security benefits and no other reason, for as soon as they were born she gave them *no* maternal love at all.

Digging a little deeper in the warped and twisted mind of this female monster, one learns of another of her lies. She has always maintained that she would never hurt a dog. I take this with a pinch of salt. It is true to say that when she first met John Treanor he was walking his dog, a German Shepherd, which he left with his mother when the couple ran away to Luton. She attempted to kill Robin Bereza and John Rogers, both of whom were walking their dogs. In fact, following the stabbing of Rogers she actually took his dog, Archie, away with her in the car. All of which illustrates an utter contempt for dog lovers and their animals, anywhere at any time.

There will be readers of this book, indeed even those within the psychiatric profession, who will argue that some form of mitigation might be found in the fact that she started using drugs and hard liquor at the tender age of fourteen years, and that this chemical onslaught affected her developing brain. This is a perfectly feasible point to make, however, millions of youngsters start using drugs and alcohol much earlier in their lives than Dennehy did and they don't turn into serial killers without a conscience and with a love of human blood, do they? Therefore, I would say, 'So what?'

Women who kill up close and personal with a knife can be found in numbers throughout the black annals of criminal history, but to my knowledge none of them can equal Dennehy, and this is saying something too. I will go further adding: I have interviewed many one-off female killers and even the notorious American serial killer, Aileen 'Lee' Carol Wuornos, and none of them hold a candle to the fiend that *still* exists in Joanna Dennehy.

In my opinion, she *will* kill again.

Suzanne 'Sue' Margaret Basso

Method of killing: 'sustained torture'.
Her aims were to cause extreme physical pain, to give
mental and physical anguish, and to cause mental agony.
Victims
Carmine Basso (forty-seven) and Louise 'Duddy'
Musso (fifty-nine)

When Christianna Hardy, *née* Basso, daughter of Suzanne
Basso, heard that the death sentence had been passed down on
her mother she commented: 'It's wonderful. It's wonderful.
Justice has finally been served. She is off the streets. She can't
hurt anybody any more.'

There is evil and a malevolence that transcends evil; such
is the following case, one that will make your stomach churn
for if any woman deserved the death sentence it is Basso.
And on Wednesday 5 February 2014, at 'The Walls Prison'
Huntsville, she was executed by lethal injection.

Louis 'Buddy' Musso's body was found on Wednesday 26 August 1998. According to court documents from Harris County, Texas, Mical Renz was jogging on North Main Street in Galena Park, a city east of Houston, at around 6.15 a.m. when he saw what he took to be someone lying on the embankment at the side of the road. Renz didn't investigate the matter any further and continued on his way. However, after finishing his morning run and preparing for work, Renz went back to the place where he had seen the recumbent figure. It was, by then, a few minutes before 8 a.m., and when he got close up to the figure he discovered that it was the dead body of a man. He phoned the police.

Within minutes, Officer Kevin Cates of the Galena PD arrived at the scene. Cates observed that the deceased man was dressed in clean clothes, despite the fact that his body was bloody and very badly bruised. This macabre state of affairs led Cates to conclude that the body was that of a murder victim who had been moved to that location and dumped, rather than having been killed there.

Shortly afterwards, Assistant Chief Robert Pruett also arrived and he arranged for a police despatcher to check neighbouring cities for reports of missing persons. Information from Jacinto City, which borders Galena Park, indicated that a woman by the name of Suzanne Basso had recently filed a missing person's report. On receiving this information, Robert Pruett headed out to Basso's address, hoping for a lead on the as-yet unidentified victim.

Born Schenectady, New York, on Wednesday 15 May 1954, Suzanne Basso was forty-four years old and lived in an apartment in Jacinto City with her son, James O'Malley. When Chief Pruett arrived there, Basso wasn't at home; she had gone to the police department to give officers an identification card belonging to the missing man, Louis Musso.

Pruett waited, and within a few minutes Basso returned. From the initial conversation, Pruett learned that Musso lived there along with Basso and her son. Basso invited the police officer into her home, where he was introduced to O'Malley, and where he was surprised to see some bloodstained clothing and a sheet near a temporary bed in the living room.

In response to Pruett's questions regarding the bloodstained articles, Basso said that Musso slept in the living room and that the clothing was his. The officer then asked her and O'Malley to accompany him to where the body was, in order that they could identify it, which they did without expressing any surprise or emotion. Pruett then asked the pair to accompany him to the police station to give written statements. Both had little option other than to agree.

O'Malley very soon confessed to involvement in the murder. He gave written and oral statements which outlined the events surrounding the killing and named all the other people involved, and what emerged from that initial confession and the subsequent murder investigation was a horrific story in which a mentally retarded man had been subjected to an appalling catalogue of torture and violence at the hands of six people, all of which was orchestrated by Suzanne Basso.

In life, Suzanne Margaret Basso was five-foot two-inches in height, with grey hair and blue eyes. According to the Texas Department of Corrections records listed prior to her execution she listed her occupations as office clerk, seamstress and labourer. At the time of her arrest she had no prior criminal convictions.

It isn't easy to piece together a reliable personal history of Basso, for much of what she would have the world believe about her has been discredited and exposed as downright lies. What, however, is true is that she was born 15 May 1954 to Florence and John Richard Burns. She had seven siblings. As a side note, Florence was the eldest sister of spree killer, Robert Garrow, who killed four people throughout 1973. Suzanne Basso's uncle Robert was a sadistic rapist and burglar with a rap sheet as long as his arm. He was shot dead trying to escape from Fishkill Prison in 1978, aged forty-two.

In the early seventies, the then attractive Suzanne married a US Marine by the name of James Peek. The couple had a daughter, Christianna, and a son, whom they called James Kirby. Peek was subsequently arrested in 1982 for molesting his daughter and charged with taking indecent liberties with a child. He served eleven months in prison, during which time the children were placed in foster care.

What is also beyond dispute is that this middle-aged woman is one of the most evil female killers of modern times and was as deserving of the death penalty as any man, but whatever she did in the forty-four years before she was arrested for murder, it is certain, having been attested to in court, that Basso frequently demonstrated a penchant for cruelty and deviant behaviour. Her twenty-three-year-old son James 'JD' Peek (his name later changed to O'Malley for some obscure reason), professed to be terrified of her, and her now married daughter, Christianna Hardy, said that her mother had abused both her and her brother both emotionally and sexually.

In fact, there can be no more vivid indictment of this evil woman than that provided by Christianna, who said jubilantly, when the jury voted in favour of the death sentence, 'It's wonderful. It's wonderful. Justice has finally been served. She is off the streets. She can't hurt anybody any more.' She went on to say, 'Let the inmates kill her. I don't care. She didn't feel any sadness for Buddy. She didn't feel any sadness for anybody else that she's hurt. Why should we give her sympathy?'

The first recorded reference to Basso's earlier life comes from the *Houston Press* in an article concerning the circumstances surrounding the death of her second husband, one Carmine Basso, whose body was found on Tuesday, 27 May 1997, in an office suite, No. 215, of a building at 6633 Hillcroft, in southwest Houston. It appears that she had previously placed a wedding announcement in another newspaper, the *Houston Chronicle* on Sunday 22 October 1995. The grandiosely worded and wildly inaccurate announcement said that 'Suzanne Margaret Anne Cassandra Lynne Theresa Marie Veronica Sue Burns-Standinslowski' and Carmine Basso had tied the knot. The newly wed Mrs Basso, as well as having eleven forenames, claimed to have eleven brothers and to be heiress to the 'Oil Dynasty in Halifax, Nova Scotia'.

As if this spin of bullshit were not enough, this heiress to an empire in 'black gold' claimed to have been educated in England, at no less a seat of learning than Saint Anne's Institute in Yorkshire, where she obtained a degree in Home Economics and Trade Sewing. A model of all virtues, she rounded off her education by entering a convent and becoming a nun, where she was known as Sister Mary Theresa.

Perhaps her role model was Mother Teresa of Calcutta, although she in no way resembled the saintly winner of the 1979 Nobel Peace Prize. Weighing in at an impressive 365 pounds, the porcine Basso was built for the world of gridiron football rather than a convent and, very clearly, had never followed a regime of fasting and abstinence. In any event, convent officials soon disabused the *Houston Press* of any notions that this may have been true. As for St Anne's Institute in Yorkshire, it didn't exist!

What is more, that may not have been all that was untrue in this female Pinocchio's curriculum vitae, richly embroidered as it was in merit and distinction. According to Carmine Basso's stepmother, Suzanne's new in-laws were far from sure that Carmine and her were even married at all. The stepmother, Arlene Basso, is quoted as saying to a reporter, 'Believe me when I tell you, *she* is off the wall.'

Arlene also said that the alleged newly wed Suzanne had claimed to have twin daughters. She sent a photo of the twins to the Basso family, who could instantly see that the picture was, very obviously, one girl looking into a mirror, and a surefire candidate for receiving *A Dummy's Guide to Photography Award*.

Therefore, to my mind, and to the minds of all of the readers of this book, we may safely assume that not only was Suzanne Basso a pathological liar but one who lived in a world where elephants fly, lead balls bounce and fairies reign supreme, all of which is confirmed when she concocted Carmine's own pedigree. In a pretentious quarter-page newspaper advert she stated that her spouse was the holder of the Congressional Medal of Honor. He was not! However, her assertion that he was the owner of the firm Latin Security and Investigation proved to be true. The company's seedy office was registered at Suite 215, 6633 Hillcroft Street,

Houston, which is precisely where Officer J.R. Martinez found Mr Basso's malnourished, slowly decomposing corpse.

Although the autopsy showed no apparent trauma to the body, the subsequent murder of Louis Musso did cause the police in Houston to take a fresh look at Carmine's death and the circumstances surrounding it.

According to the medical report, it seemed that Suzanne Basso was the last person to speak to her husband, and that was at 11 a.m. on Tuesday, 20 May 1997. She'd phoned him from New Jersey, where she claimed to have been visiting her mother. The report also says that, although there were no rest rooms or hygiene facilities in the office suite, the couple had been apparently living there for several months and the results were 'not pleasant'. It goes on to state that 'there were several trash cans with faeces and urine in them'. In truth, the office was so dirty that the cleaners would not go near it because of the horrendous smell coming from within. And Carmine's rotting body cannot have helped matters either!

Although Suzanne Basso was never convicted, or even charged with being involved in some way in Carmine's sudden demise, for my part I suggest that she most certainly was. The autopsy was carried out by Harris County Medical Examiner, Joye Carter, who ruled that Carmine Basso had died of natural causes – this was a determination which she would later modify after she learned of the murder of Buddy Musso.

Initially, Joye Carter concluded that Carmine's death was the result of 'erosive esophagitis (inflammation of the lower oesophagus due to the regurgitation of gastric acid contents – in laymen's terms a serious case of 'heartburn'). This erosion extended to the trachea and a portion of the cervical spine area. The only other 'major abnormality' noted was 'a strong smell to the body'.

In short, it seemed that Carmine Basso died, at the age of forty-seven, from a fatal case of acid indigestion and nothing more. Nevertheless, Dr Carter was prompted to say, two years later: 'When Mr Basso was found dead, it did not appear to be foul play, but it did appear to be a little strange. In the light of the Musso case, I think it may warrant a second look.'

While the debate over whether to exhume Carmine Basso is, still at the time of writing, unresolved, there is no doubt that there was nothing unnatural in the cause of Buddy Musso's death, for he had most certainly been murdered.

'I made a promise to Buddy that I would always take care of him, and I hurt, and I will always carry that guilt.'(Mimi Averill, at Basso's July 1999 trial.)

Although Buddy Musso was fifty-nine years old, he was mentally retarded, described by those whom knew him as a trusting soul, but with the mental capacity of an eight-year-old child. He was born and raised in 'The Garden State', New Jersey. He was a regular churchgoer, and it was at church were he met Mimi Averill, about twenty years prior to his death. Mimi, who had a mentally retarded grandson herself, had warmed to Buddy and he became something of an adopted member of the family.

It was 1998. Very little is known precisely how Musso and Basso came into contact, however, we do know that he had previously been married, he had a son, his wife had died of cancer in 1980, he was residing at an assisted living house in Cliffside Park, New Jersey and he worked as a bagger at a Shoprite supermarket. It is also known that they first met at a church bazaar; she was with her son James, with an IQ of

only 70, and her mother, Florence – another churchgoer –
and Buddy was probably accompanied by Mimi Averill, the
two older women having known each other through their
Faith. Therefore, the mutual introduction was, at that time,
all perfectly innocent.

The deviously cunning Suzanne Basso soon zeroed in on
the fact that Buddy had money in his bank account and was
the recipient of Social Security cheques. She flirted with him,
soon convincing him that it would be a good idea if they
would marry and, in the June of that same year, without any
word to the Averills, Buddy upped sticks and headed south
for Texas to live with Basso and her son in Houston.

The trio lived in Basso's apartment and, immediately, the
bride-to-be took control of Buddy's life, beginning with his
finances. She tried to get his Social Security cheques sent
directly to her, and she wrote cheques to herself from his
bank account. Within a month of his arrival, she made out a
will in Buddy's name, which he signed, naming her as the sole
beneficiary of his estate. This nefarious scheme, as patently
shallow as it may be, was devised so that Basso might collect
on Buddy's life insurance policy. In fact, by the terms of the
policy, the insurance company would pay $65,000 if he were
to meet a violent death, which is exactly what the wicked
Basso intended to happen.

During the time between his arrival in Houston and
his death, a mere two months had passed. Buddy was only
allowed to speak to his friends, the Averills, on one occasion.
During the call he wept and told them that he missed them,
so no further calls were allowed. Basso herself phoned the
Averills, but despite their requests they were not allowed to
talk to him.

Basso and her son were friendly with Bernice Ahrens who lived in a nearby apartment with her adult children, Craig (twenty-five) and Hope (twenty-two), along with Hope's boyfriend, Terence Jermaine Singleton (twenty-six) – and a rum bunch they were indeed.

On Saturday, 22 August 1998, in response to a phone call, Houston PD sent patrol officer Jeffery Butcher to a reported assault in progress. When he arrived at the scene he was met by the complainant, one Jeffery Jones. Also present were Buddy Musso, James O'Malley and Craig Ahrens. Jones told the policeman that O'Malley and Ahrens had been forcing Buddy to run on the spot, against his will. The officer noticed that Buddy had two black eyes and various other signs of violence about his body. He noticed also that Buddy was mentally retarded and seemed to be suffering from exhaustion.

On questioning, Buddy explained that some Mexicans had beaten him up. He denied that O'Malley and Ahrens were responsible for his injuries. With little else to go on, the officer drove Buddy to the apartment of Bernice Ahrens, where he met Suzanne Basso. Wearing the most plausible of her psychopathic masks, she explained that she was Buddy's guardian, adding that Buddy had been abused when he was living in New Jersey. The self-styled 'Angel of Mercy' went on to say that she had sent O'Malley and Ahrens to take Buddy running, as he always wanted to run around in her apartment (probably in training for an attempt to get away from her and get back to the Averills as fast as his legs could carry him). At this point, Buddy went up to Basso and put his head on her shoulder in an affectionate manner.

Convinced by this that Buddy was now in safe hands, Officer Butcher went away, leaving Buddy in Suzanne Basso's care. It was a cunning deception by this mentally twisted woman and a fatal, but an innocent misjudgement by the lawman, as, from the moment he left the Ahrens's apartment, Buddy was subjected to a regime of inhumane and cruel torment and violence which would end only when he died, some three days later.

At this point, I would ask the reader to imagine that their own eight-year-old innocent child – for that was what Buddy Musso mentally amounted to – was going to suffer what followed. Imagine the pain, the terror, if you will, then look deep into your own soul and tell me that Suzanne Basso didn't deserve the death sentence?

The extent of the brutality which Buddy was forced to undergo, and his misery during those final days of his life, is graphically documented in the court records of Harris County. For the next few days, Buddy, Basso and O'Malley stayed at Ahrens's rooms, and during that time all the occupants, egged on by the evil and avaricious Basso, subjected this trusting soul to beatings and abuse that no Stephen King horror story could invent.

Buddy was forced to sit in what is described as a 'hurricane position' with his knees on a mat and his hands clasped behind the back of his head. Any time the hapless man failed to hold this position, he would be punished. This chastisement involved such things as Jermaine Singleton kicking Buddy 'in the tail' with force and Basso hitting him about the head with a shoe and a metal part of a vacuum cleaner, which caused the first of seventeen gashes to his head. At one point, Craig Ahrens suggested that they take Buddy to hospital to have his head stitched, but the idea was not taken seriously and the beatings continued.

Throughout the entire period until he died, Buddy was denied food of any sort and, as time progressed, the beatings and abuse intensified, with baseball bats, a leather belt and steel-tipped boots being used. At trial, one of the defendants also admitted that they had bathed him with caustic cleaning fluids and bleach and they scrubbed him with a wire brush.

At some point, an argument erupted over whether Basso had told Buddy that she wanted to have sex with him. Craig Ahrens, O'Malley and Singleton confronted Buddy about this and began to beat him. O'Malley, wearing steel-tipped boots, kicked him in the head and chest and stomped on his arms. According to testimony from Bernice Ahrens, who apparently just stood by and did nothing to intervene, Buddy was pleading for relief from the constant beatings and asking to be taken to a hospital because he wasn't 'feeling well'.

On the Tuesday evening, before dinner, O'Malley and Singleton took Buddy for a bath. He slipped in the tub and hit his head. At this, O'Malley jumped in the tub and stamped on his head and chest causing him to bleed from a deep cut on his skull. Hope Ahrens then entered the room and the three combined to punch and kick Buddy, which made his 'ear puff' and his head bleed even more. Then they dragged him out of the bath and left him on the floor while they went into another room to eat dinner.

During the meal, the 365-lb Basso went into the bathroom and hit Buddy on the head with a Mickey Mouse ornament, leaving an x-shaped cut. Singleton joined her in the attack and, as Buddy was by this time barely responsive, they put him back into the tub and savagely poured surgical spirit and peroxide onto his cuts before returning to the dinner table.

Shortly after dinner it was discovered that Buddy who, remember, saw life from the viewpoint of an eight-year-old child, had given up the struggle and had mercifully died.

> But, Mousie, thou art no thy-lane
> In proving foresight may be vain
> The best laid plans o' mice an' men
> Gang aft-agley
> An lea'e us nought but grief and pain
> For promis'd joy.
> (Robert Burns – poem *To The Mouse* 1786.)

There are few things more disaster-prone than the designs of petty criminals who have aspirations above their ability. Influenced by what they read, or see on TV, these over-ambitious mediocrities consider that they are capable of emulating the exploits of those whom they perceive to be eminently more successful than they themselves have been. Fuelled by the wrong motive, often greed or revenge, they lay plans which are ill conceived and, almost always, destined to end in failure, and make a mega cock-up. 'Team Basso' most certainly did.

To distance herself from the murder, and with the insurance payout in her tiny mind, Basso arranged that they clean up Buddy's corpse, dress him in clean clothes, put him in the trunk of Bernice Ahrens's car and drive to the location where his body was found – Main Street, Galena Park, where Mr Renz found it the following morning.

This majestically supreme example of incompetence

required police to believe that Buddy had dressed himself *after he was dead*. Then came another remarkable act of gross stupidity. The bungling lowlifes left handcuffs and two baseball bats, all splattered in Buddy's blood, in the Ahrens's apartment. There was blood all over their carpet. There were bloodstained towels, plastic gloves and bloodied razors. There was blood splashed around the bath and even more found inside Bernice's car; all of which the police found very quickly.

Musso's first Will had been written in 1997, but a more recent Will leaving his entire estate to Basso found on a computer was dated 13 August 1998, just twelve days before he was murdered.

Bank statements were found showing that Basso had been cashing Buddy's Social Security cheques. Other documents indicated that this evil woman had tried unsuccessfully to arrange to take over the management of his Social Security income. It also appeared as if someone had fought Basso's request; this was possibly Buddy's niece who was close to him, or his trusted friend, Al Becker, who had been handling Buddy's benefits for twenty years. And, to top it all, there was also a copy of a Restraining Order made by Basso forbidding Buddy's friends or relatives from making contact with him.

But now let's turn to Buddy's autopsy, which makes for sickening reading.

Among the many injuries that the medical examiner, Dr Shrode, detailed at the trial were fractured ribs, a broken nose, a skull fracture, cigarette burn marks, chemical burns and bruises extending from the bottom of his feet to his upper torso, including his genitals, eyes and ears. Blood was found in the oral cavity and windpipe. The autopsy revealed that the immediate cause of death had been 'skull fracture from multiple blunt impact trauma', but the injuries to the genital area were so serious that they themselves could have resulted in death. Testimony was also presented that the tragic victim had lost up to thirty pounds in weight during the few weeks that he had spent with the sadistic Basso.

Although all the participants were found guilty, the death penalty was not sought for Basso's five co-defendants. Only she was singled out for the ultimate punishment, since she had masterminded the entire plot to gain the insurance payout. The state's attorney painted a picture of an evil and unscrupulous confidence trickster who used many aliases, and police discovered that Buddy was not the only one whose death would be of benefit to Basso: she had taken out life insurance policies on several people, including an eight-year-old child who didn't actually exist – all of which brings me back to the 'death from natural causes' attributed to Carmine Basso.

This chapter has taken us right into the devious, cold-blooded mind of one of the most sadistic female killers in US criminal history. We can trace Suzanne Basso's bad bloodline right back to her uncle, spree killer Robert Garrow, who killed four people throughout 1973. As mentioned before, he was a sadistic rapist and burglar with a rap sheet as long as his arm. Basso's first husband, a US Marine by the name of James Peek, was subsequently arrested in 1982 for molesting his own daughter. Her own son, James, with an IQ of 70, was mentally challenged from start to finish.

We know that Suzanne Basso was a con artist, a woman who used numerous aliases and presented false credentials to get whatever she needed at any given time. Whether she was actually legally/illegally married to Carmine Basso matters little in her scheme of things, but certainly no record of marriage between them has ever existed – the reason being she still was not divorced from James Peek, remaining married to him until they strapped her down onto the gurney in Huntsville and gave her the lethal Decree Nisi.

It is true that Carmine ran a company called Latin Security and Investigation, but this was a fly-by-night set-up bringing in no money at all. The offices were crummy at best, however, what assets Carmine did have was a life insurance policy, probably arranged by the devious Basso, and which as far as I can determine did not pay out on his demise. Where and how Basso met Carmine Basso is not known, however, what has been established is that the couple became romantically involved in 1993 and Carmine moved in under the same roof with Basso and her husband. Nevertheless, what raises red flags with me, and this is why I attribute his death to the hands of Suzanne Basso is easily understood now that we know how she enticed Buddy Musso into her web, kept him under her control, stole his money, tried to cash in on his life insurance policy and then subsequently killed him.

I suggest she did exactly the same with Carmine Basso!

Houston PD records show that on Tuesday, 27 May 1997, a Suzanne Basso telephoned police to say that she was concerned about her 'husband' Carmine Basso, as she hadn't heard from him since she'd called him from New Jersey at 11 a.m., on Tuesday 20 May. Given the great benefit of hindsight, this might have raised a red flag for you and me because she professed to love Carmine very much. And most loving couples chat to each other at least every day or so.

Secondly, again with the benefit of hindsight, and with no evidence of foul play to incriminate Basso at the time, police never asked her to account for her alibi – that of being in New Jersey when she made her last call to Carmine.

But it is the state of Carmine's office and that of his corpse that raises other red flags for me. To begin with, due to the deteriorated state of the body the medical examiner could not give even a remote guess of time of death – most certainly the man had been deceased for at least a week, if not more. The examiner did note that the man was 'malnourished', much in the same way as Buddy Musso was at the time of his death – all of which indicates that he had been denied food.

So, imagine, or sniff if you will, a scene from the gruesome 1995 thriller movie *Seven* starring Morgan Freeman and Brad Pitt. Now try and place yourself in the office at Suite 215, 663 Hillcroft Street, Houston, where, in May, the temperature rises most days to over eighty degrees. Think of what this unrelenting heat will do to a corpse, all enhanced by the stench of rotting garbage, plus trashcans filled with human excrement and stale urine? The point I am making is that no one in their right mind, not even the Bassos would *voluntarily* use their office as a toilet when there are several gas stations and other public conveniences close by, but Carmine did because he, like Buddy Musso, had no other choice until Suzanne forced cleaning fluid down Carmine Basso's throat and killed him.

The title of this book focuses on female serial killers, and, it would be fair to say that Suzanne Basso does not qualify as being one, who is by definition an offender who kills three times or more with a cooling off period between the 'events'. What I can say with a degree of certainty is that she was an 'emerging serial killer' because her murderous and deviant psychopathology is writ large throughout her history from cradle to grave. And, there is no smoke without fire, what with her motive being financial greed, as I hope you will agree. I also say that having got clean away with the killing of Carmine Basso, she attempted to do exactly the same with the murder of Buddy Musso. Like all 'Black Widow' killers, they never stop until they are apprehended, and this is a statement no one can deny.

Perhaps a final word on the matter should go to Basso's daughter, Christianna. Shortly after her mother's conviction and sentencing, she said: 'I might just sit at home and pop a bottle of champagne when the lethal injection is given. I have no remorse for her.'

This murderous and manipulative freak of nature even attempted to exact misplaced sympathy from the jury at her trial after having shed an enormous 200 pounds in weight in an attempt to look frail. Her ploy failed. When asked by the death house warden if she had any last words to say before she died, she replied: 'No Sir!'

At the time of writing the current status of Basso's co-defendants is, as follows:

PEEK (O'Malley). James Kirby. # 04458396. Earliest possible release date given parole: 24.09.2017. French Robertson Unit, Abilene, TX.
SINGLETON. Terence Jermaine. # 00875656. Natural Life. Jim Ferguson Unit, Midway, Madison County. TX.
AHRENS. Bernice. # 00875450. Earliest possible release date: 26.08.2078. Carol Young Medical

Complex, Attwater Ave, Dickinson. TX.

AHRENS. Hope. # 00895931. Earliest possible release date given parole: 26.08.2018. Lockhart Work Facility, Caldwell County, TX.

AHRENS. Craig. # 00875656. Earliest possible release date: 26.08.2058. Jim Ferguson Unit, Midway, Madison County. TX.

Patricia 'Pat' Wright

This killer stabbed her victim, who was Willie Jerome Scott (thirty-seven)

Arletta Wright wrote to me an email on Friday 30 May 2003, in which she stated: 'Chris, thank you, I appreciate your help. I spoke to my sister Patricia Wright on Wednesday by telephone. I advised her that I needed the truth. My sister did say that, yes, she got all the insurance money [from Willie Scott's life insurance policy]. And I knew all along.'

Once in a blue moon a case comes across my desk, a matter which is not strewn with bodies dumped in ditches, blood drenched walls, smoking 'Saturday Night Specials', the terror of a serial killer still at large, but which is something more mundane, more prosaic, so pedestrian that it seems hardly worth a second glance. However, what follows most certainly *was* worth a second look for it concerned the desperate pleas of a 'Black Widow' who, sentenced to serve life in prison, was now claiming that she was innocent – and her entire family and thousands of her Internet supporters thought the same way too. But is she a 'piece of work'? Oh, yes, indeed she is!

This homicidal piece of work is a canvas of no routine amateur, for the mind-twisting case of Patricia Wright may be likened to a masterly woodcut completed by Maurits Cornelis 'MC' Escher, the Dutch graphic artist most recognised for mind-bending visual illusions and impossible buildings. To get my drift, please take a look at some of MC's illustrations on the worldwide web. You will see exactly what I mean. Like Escher, Patricia Wright was a wizard at almost mathematically deceiving the eyes and minds of whoever looked at the pictures she painted. Hers is also one of the most interesting cases I have come across.

I am no stranger to the California correctional system, having been a one-time visitor to Alcatraz, several times to San Quentin State Prison (SQ) and other facilities too. However, until I took an interest in Patricia Wright I had never been to the Central California Women's Facility (CCWF), Chowchilla, which was opened in October 1990.

Housing over 3,200 female inmates – many of whom are serving life – CCWF is the largest female correctional facility in the USA and covers a massive 640 acres, which is, by my reckoning, larger than 320 UK football pitches. Amongst other inmates, I was here to pay Patricia just the one two-hour visit. She is serving a natural life sentence for the brutal stabbing to death of her husband, Willie Jerome Scott.

Patricia Scott (*née* Wright) has always firmly denied this murder; moreover, in letters to me she claimed that a *single* 'double-indemnity' insurance policy covered her husband's life, and that, after his death, she collected just over a mere $30,000. More to the point, Patricia was going through an extensive appeals process. On balance she was on a 'winner' because there were loopholes in her conviction that the state's attorney couldn't close. Given some time, the support of her family and countless friends, Patricia *might* have walked free without the proverbial stain on her otherwise black character.

To garner further support for 'Innocent Patricia's' cause, Arletta Wright emailed me. She was hoping that after a careful examination of the case I would come down on Patricia's side, and after sending me thousands of documents at her own expense and with Patricia's grace and favour, I settled down for a riveting read. What they received in return was not at all what they'd expected!

Arletta, Patricia's sister, is adamant, too, that her sister is innocent. Indeed, in a letter from prison dated 15 March 2003, Patricia Wright wrote these words to me:

Now, I not only know that I did not kill my ex-husband, the actual killer has now confessed to doing the killing. He is my brother [Larry Wright]. This saddens me greatly. He has now told the family. While I do not wish to harm him, he did this, not me. I want my life back...I have been incarcerated about six years for a murder I did not commit. I am innocent. My brother has now told why he had to kill him [Willie Scott]...because he [Larry] is a straight man and this gay man [Willie] came on to him and he couldn't allow that. So, I am at another loss here. Now, that of my brother as I cannot forgive him for what he has done to my family, my children and me, I am a good person. I don't deserve this. Please help me.

Fascinating, heartbreaking stuff, certainly. Yet she went on to say this:

My brother says he'll never go to prison for this murder; that he's sorry but he can't do it – confess for this murder. Rather let me rot. I don't know what to do about him and his confession. How can I tell the authorities? He'll get life in prison and it may not even exonerate me and set me free. All this is really upsetting.

Can the reader smell bullshit piled upon even more bullshit here? Sadly, however, hundred upon hundreds of this woman's supporters believed every word of this killer's claims of total innocence, yet one need not be a psychiatrist, even a psychologist or even a road sweeper or a traffic warden to smell a rat here, that is unless one doesn't live on Planet Earth. Period!

Oops. I may have slipped up here. As all of my loyal readers will know, I speak my mind. I thoroughly enjoy involving you all in each and every case so that you can form your own opinions as to motive, guilt or innocence. Therefore, at this point I apologise for any inference, one where I am prejudging dear Patricia Wright. God forbid! But, please read on and enjoy the ride. Take the role of Peter Falk, the actor in the TV detective series *Columbo* if you will.

Patricia Wright forcibly maintains that she was 'fitted up' for the murder by relatives and crooked detectives. She says she is mentally ill and 'legally blind'. She is not mentally ill, far from it, but she is certainly almost as blind as a bat.

I soon discovered that some of Wright's claims are true, notably that, on Monday, 17 September 1990, she was examined by Raymond E Gaylord, QD, who confirmed in a medical report that she was 'blind due to pigmentary degeneration, with a best-corrected visual acuity in both eyes at 20/400'. Because of her poor eyesight, since 1974, Wright had 'qualified for supplementary Social Security Payments until her monthly payments of $705.40 were terminated as from Sunday, 1 March 1998'.

It is also true that, by the time of her trial, which took place eighteen years after the murder had been committed, the police had destroyed the murder weapon – a knife. And, it would be correct to say that the 911 caller who had alerted law enforcement to the body was never located and the tape of the call had been misplaced or lost, or even, like the knife, destroyed.

Even more to the point, and in favour of Patricia Wright, no fingerprints or blood were found linking her to the murder. Then, to add more weight to her pleas of innocence, two material witnesses had since died, along with the coroner and the arresting officer.

Nevertheless, this I soon discovered, was where the truth ended. In a nutshell, Patricia is quite sane and arguably earns the distinction of being one of the most duplicitous female killers in the US prison system today.

I mentioned previously that Wright claimed that she only profited from the one life insurance policy taken out by her husband Willie. Unfortunately for her, and the thousands of people who support her, I was to discover that this was a bald lie. Nevertheless, with no evidence, physical or otherwise, to link anyone to this brutal murder, the trail leading to Willie's murder ran cold. Although the police had their own suspicions, nothing else had happened, although Chinese Whispers indicated that Patricia Scott and Lawrence 'Larry' Slaughter had murdered the man for an insurance payout. Then someone 'coughed' to the law. On the evidence provided, Patricia Wright and Larry Slaughter – the latter of whom's single fingerprint was found in the van where the victim was found – were arrested and found guilty of conspiracy to murder. Currently, they are both serving natural life terms in the California penal system.

Slaughter has said nothing and he has refused to discuss the case with me or anyone else. Conversely, the garrulous Patricia claims she is innocent. She says that although she collected on the *one* double-indemnity life insurance policy, the money was never a motive. She argued that she stood to gain nothing from Willie's murder, but this is where the wheels fall off her truck.

First-degree homicide frequently visits 'The City of Angels'. I know because I have a shared apartment in Toluca Lake, Studio City, LA, and I know more cops and homicide detectives than I can count. Nevertheless, at the end of Fall, 1981, another murder was added to the statistics topping off at around 300 per year.

At about 2.15 p.m., Tuesday, 22 September, following an anonymous 911 call from a woman, LAPD Sergeant Thompson was tasked to investigate a 1977 Dodge 'Harvest' three-door motor home parked facing east at the south kerb in front of 436 E Temple.

The veteran cop knew that this ropey downtown location was a well-known hangout for gays and male prostitutes, yet on this stifling hot afternoon the area was uncharacteristically deserted.

Pulling his sleek cruiser to the side of the street, Thompson stopped. He had just finished a high-speed pursuit that had resulted in a drunk driver high on smack, being forced from the highway. Hot engine oil from the police car dripped onto the road, and one of the hubcaps was now missing

Leaving the V8 ticking over and the air-con running, the officer switched on his strobe bar, made a note of the camper's plate – 407 YSZ – and he called it in.

Sergeant Thompson tried both front doors of the camper; they were locked with the windows up. Fingering the grip of his sidearm, he cautiously walked around the vehicle and found that all of the other windows were open. The rear door was unlocked but closed. He had been around dead bodies all of his career and he could not fail to smell the unmistakable sweet, gullet wrenching stench of rotting flesh emanating from inside.

Placing a handkerchief over his nose, the officer peered through one of the windows and saw the badly decomposing body of a white male. The deceased was grotesquely slumped on a bench next to a fold-down table.

Even from where the cop stood, the cause of death seemed obvious – a black-handled, nine-inch knife was sticking into the man's chest, and a plastic trash bag had been thrown over his head. The sergeant immediately realised that he was dealing with yet another homicide and that the victim had suffered an appalling number of stab wounds.

After calling for backup, Thompson was soon joined by

other blue uniforms to secure the crime scene and, according to police statements, at 3.30 p.m., detectives Timothy Dotson and William Adrian from Central LAPD Homicide turned up. Inseparable in their work, the two men were now destined to become the lead investigators in a case that would take eighteen years to come to trial.

A driving licence, number JO809154, revealed that the deceased was thirty-seven-year-old Willie Jerome Scott. A check through vehicle licensing records showed that he had owned the beat-up camper for four years. The VLR clerk pointed the officers to an address at 4331 Alonzo Avenue, Encino. So, while the police contacted the residents at that address, the vehicle was taken away for impounding at Viertals Towing Services, at 1155 W Temple Street, where it would be forensically examined.

Detective Dotson would later say to colleagues, 'The guy looked and smelled like he'd been cooked in a fuckin' oven. It [the inside of the camper] stank to hell.'

Miss Doreen Hudson had been a supervising criminalist employed by the LAPD Criminalist Laboratory for approximately twenty-one years. It fell upon her shoulders to gather evidence from the camper that might assist investigators. Once inside the vehicle, and directed by other detectives, she collected up 'numerous items including several towels, cloths with stains on them, various items of clothing, and two shoes…49 cents, a brown purse, pills, a key, toothbrush, various papers and checks. (cheques).'

Moving slowly through the cramped interior of the camper, Miss Hudson searched a small washroom and the kitchenette area where she reported finding 'a stove'. But many years later at trial, she said that she 'could not remember if I looked in any of the drawers containing the utensils and knives'. That meant a crucial question could not be answered. Had the knife come from the camper's kitchenette drawer, or was it the property of the killer?

People who plan to kill someone usually bring a weapon with them. If the knife had not belonged to the deceased, it would have indicated that the murder might have been planned in advance. Had the knife belonged to the dead man, it could have indicated that the killer and the victim were acquainted, thus narrowing down the search for a suspect. This issue would remain unsolved for seventeen years.

But matters got worse. An officer searching the sweltering van pointed to an ashtray in the console of the engine housing. Miss Hudson took out the butt it contained and placed it into a plastic evidence bag. The theory behind this recovery was that someone other than the victim might have smoked the cigarette, and perhaps saliva typing might reveal the identity of the smoker and his brand of cigarette. This saliva testing was not carried out!

While all this was going on, the camper was being dusted for fingerprints. Thirteen different sets of prints were found and it goes without saying that the owner's dabs were all over his property – inside and out. The knife handle was clean of prints, however, on the left-hand-side rearview mirror a crime scene technician found a single print, which later proved to have been left by a man with the entirely appropriate name of Lawrence 'Larry' Slaughter.

Later that afternoon, detectives Dodson and Adrian arrived at 4331 Alonzo Avenue. This was a leafy suburb, a predominantly black neighbourhood squatting close to Ventura Boulevard located off Highway 101 in the San

Fernando Valley and close to the Encino Reservoir. The property was spacious with a drive leading up to the front door. The detectives knocked and it was opened by a slightly built, not unattractive woman, who introduced herself as Patricia Wright.

'We are making enquiries about Mr Jerome Scott,' said Dotson, flashing his shield. 'He lives here?'

'No!' came the blunt and somewhat suspicious answer. 'Willie and I were married once...he comes here a lot, but he ain't here at the moment.'

'You know where he is right now?' asked the beefy Adrian, who resembled the actor Brian Dennehy.

'Nope. Last saw him Saturday...something wrong, uh, huh?'

'Yes, ma'am. May we come in?'

Patricia Wright's statement to the two detectives follows, verbatim:

The last time I saw Jerome [Willie Jerome Scott] was last Saturday morning at about 10.00 a.m. at my house, here in Encino. Jerome was with another black man in his early 20s. They were both in the motor home, and they were drinking. The other man was a sissy that Jerome met.

Jerome is a homosexual and has been hanging out with a lot of sissies. He has not been living with me for some time now because of the men he has been seen with. He met this man he was with Saturday about three weeks ago. I think his name was Ralph or Roger. Just before they left, Jerome came into the house and got a bucket because he wanted to wash the motor home. They left about 11.30 or 12.00 and he said he would be back later, but I never saw him again.

I don't know too many of his friends because Jerome would never tell me much. His cousin, Lillian Black, aka McConico, knows them, and his play mother, Billie Neil, knows some of them, too. There are others who know some of his sissy friends, but you will have to check with them. I can't think of anyone who would want to kill him. He did live with a homosexual named Herman Cross for a long time, and another man by the name of John Bell from Atlanta, Georgia.

Jerome's mother, Mable Goffe, may know some of his homosexual friends. I think Lorenzo introduced Jerome to Ralph, but you will have to talk to Billie to get Lorenzo's address.

The remark 'I can't think of anyone who would want to kill him', aroused the detectives' suspicions because they had made no mention of Jerome being dead, and they had not identified themselves as homicide cops either. Nevertheless, over the following days the officers interviewed a number of witnesses who knew the deceased man. Betty Joyce Hill, a family friend, said:

On 15 September 1981, Jerome and Lillian came over to my house for a visit. They got here about 7.30 p.m. and stayed for approximately one-and-a-half hours. When they left, they were in Lillian's car, and that was the last I saw of them.

Jerome lived here for about a month-and-a-half in June and July. The next time I heard anything about Jerome was when Pat [Patricia Wright] called on Tuesday night about 9.00 p.m. and told me that Jerome was dead. On Saturday morning, 19 September 1981, at approximately 10.30 or 11.00 p.m., Pat called me and asked if Jerome was here. I told her 'no', and she said that he left her house to wash the camper and he never came back. She also said that he was with a black Negro with an earring, and that he was with Jerome when they left the house.

When Pat called me Tuesday night, she was at her sister's house on 64th Street. She said that [the] Coroner called her at her sister's house.

A Lillian McConico told detectives:

Willie Scott spent the night at my house last Wednesday, 16 September 1981. He left in his camper on Thursday at about 12 noon. That's the last I saw of him. He said he was going to Pat's house. She lives in Encino. On Saturday, 19 September 1981, at about one in the afternoon, he called me. He was in Encino because he said he was at home. That's the last I heard from Willie.

About one hour later, Pat called me. She said she would be over as soon as Willie had done washing the camper. Willie told her 'no', that the kids would just be in the way. She told me there was another 'little black dude' with him that had an earring in his ear. She said that she thought it was strange that this guy was with Willie, but she didn't get a good look at him.

About five minutes after 8.00 p.m., Pat called me again. She asked if Jerome had got there yet. I told her 'no'. She then said she was at her sister's house on 64th Street. She told me she had left a note at the house for Jerome. She told me to tell Jerome if I saw him. On Sunday at about 8.00 a.m. or 3.00 p.m., Pat called again and asked if I'd seen Jerome. I told her 'no'.

After taking their statements, Detectives Dotson and Adrian considered if one of Scott's male prostitutes could have robbed and killed him – his jewellery, wedding ring, 18-carat gold necklace, expensive diamond watch and diamond rung on his right finger were missing. They also learned that he had just cashed his IDS American Express Disability Insurance. It amounted to just over $4,350, and that money had gone too.

The cops now reasoned that it was highly possible that someone close to the deceased had known about the money, and murder for financial gain was now very much a possible motive. However, perhaps the blitz-style overkill of the murder ominously added another dimension. If robbery were the motive, just a few stabs – the first of which was lethal anyway – would have been sufficient to terminate Willie's life. However, the person who murdered him had done so in a homicidal rage. In other words, the killer did not like Willie at all!

At autopsy, it was established that Willie Scott was terminally ill from cancer and he had just a few months to live. The medical examiner also determined that the man would have lost consciousness within a minute of the first stab to his throat: the carotid artery had been severed, blood loss would have been immense and anoxia (lack of oxygen to the brain, resulting in blacking out) would have quickly ensued. This first stab, however, was followed by a 'blitz of 15 other stabs to his body', the ME noted. 'There was no evidence of a struggle and no defensive wounds are to be found on the deceased man's hands or arms.'

The crime scene investigation report stated that '... there was little blood splashing around the camper, which is usually associated with such a ferocious attack. There was no evidence of a struggle. Mr Scott had been helpless when the knife was driven into his body time and again. In scenarios such as this, it is highly probably that the attacker would have been splashed with blood and his clothes either had to be washed or thrown away.'

With all of this evidence, it was now clear that someone hated Willie with a passion. The killing was 'up close and very personal', and only a person who despised him could have committed such a heinous crime.

As the picture started to unfold, it became obvious to investigators that the deceased had been drinking heavily, and he might have fallen into a drunken stupor, dying without putting up a struggle for his life. Willie could have been murdered at the location where the camper van was discovered, or murdered elsewhere and the vehicle driven by the killer/s to 436 Temple, where the police found it.

Semen recovered from the dead man's enlarged rectum, which suggested that he had had gay sex with someone before he died, was not tested for a DNA profile. Two tests on blood found in the camper proved that one of them matched Scott, and the other was from an unknown person. The latter was never traced.

But what of the 911 call alerting police to the camper and the decomposing body? Of course, anyone could have peered in through the window and seen the carnage after noticing the smell of rotting flesh. However, the police could not rule out the possibility that, as the corpse had been there for some days, someone wanted the body to be discovered. If so, why?

Born on Wednesday, 29 December 1943, in Texas, five-foot-nine-inch Willie Jerome Scott enjoyed a bisexual lifestyle, getting drunk, picking up male prostitutes and having sex with them in his camper van. In fact, he even made sexual advances to male members of his own family, including one Gerald Singleton, the husband of his sister-in-law, Sherry Wright Singleton, and he had made other sexual advances to young Larry Wright, Patricia's brother. Eventually, Willie's behaviour prompted the divorce.

In a 26 April 2003 letter to me, Patricia Wright's sister, Arletta, wrote:

Jerome was a 'flamer'; at times he wore lipstick, nail polish, ladies' earrings, and he tried to hit on any man who he could talk to in private. My first husband was a Minister so Jerome would never have had success in picking up on my husband but Jerome tried to pick up on Gerald Singleton and every man that crossed his path. He even tried to pick up on my sister Carvette's husband, named Agee. He went through our family trying to pick up on different sisters' husbands and boyfriends. He drank a lot.

So, now we turn our attention to Patricia Wright. Born on Tuesday, 17 July 1951, marriage documents show she married Willie Scot in June 1978, and they initially lived along tree-lined South Highland Avenue, between Wilshire and W Olympic Boulevards, Los Angeles.

The documents sent to me by Arletta Wright show that as early as Thursday, 5 June 1980, and just two years after his marriage to Patricia, Willie took out a double-indemnity life insurance police – No. 40163159 – with the firm New York Life. The $15,000 cover included 'Accidental Bodily Harm' to be paid, even in the event of murder, to the beneficiary, his wife Patricia Scott, who would receive the then tidy sum of $30,000. The premiums were $26.95 per month.

I could also see from New York Life documents, that throughout the period of the policy it was Patricia who paid the premiums through her own bank account. And, it is here the first red warning flag pops up. In letters to me from Patricia Wright, she was adamant that this insurance policy was taken out by Willie Scott '...years before we even met', while the insurance company's records conclusively prove otherwise – that the policy was taken out two years *after* they married.

This is puzzling, though, for the Wrights and their legal advisors had had this insurance policy document in their records for years. One might have thought that surely someone, at least one professional by the pro-Wright campaign since her incarceration, or even police investigators, would have noted this glaring contradiction? It is almost inconceivable that no one had spotted it before I did, for it clearly shows a deception on behalf of Patricia Wright.

This was an issue that I needed to put under the glass

and examine more closely and it was worth the effort, for I then noticed something else. Arletta and Patricia had inferred that Willie had taken out this policy years before the couple met. If Willie had taken out the policy before he had even met Patricia, who had been the original beneficiary? There had been no previous beneficiary recorded in the insurance company's files; the only beneficiary was Patricia Wright. So, I hope the reader will agree with me, that you do not make someone a beneficiary of a life insurance policy if you have never heard of them, or even met them before! They don't do it on this planet anyway, I dare to say!

Now I knew that I was being spoon-fed a red herring. This was a wake-up call. Now I was under no illusion that the thousands of pro-Wright supporters were being led up the garden path, too. In chucking their hard earned cash into the 'Save Patricia Fund', they were throwing good money after bad.

On Tuesday, 30 September 1980, the address for all insurance company correspondence was changed to PO Box 78431, Los Angeles, and, on the very same day, Patricia's bank bounced a cheque payment for $29.65. There were insufficient funds in her account to pay the premium.

On Monday, 5 January 1981, a second cheque for the same amount failed to clear, and again, in March of that year, a third cheque was dishonoured.

So, it is patently clear that during this period, Patricia and her husband, Willie, were suffering financial hardship and, around this time, they learned that he had terminal cancer.

On Thursday, 26 March 1981, the couple moved to 3617 West 64th Street, LA, and Patricia brought the arrears up to date.

In 1995, fourteen years after the murder of Willie Jerome Scott, Patricia's brother, Larry Dion Wright, started a twelve-year stretch at the Corrigan Men's Facility Maximum Security Prison in Connecticut. He had been convicted of threatening the life of a social worker called Judith Castonuary at the Department of Children and Family Services. He had also been charged with physically abusing his son Larry Jr.

Larry Wright Sr. wanted out of prison and because he couldn't write, he dictated a letter to a cellmate who then posted it to the LAPD. In the letter, Larry, through his 'cellie', explained that he had information about the Scott murder. He told visiting detectives that, when he was a thirteen-year-old lad, he was watching television one evening and thought he heard a loud noise outside. He assumed that it was Jerome's motorhome 'rocking and rolling' in the driveway at 4331 Alonzo Avenue, although he didn't bother to investigate until the following morning.

Larry Wright gave the following statement to investigators at 11.30 a.m., Thursday, 30 March 1995. It is reproduced, verbatim, below:

> I began living with Patricia Wright shortly after my mother's death. Since that time, Patricia was my legal guardian. Over the years, I have heard from different family members that Patricia had been involved in the death of my father, Charles Wright. My father died of an overdose of drugs.
>
> In 1981, I was living with Patricia Wright at 4331 Alonzo Avenue, Encino, California. On the day I last saw Jerome Scott, I was in the house with Patricia Wright, Larry Slaughter, 'Billy' Torr, Lorenzo King

and Jerome Scott as he talked with Patricia and Larry in the dining-room area.

Some time during the evening, I saw Jerome walk out of the front door toward the mobile home parked outside. Patricia and Larry got up and walked out of the front door toward the mobile home. I don't recall when Patricia left the house, but I believe she walked outside shortly after Larry Slaughter walked outside.

I remember hearing the mobil [sic] home rocking back and forward like if there was a great deal of movement inside. The noise from the mobile home was much more noise then I would hear of a person was just walking inside it [sic]. Not long after I heard the noise from the mobil home [sic], Patricia came inside the house and directly told me "Larry was not hear tonight" [sic]. I later realize that she was telling me not to tell anyone that Larry Slaughter was at the house that night. Patricia looked like something had occurred that made her cautious and suspicious. I felt that something had occurred, but I didn't know what. I went into my room and I again heard the noise of the mobil home rocking [sic]. I think Patricia went back outside and I went to sleep.

The detectives then asked Larry Wright if he had ever seen Larry Slaughter carrying a knife and he made this startling allegation:

I recall that Larry Slaughter would carry a large knife stuffed in a cardboard case in his right rear hip waistband. Larry Slaughter had carried the knife in his

133

waistband for several years. The knife had a wooden handle dark in colour and the blade was very long. In all the time I have known Larry Slaughter, I have never seen him without that knife until Jerome turned up missing. Since the day that I found out that Jerome was dead, I noticed that Larry wasn't carrying the knife that I had seen him with in the past.

The next morning I saw Larry Slaughter walking down the hill toward Patricia, who was waiting for him. I had not see the mobil home [sic] or Jerome since the night before.

The police eagerly seized on this information, but failed to ask the obvious question: 'Why did it take you fourteen years to tell us?'

Of course, the detectives and scenes-of-crime investigators who had initially entered the camper shortly after the murder found no evidence of any struggle at all. It had appeared that the victim had been stabbed to death as he slept or was incapacitated with drink, all of which might discredit Larry Wright's story…unless, or course, the man, unable to defend himself under any circumstances, surrendered after the first knife blow – which the autopsy confirmed – and this was followed by the stabbing and accompanying commotion Larry Wright was referring to.

There was, however, another problem with Larry's statement. I have since learned that, at the time of the murder the Wrights rented the home – they didn't own it. It was an old property and Patricia and Arletta Wright strenuously claim in a document dated Thursday, 20 February 2003, 'not even a small car would fit into the narrow walkway to the front door, that it was common knowledge that Willie's motor home was always parked across from the residence in Alonzo.' Today, all of the properties in Alonzo Avenue are upscale, but 4331 is still situated at the top of a narrow driveway with a garage.

When I explained to Arletta and Patricia Wright, Larry's claim, that he had heard the commotion in the camper van from inside the house, they went very quiet on the subject. And, their recollection of the parking situation was completely at odds with the statement of Ephesian Waters, who remembered: 'When I got to the house on Saturday, there was a gold Cadillac in the garage and a two-door grey or silver Toyota in the driveway. On Monday, the Toyota and Cadillac were still there. Also I saw a black Lincoln parked in the driveway.'

Also completely contradicting Arletta and Patricia Wright – and simultaneously confirming the statement made by Ephesian Waters – was neighbour, Lois Levy. She told police: 'Later that Saturday night I heard a lot of cars driving up their driveway.'

In an effort to now dig themselves out of a hole, Arletta and Patricia explained to me that shortly after the murder Patricia vacated the premises. New residents moved in and a contractor was hired to enlarge the walkway, converting it into a drive 'where they could park their small car', which is simply another lie. It is also completely at odds with the statements made by Mr Waters, Lois Levy and Larry Wright. Indeed, when I visited the property some years ago it was patently obvious to me that the driveway today is exactly the same width as it was back in 1981.

However, for a moment let us look at Larry Wright more closely. For most of his school years he was placed in a special education class for the emotionally disturbed and mentally retarded. He dropped out of school in the seventh grade (for those aged between twelve and thirteen in the US). Patricia had raised Larry from the age of nine after their mother, Jeanette Wright, died.

After speaking to the LAPD, and having served just two years of the twelve-year sentence, Larry Wright was out of prison and a free man, only to start confessing again, this time saying that LAPD detectives had beaten him up in prison and harassed him into signing his statements.

So, might we safely assume that Larry Wright isn't the brightest button in the box?

The LA District Attorney and the police have denied cutting a deal with Larry Wright, who, as might be expected, says otherwise.

With one informant now prepared to offer 'new' evidence before he subsequently withdrew his statement, the LAPD wisely started fishing around for someone else to corroborate Larry Wright's account, so detectives decided to arrest Patricia's brother-in-law, Gerald Singleton, on suspicion of murder. Despite this being a long shot, they held him in custody for seventy-two hours and sweated him out. The Wrights' claim that his photograph was flashed on every major news channel, and on the front page of the *Los Angeles Times*, until his release. Try as I could, I was unable to verify this claim, probably because murder is so commonplace an event in LA that Singleton's arrest would hardly have been front page news. But now he said to investigators that Patricia Wright had asked him to take a brown paper bag to Lawrence Slaughter as payment for the killing of Jerome Scott. After Singleton had signed his statement, he was immediately released. So I think we can all agree that the evidence suggesting that he might have committed murder was flimsy at best.

Singleton's statement to the LAPD was taken at 5 p.m., Thursday 18 May 1995. In it he starts by highlighting just a part of his rich criminal CV. Well done, Gerry!

Back in 1981, I was just released from Orange County Jail for conspiracy to commit robbery. I was out of jail for about (1) week when Pat (my wife's sister) asked me to do her a favor. She said that this man (I know him as Larry Slaughter) is bothering her for his clothes. Pat said that she would pay me $25 to take a brown paper bag, with clothing in it, to Larry Slaughter. I was to deliver it downtown, somewhere on Broadway, where Larry would meet me. I did the job. She gave me the bag but I never looked in it because I really respected Pat. I got off the bus and he was right there waiting for me. I handed him the bag and he just took off running. This really surprised me because Larry and me were friends. I hadn't seen him for a while and I wanted to talk to him but he just took off running so I just got back on the bus. I seen Larry on and off for years after that happened [sic].

Then in 1990 or 1991, I end up in the same jail dorm with him out at Wayside [the Pitchless Detention Center, Castaic]. I confronted him and I told him I was pissed off about the way he has been treating me, and the time I took the bag. He tells me, "Man, there was about $25,000 in that bag. I was in a hurry."

At this point, we got into a conversation about Willie Scott's murder. Slaughter said, "Man, I'm tired of Larry Wright, Billie, Sandy, and them discussing this murder. They don't know how serious it is. The only ones who were there was me and Pat. Pat took the first swing. Pat's a crazy bitch. She acted like she enjoyed it."

Slaughter said that we...Willie, Pat and I, were all together in the camper somewhere downtown. Pat takes some kind of knife and starts stabbing Will in the chest, calling him a motherfucker every time she stabs him. Slaughter said that he just stood by and watched. After the stabbing, they just left him there and took off.

This statement partially demolished the information given by Larry Wright, whom we know led police to think that the murder might have taken place in the driveway of his home, for Singleton claims that Slaughter confessed to the murder taking place 'somewhere downtown'.

Singleton very soon retracted his confession, yet undeterred the police turned their attention back to the camper van and the earlier fingerprint evidence. On the left-hand-side rearview mirror Slaughter's single print had been found. In itself this was of little evidential value because Patricia Wright and her sister, Arletta, claim in a letter to me:

Lawrence Slaughter was a close friend to Jerome Scott. Mr Slaughter had been in the 1977 Dodge motor home hundreds of times also before Jerome Scott got murdered. No one can tell what date or time a fingerprint got on a object that's a well-known fact.

However, this claim by the Wrights is of interest insomuch as one obvious fact appears to have been overlooked. If Slaughter had been in the camper 'hundreds of times', why was only *one* of his prints found on the *outside* of the vehicle? Presumably, Patricia Wright had been in the camper many times, too. However, also mentioned in the letter above, Arletta states: 'Thirteen fingerprints (sets of) were recovered from inside and outside the 1997 Dodge motorhome, none of the fingerprints matched Patricia Wright.'

Yet again, more red flags pop up as a result of claims made by Patricia and Arletta Wright. Research by me proved that Slaughter had not, in fact, been in the camper 'hundreds of times'. Slaughter was 'straight' and he had no time for Willie Scott – he hated him with a passion.

Several times during my lengthy career I have taken on cases in support of a convicted killer protesting his or her innocence, and, if Patricia and Arletta Wright were being truthful then I would have no hesitation in batting on their side and trying to get Patricia off of the hook, so-to-speak.

In summary, so far all the 'Patricia Is Innocent' campaigners had was a lot of convicted criminal and proven liars who wouldn't know the truth if it stared them straight in the face, added to which is the botched scenes-of-crime investigation, lost material evidence, destroyed vital evidence, and material witnesses dying over the passing years, and here I was, sitting at my desk, with a pile of documents and letters and the complete police file and getting nowhere.

And, it is at times like this I recall the fictional Lt Columbo, of the eponymous TV series. Does he ever give up? Not on your life he doesn't. So I decided that since I had come up against these many inconsistencies, perhaps it was now time to think laterally.

Rewinding a bit, it seems worthwhile focusing on the obvious inconsistences, mainly those of Patricia and Arletta Wright.

If Mr Slaughter was a regular visitor to Willie's camper, then surely at least one of Slaughter's dabs, a fingerprint, or a palm print, even one of his hairs, would have been discovered in the interior? Nothing had been found except just one fingerprint on the outside left-hand-side rearview mirror.

Despite the statements given by Larry Wright and Gerald Singleton – both statements retracted almost as soon as these men were released from custody – not a shred of physical evidence was found to say that Slaughter had ever been in the camper, let alone killed the man in a pique of homicidal rage.

Nevertheless, armed with these dubious statements, the police started digging deeper, as did I. One not insignificant issue that caught their attention was Patricia Wright's unusual behaviour shortly after Willie disappeared.

Strangely enough, the first hint came from Larry Wright, who had told detectives that, within a day of Willie's disappearance, Patricia started calling various hospitals trying to locate him. Larry claimed that this all seemed strange because he had a habit of vanishing for days on end, indeed weeks at a time, and that Patricia Wright had never seemed concerned about his whereabouts until the day he went to wash his van.

A family friend, Betty Joyce Hill, had told detectives that, on the day Willie disappeared, Patricia had phoned her to say that he had gone off to wash his camper and hadn't returned. Patricia said that she was worried about him.

Betty Hill's recollection corroborated Larry Wright's observation.

Detectives had also interviewed Lillian McConico who claimed that Patricia had phoned her, too – not once, but on two occasions, asking if her former husband was with her. He was not, but this was again highly unusual behaviour for a woman who knew that her former husband would take himself off trawling for gay sex for lengthy periods and had never concerned herself about his behaviour before.

If the police were going to tie this somewhat creaky case up, it would be by finding proof of a motive for the killing.

Larry Slaughter and Patricia Wright say they certainly were not lovers, while, as might be expected, other members of the family say they were. Nevertheless, this matters little because Willie and Patricia had already parted company before the murder, and there was apparently no degree of animosity between them.

Sniffing around, although it could be said somewhat belatedly, the police finally got wind of the insurance payout to Patricia Wright. This alleged motive supposition – killing for financial gain – was slightly rocky from the outset, for why murder a man who was suffering from terminal cancer who only had a few months left to live? Nevertheless, when detectives made more thorough enquiries at New York Life, the company who had issued the policy, they were surprised to discover the existence of a *second* double-indemnity policy – No. 37645648 – a policy that, till the time I started working on this matter, the Wrights argue never existed.

The police officers' suspicions were further aroused when they learned from New York Life that Patricia had made the claim on the first policy with somewhat indecent haste on Tuesday, 23 September 1981 – the second working day after the murder – and before Willie Scott was cremated on Monday, 28 September at the Forest Lawn Cemetery in Glendale.

Records show that Patricia picked up a cheque for $30,352.81 less than a month later, so this insurance policy was paid out. When I asked Patricia how she had spent this windfall, she wrote to say that she had reinvested it into an annuity and, with the balance of $10,000, she had bought a car. This was a complete lie and yet another red flag was hoisted.

We know of Patricia's unusual concern about Willie's whereabouts the day after he vanished – she had never worried before. We also know of the anonymous 911 call alerting police to the camper and a decomposing body. I asked myself, could Patricia Wright, who wanted the money as soon as possible, have made this call? The answer has to be, yes!

In investigations where circumstantial evidence plays a large part in justice being meted out, a jury takes into consideration acts indicative of guilty consciousness or intent; the anonymous 911 call and Patricia's unusual concern for Willie certainly fits into this category.

Now scanning the second insurance policy (the one that Patricia and Arletta claim never ever existed), the detectives took down details and followed up a few leads. It transpired that one James Alley, the insurance agent who sold the policy, hadn't even seen Willie Jerome Scott complete the application – let alone sign it.

Alley, who knew Patricia and Willie, took Pat's word that Willie would sign the application form when he returned later in the day. However, the strong circumstantial evidence points to the conclusion that Patricia Wright forged the signature and passed it off as genuine, saying that Willie had come home, eaten a meal, signed the form, and 'had to rush off out again on business'.

Not only that, but the duplicitous conniving forger failed to tick the appropriate box indicating that Willie was something less than 100 per cent fit. He was dying of cancer with just a few months left to live on Planet Earth.

Now the homicide cops finally had something to get their teeth into, and they bit down hard when they noted that the second double-indemnity life insurance policy – this time to the merry tune of a cool $55,189.77 jackpot in the case of accidental death or murder – had been taken out on Wednesday, 26 August 1981, a year after the couple divorced and just twenty-four days before the murder.

The investigators also learned that it was Patricia Scott, *not* Willie, who had paid the first and only premium payment. Coincidentally, too, she was the sole beneficiary. She had received the full payout of $55,189.77 on Friday, 21 January 1983. She had not told a soul.

Further detective work proved that Patricia had reinvested $30,189.77 of this money back into an annuity with New York Life, and had spent the balance on, among other things, a mini-van.

Technically, and this is another red flag, Patricia and Arletta Wright are correct when they say that 'the second policy never existed'. I have since confirmed that the second insurance policy document was not issued before Willie

Scott's murder. Indeed, the document was never issued at all because, by then, the man was dead and cremated.

However, despite their knowledge to the contrary, what the Wrights conveniently failed to point out to the police, or me – and they most certainly have not informed their thousands of supporters – is in fact that Willie's life *was* covered under New York Life's 'TEMPORARY CONDITIONAL COVERAGE AGREEMENT' from the date of the signature and the first payment.

This was a slippery move because in her own letter to me, she states: 'The DA said I had two insurance policies, yet they could not find a second insurance policy anywhere because there was always only one.'

Obviously, and crucial to her claims of being an innocent woman, Patricia is trying to hide from everyone the existence of the second policy that was fraudulently taken out shortly before the man's murder. In a document supplied to me by the Wrights dated Wednesday 19 March 2003, item # 34, Arletta poses this interesting question: 'Why would Patricia Wright want to murder her husband – in fact they were divorced – knowing that he was the sole financial source of income for their two children and Patricia at the time?'

This observation was somewhat disingenuous because Willie Scott *did not* support his family at all. Patricia was receiving $705.40 a month in social security benefits.

Of course, we recall that the claim on the first policy was made just three days after Willie Scott's murder and, maybe because of financial hardship, Patricia did need the money urgently. And we know that Willie had terminal cancer which Patricia was well aware of, so why did she and Slaughter kill him? This highlights the terms or the double-indemnity clause. $30,000 would only be paid out if cause of death were accidental bodily harm or homicide. If the man had died through natural causes, and he did have terminal cancer with a short time to live, then the payout would have been a mere $15,000. The very existence of a second double-indemnity policy being taken out under extremely dubious circumstances points to the conclusion that it was without Willie's knowledge, and if so it definitely sets Patricia Wright's motive in stone.

It was confirmed by several witnesses and supported by police documents, that Larry Slaughter paid a number of unannounced visits to Patricia Wright's residence directly after the murder, demanding that some of his clothes be returned. When he turned up, she hid behind locked doors. Patricia Wright had never washed Slaughter's clothes in the past, although immediately after the murder she had washed a pair of his trousers, a sweatshirt and a lightweight jacket. Arletta and Patricia further confirmed this in letters to me, as did Slaughter and Singleton in the statements to police.

The suggestion is that these items could have only been the bloodstained clothes worn by Slaughter at the time of the murder. However, this being the case, one has to ask why Patricia did not give them to him, rather than hide behind closed curtains? Indeed, Slaughter was extremely keen to have his clothes returned to him because they had been contaminated with physical evidence that tied him to the murder. Was he fearful that the cunning woman – as another form of insurance – might use this against him?

But was it just his clothes Slaughter wanted? The circumstances suggest he wanted money, possibly his cut of the first insurance policy payout, and this dovetails somewhat neatly into the statement given, then retracted, by Gerald Singleton, who told detectives that, after his early release from prison in 1981, and after the payout of the first policy, that he ran an errand for Patricia Wright, which was to deliver something in a brown bag – presumably the clothes and $20,000.

Singleton also claimed that Slaughter later confessed to the murder. Whether the $20,000 figure is correct we may never know. If true, Patricia Wright would have been left with just $10,000 from the first policy she herself asserts she used to buy a car, which was yet another lie. Documents prove that she bought the car after the second policy paid out – the policy she said never existed.

Along with Slaughter, this extremely devious, cunning and manipulative woman had possibly been plotting the murder of Willie Scott for some time. And, Scott had to be murdered before he died of natural causes, thus increasing the payout to $30,000. However, she would have been wise not to inform Slaughter of the second policy that circumstances point to her having discreetly taken out just twenty-four days before Willie was killed. If Slaughter had known about the second policy how do you think he would have reacted?

Patricia Wright claims she is a good woman, and wouldn't you say you were an angel if you were trying to extract yourself from a life sentence? She says that she loved Willie and that she would never have harmed him. But the fact remains that whoever conspired to murder Willie Jerome Scott for the purposes of collecting his life insurance, and other monies, as well as the expensive jewellery, were very devious and evil people indeed.

Having completed my investigation into the case of

Patricia Wright, out of courtesy I emailed a copy of my indings to Arletta Wright for her comments, and the reply was truly amazing.

She stated that I was 'absolutely 200 per cent right', and that she [Arletta] had written all of her letters to me, and compiled her meticulously presented files 'believing 200 per cent' that the information she had received from Patricia Wright was honest. She added:

> Please forgive me if you feel I have deceived you. I didn't mean to be taken that way. I have asked my sister how much insurance she got and she guaranteed me it was only $30,000. She said someone else must have cashed it [the second policy].

All of which proved that, even at such a late stage, the duplicitous Patricia Wright was still denying the existence of a second policy payout – even to her own beloved sister. Nevertheless, when I pointed out in reply that for someone else to cash in the policy was impossible – the insurance company's records were accepted by both prosecution and defence as totally accurate, and that Patricia had cashed in on the two policies because the money had been deposited in her bank account – Arletta had to concede:

> I agree. I believe you 100 per cent. My sister should have been straightforward right up front. It makes me look like a fool to go to bat with my sister if I don't have the truth. It definitely hurts a lot. Patricia should have been straight from the beginning and said 'Yes, I got the insurance but I didn't kill him'.

I reminded Arletta, a deeply religious person who quotes scripture in her letters, that she'd obviously carefully studied the court transcripts because she always had any other information I required at her fingertips. Surely, I suggested, she *must* have noticed the discrepancy over the insurance policies; she had, in fact, been a fraud investigator for a telephone company in the past. Did she not attend the trial and hear all of this before? Obviously, I suggested, motive for financial gain lies at the root of the matter.

Arletta's reply was interesting:

> I didn't get a chance to read the transcripts all the way through, though I do my best. I had my hands full for the past two years. My daughter had a baby girl. I didn't read all the transcripts. But I believe in my sister's innocence. I strongly believe the truth will come out.
>
> The truth will set Patricia free. This is the first time I have heard about my brother Larry Wright confessing to a murder. I have never ever heard of such. Where did you get that statement from? My brother was a little boy when Willie died.

I told Arletta that this statement had come from none other than Patricia Wright, who told me in a letter that Larry had confessed to the murder.

Arletta's reply was immediate. 'My sister never tells what she writes in letters.'

Like an insect struggling to extricate itself from a Venus Fly Trap, Patricia Wright is also fighting for her freedom. However, in doing so, she attempted to conceal the truth, not only from me, but she is still concealing the truth from the thousands of people who believe she is innocent – including the person she claims to love above all others, her sister, Arletta.

First, Patricia lied about the insurance policies and, it seems deceived Arletta into the bargain. Then she lied about Larry Wright admitting to the murder, and that all the family knew that Larry had confessed, when he had not and they hadn't either.

These days, Arletta remains deeply shocked; especially as for years she had convinced herself of Patricia's innocence, and she has gone to considerable lengths and financial expense through well-meaning efforts to prove it. Indeed, such is the deep-seated belief in Patricia's innocence that, even now, Arletta says she holds out hope that her sister is telling the truth and prays to God that this is so.

In one of Patricia Wright's letters to me from prison, she states, clutching at straws, 'There was no physical evidence, real or imagined, to say that I had committed the murder.'

At face value, Patricia Wright seems convincing enough. But, may I remind the reader of the letter written by the serial killer, Judy Buenoano, earlier in this book. She wrote this shortly before her execution:

Don't be fooled by me. Don't be fooled by the face that I wear for I wear a thousand masks; masks that I'm afraid to take off and none of them are me. Pretending is an art that is second nature to me but do not be fooled. For God's sake don't be fooled.

If the cap fits, wear it, and this all so true of Patricia Wright, but it was not physical evidence that convicted this utterly despicable woman – it was circumstantial evidence. It is the cumulative effect, the 'arithmetic of circumstantial evidence', which causes so many juries to say that, even though the evidence before them is entirely indirect, they are 'satisfied beyond any reasonable doubt' of the safety of convicting, as was the case with Larry Slaughter and, at a separate trial, that of Patricia Wright, whose final plea to me was:

> I am fighting for my life, Christopher. I simply received insurance money, now long gone, because of his death. I never wanted him gone or dead. We loved each other. We have a son who needs both his parents. We stayed friends till the end. I did not commit murder. I am innocent. I am a good person. I don't deserve this. Please help me.

In desperation, Arletta phoned her sister in prison. During the short conversation, Patricia finally admitted to the second policy, and Arletta confirmed this in an email to me dated Friday, 30 May 2003:

> Chris, thank you. I appreciate your help. I spoke to my sister Patricia Wright on Wednesday by telephone. I advised her that I needed the truth. My sister did say that, yes, she got all the insurance money. And I knew all along.

Having seen the meticulously presented files and documents sent to me by Arletta Wright, and having received much correspondence from her and speaking with her over the telephone, I am sure she is, or was, convinced of her sister's innocence. 'And I knew all along' might also refer to her own private suspicions.

Like a visitor viewing one of Monet's grand works, and as the closest relative to Patricia Wright, Arletta, a God-fearing woman, stood too close to the larger picture and, through no fault of her own, she couldn't see the wood for the trees.

Arletta Wright comes from homegrown and simple stock, and it is not uncommon for relatives – even faced with the obvious fact that one of their family is guilty as sin – to revert to denial. They simply cannot allow themselves to imagine that someone they love and hold dear to their hearts could commit such terrible crimes for such cold-blooded reasons. I am of the belief that Arletta is no exception. For years, her thoughts and feelings would have cemented into one of almost total belief in Patricia's claim of innocence. She has been surrounded by citizens, various journalists and lawyers who have supported Patricia Wright, and all of this had combined to strengthen Arletta's resolve. But herein lies the problem.

Arletta, and all of Patricia's supporters, have been predisposed – for their own personal and professional reasons – towards believing the protestations of this woman who is in prison. They have, in effect, their own well-meaning agendas. The newspaper articles reporting on the case are most certainly biased towards injustices perceived – rightly or wrongly – to have been carried out by a largely white California law and criminal justice system upon the black community. Nothing much has changed today.

Larry Wright insisted that he wanted to help his sister get out of jail. Then, in his second letter to me, he said he would only do so for $10,000 up front!

I believe that, in desperation, Arletta Wright turned to

me in an honest attempt to finally uncover the truth. She even offered to pay me up front for my time. I declined any payment, saying that, if I took the case, I would remain unbiased and I did not want to be influenced in any way. I explained that the chips would fall as they may, that my findings would be published for the public record, either to support Patricia's claim of innocence or to confirm her guilt.

This chapter is based upon 1,800 case documents and personal correspondence.

Patricia Wright (CDCR # W79941) now sits in a cell at the California Institution for Women (CIW), 16756 Chino-Corona Road, Corona, CA. For her there is no possibility of release.

Lawrence Slaughter (CDCR # J14215) is incarcerated at the California State Prison, Solano, 2100 Peabody Road, Vacaville, CA. For him there is no possibility of release.

I wish Arletta Wright all the best for the future, while this example of killing for an insurance payout reminds me of the next character who is, undoubtedly, as deadly as any male – Marilyn Kay Plantz./

Four More Killers

MARILYN KAY PLANTZ

Before her execution in May 2001, this killer made a statement: 'I want to tell all of my family that I love them very much, especially Trina and Chris. What God has given me is love and I have to overcome the world. And I just want to tell y'all to know that nothing, absolutely nothing, can separate us from the love of God. And if y'all want to see me again, you must be born again.'

Unlike the United Kingdom, US criminal history is littered with examples of women like Patricia Wright who kill for financial gain. Take Marilyn Kay Plantz for example.

Almost thirteen years after her husband James 'Jim' Earl Plantz was beaten and burned to death in a murder-for-insurance money scheme, thirty-nine-year-old Marilyn Plantz died by lethal injection on Tuesday, 1 May 2001 for her part in the murder. Plantz was pronounced dead at 9.11 p.m. after being injected with a poisonous mixture of drugs at the Oklahoma State Penitentiary 'Big Mac', McAlester.

Her death sentence came after her plot to kill her husband and collect $299,000 from a life insurance police taken out in his name.

On 26 August 1988, thirty-three-year-old Jim Plantz, a night shift press supervisor for *The Oklahoma* newspaper, was ambushed by William Clifford Bryson and Clinton Eugene McKimble as he came home from work with groceries in 1988. Marilyn had recruited the pair to carry out the murder. They attacked him with baseball bats and left him on the floor of his bedroom, bloody and in great pain. After pulling his vehicle around to the back of the house they threw him into the truck before driving to an isolated spot. Placing the semi-conscious Jim behind the wheel, McKimble stuffed a rag in the gas tank filler pipe and lit it. But the truck failed to explode. Bryson then doused their victim in petrol and set him on fire. As they sped off, McKimble said that when he looked back he saw Plantz struggling and rising up in the seat while flames shot out all around him.

Relatives said they initially believed the accident story she had concocted, and she was so convincing that they offered to help this seemingly distraught and plausible woman – even after her arrest.

'That's how believing we were,' said Karen Lowery, Jim's sister. 'We even tried to get a lawyer for her. Then the detectives started telling us what they found.'

The couple had been married for eleven years, and their two children, aged six and nine, were in a bedroom when the attack occurred. McKimble testified against Plantz and Bryson in exchange for a life sentence. Bryson was executed on 15 June 2000. Plantz was executed on 1 May 2000 to become the eleventh condemned inmate, and the second female, to be put to death in the 'Sooner State' in 2001, and the forty-first overall since America resumed executions.

For her last meal, inmate # 178478 Plantz ordered one chicken taco salad, one Mexican pizza, two enchiritos, two chicken soft tacos, one order of cinnamon twists, one piece of pecan pie and two cans of Coca-Cola.

Jim Plantz is buried in Plot # 61906061, Brown Cemetery Bethal Acres. Pottawatomie County, Oklahoma.

FRANCES ELAINE NEWTON

Born on Monday, 12 April 1965, Newton was already on probation from a 1986 probate forgery offence, when she was convicted of the murder of her twenty-three-year-old husband, Adrian, and two children: her son Alton, aged seven, and her twenty-month-old daughter, Farrah. These murders were committed on Tuesday, 7 April 1987.

The diminutive and slightly built accountant had taken out an insurance policy to the merry tune of $50,000 on her husband's life only a month before shooting her family with a .25-calibre pistol.

For the record, it was established that Newton and her husband had separated just the month prior to the killings and another policy *already existed* on her husband's life. She reasoned on a 'double-whammy' with two payouts if all went to plan. She later admitted taking a gun, which she claimed belonged to her boyfriend and who did the killing, to her estranged husband's apartment on the night of the murders, but told police that she took it only for protection, and that her family members were alive when she left.

Just like Patricia Wright and Marilyn Plantz, Newton filed insurance claims with somewhat indecent haste just nine days after the killings and was arrested and charged with capital murder the very next day, being Wednesday, 22 April.

Those who murder for insurance payouts are motivated by greed, and it is this avarice that almost always catches them out. They can conceive the start and finish of an enterprise but, in their haste to get their hands on the money, they frequently overlook the details and the many pitfalls that lie between: a description that fitted with Frances Newton like a glove.

Despite lengthy appeals, Newton finally met her 'Maker' on 14 September 2005. She became the third female to be executed in Texas since the resumption of capital punishment in 1982. The first and second were Karla Faye Tucker and Betty Lou Beets. She declined a final meal and made no statement after she was strapped to the lethal injection gurney, at 'The Walls' prison, Huntsville, to become the first African-American executed in 'The Lone Star State', since a slave named 'Lucy' was executed there on 7 March 1858.

Unlike most offenders who are executed in Texas, someone thought enough of her to pay for a private burial rather than have her placed in a common grave; the latter being in the Captain Joe Byrd Cemetery run by the Texas Department of Criminal Justice (TDCJ), colloquially known as 'Peckerwood Hill' – which when translated is an insult to poor white people – in Huntsville. Instead, Frances Newton's final resting place can be located as # 11771305, Plot 891N, Space 4, in the Paradise North Cemetery, Houston, Harris County, Texas.

However, let us not forget that the seemingly open,

smiling and honest face that Newton exhibits itself on any Internet search masks true evil.

But monetary gain was not quite what the next female killer had in mind. All she wanted was her victim's car!

ERICA YVONNE SHEPPARD

'Thou shalt not covet thy neighbour's car.' Certainly, Moses was not quite as specific as that, but nineteen-year-old Erica Yvonne Sheppard should have known that it doesn't do to covet things that belong to thy neighbours. In this instance the object of Erica's covetousness was a brand new Mazda 626, the property of one Marilyn Sage Meagher, aged forty-four.

Sheppard, with her nineteen-year-old boyfriend, James R. Dickerson, spotted Meagher carrying clothing from her car to her apartment at 465 Wild Indigo, Bay City, Texas, and decided to rob her of it.

The two would-be car owners tackled their victim in her apartment, demanding the keys at knifepoint. As the terrified woman begged for her life, the pair slashed her throat several times. They then wrapped a plastic bag around her head before smashing her skull with a ten-pound statue.

These two mindless, despicable morons fled in the Mazda but were later arrested. Both were sentenced to death. However, on Friday, 10 September 1999, # 999107 Dickerson died of AIDS appropriately on Death Row.

His former girlfriend awaits her Maker via lethal injection on Death Row at the Mountain View Unit, Gatesville, Texas, where she never stops complaining about the living conditions she lives under, while Marilyn Meagher is buried in Plot # 180823230, Forest Park Westheimer Cemetery in Houston.

KARLA FAYE TUCKER

Killing a woman for her new Mazda car is one thing but I simply could not resist including Karla Faye Tucker in this book. For this homicidal maniac ran amok all in the hope of stealing a motorcycle, and/or, some motorcycle parts. I cannot be more specific than this, I'm afraid – more to the point as Tucker hadn't a clue what she intended to steal in the first place!

When ordering her pre-execution meal she stated: 'Yes, sir. I'd like a banana, a peach and a salad with either Ranch or Italian dressing.'

Born Wednesday, 18 November 1959, Tucker was twenty-five-years-old, a white somewhat attractive drug addict and a prostitute, when on Monday, 13 June 1983, after a weekend orgy of indulging in methadone, heroin, Dilaudid, Valium, Placidyls, Somas, Wygesics, Percodan, Mandrax, marijuana, rum and tequila, she, with her pill-popping liquor-drinking accomplice, Daniel Ryan Garrett, aged thirty-seven, broke into an apartment on Watonga Drive, north-east, Houston.

The place was the home of twenty-seven-year-old Jerry Lynn Dean, a former lover of Tucker's, and the motive for the home invasion was the intended theft of a motorbike, and/or, some motorcycle parts. To the thieving couple's surprise, they found Dean asleep. Beside him, also asleep, but hidden from view under the bedclothes, lay his pretty thirty-two-year-old girlfriend, Deborah Thornton. What ensued was an orgy of blood-soaked violence and brutality on a sickening scale.

On seeing Dean, Garrett began hitting him about the head with a hammer, and this caused the victim to emit a gurgling sound. To put a stop to the noise, Tucker grabbed a pickaxe, which was lying in the room, and plunged it into Dean's back. She carried on raining blows on him until she became aware of Deborah cowering in terror in the bed and turned the pickaxe on her with an equally frenzied intensity.

Both victims mercifully died almost outright under the onslaught, which was about the only good aspect of the double killing. Their bodies were each punctured more than twenty times, and police had no trouble finding the murder weapon, as the pickaxe covered with Tucker's fingerprints was embedded in Thornton's chest.

Witnesses later testified that Tucker had boasted that she had been sexually aroused by what she was doing and had experienced an orgasm each time she struck her victims – all of which might seem like an overstatement, but it is certainly the first time I have ever come across a female killer who has 'enjoyed' a similar homicidal occurrence!

Nevertheless, what had begun as petty burglary had escalated tragically into a depraved slaughter. It also resulted in both Tucker and Garrett being sentenced to death for their gruesome crimes. Garrett, however – and much like the aforementioned Dickerson – cheated the executioner when he died of liver disease on Tuesday, 15 June 1993.

Inmate # 999777 Karla Tucker went on to spend more than fourteen years on Death Row. During that time she underwent a conversion to Christianity and became a model prisoner. Nonetheless, despite a widely publicised plea for mercy to the 'Whip 'em and Hang 'em Brigade', and Governor George W. Bush, she was executed by lethal injection on 3 February 1998, becoming the first woman to be executed by lethal injection in Texas since the Civil War. She is buried at the Forest Lawndale Cemetery, Houston.

Jerry Lynn Dean is buried at plot: 'Field of Flowers South, Row 7, # 37452867, at the Memorial Park and Cemetery, Tyler, Smith County.

For Deborah 'Debbie' Ruth Thornton *née* Carlson she had been a murder victim who was simply at the wrong place and the wrong time. She had moved to the Houston area from her home in Ohio with her brother Ron, to work in a trailer manufacturing company.

Deborah lies with her father, Homer D. Carlson and her mother Deborah at Section C, Plot 80, # 6843219, Mifflin Cemetery, Gahanna in Franklin County, Ohio.

And, at this very point, I feel the desperate need to digress with a 'sex change' if you will allow me; simply because I need to get some balance into this book because it is not only female killers who bungle the job – more often than not men do to. The incident springing to mind, tragic as it is, the flip being the definition of 'black humour' at its best. I'll call it 'The Tom and Jerry Case'.

On Thursday, 26 June 1997, one Derrick Wayne Frazier, unemployed and a native of Dallas, along with an accomplice called Jermaine Herron, took public transport to the suburb of Refugio and began their evening by burgling a house, from which the stole a considerable amount of property. Nevertheless, the success of their endeavours posed a problem for these two halfwits, for how were they going to get all this merchandise/swag home? On the bus?

After some heated deliberation in the well-lit street, they reached an agreement, and proceeded to the house next door, the dwelling of Betsy Nutt who was married to Jerry Nutt and which they shared with her fifteen-year-old son, Cody. Her husband was out at the time, so quite why Betsy offered her nocturnal visitors a ride back to town will always remain a mystery. However, when she went outside to start her vehicle, Frazier followed her and shot the lady in the face at point-blank range with a 9-millimetre handgun. As she fell to the ground, he fired another bullet into her back. For his part, Herron shot young Cody once in the head and three times in the chest.

Now, I would like you to picture this for the Nutt's home sat in the middle of a very quiet, respectable neighbourhood, even a lot quieter at night. After 8pm one can hear a pin drop, the only noises coming from those inquisitive enough to pull back a window blind and poke their noses into anyone else's business. Now there was shouting and arguing under a street lamp followed by gunfire, nevertheless, after looting Betsy's home of guns, ammunition, sports equipment and sports clothes, the two master-criminals loaded her brand new pick-up with the proceeds of both robberies but, before feeling the scene, yet another heated debate ensued – this time over the matter of destroying any forensic evidence of their visit. Eventually, consensus was reached and, in an ill-inspired but totally misguided moment, these two cartoon characters set fire to Betsy's house. As the place burst into flames it suddenly dawned on the two idiots that neither of them had driven a motor vehicle in their lives – all combining in yet another act of massive stupidity that guaranteed the almost instantaneous arrival of every law enforcement officer from there to Kingdom-come and the fire department! After a *very* short car chase, during which Mr Frazier decided that the fastest route to the freeway was through someone's backyard, both men were arrested.

As might be expected, Frazier was executed on 31 August 2006. His last rambling statement was this: 'Yes I do. Debbie, my Baby, I love you; do you know I love you. You are my life. You are my wife – always stay strong. Stay strong everybody. *I am innocent. I am being punished for a crime I did not commit. I have professed my innocence for nine years, and I continue to say I am innocent.* Let my people know I love them. We must continue on. Do not give up the fight; do not give up hope for a better future. Because we can make it happen. I love you, I love my son, and I love my daughter. Bruno, Chuckie, Juanita, Ray – I love you, all of you. Stay strong baby. I love you forever.' [Author's italics].

Herron was executed on 17 May 2006, but not before tucking into his last meal: Sirloin steak, spicy Worcester sauce, a bacon cheeseburger with ten slices of bacon, onion rings and fries with cheese, French dressing, a butter finger blizzard with caramel, pecan pie, vanilla ice cream and peach cobbler.

For his part, Frazier had in mind dieting for he refused any food at all – but now back to the gals.

Aileen 'Lee' Carol Wuornos

Method of Killing: Shooting
Regardless of range, most entrance wounds will be surrounded by an inflamed ring of abraded skin. This is caused when the bullet in flight indents the skin as it punches a hole through, abrading the skin around the wound as it does so. The abrasion ring varies in the width depending upon the calibre of the projectile and the location of the wound on the body. Even where there is no evidence of an abrasion ring, it will, nevertheless, be obvious which is the entry wound as it presents a circular oval punched-out hole.

Victims
Richard Mallory (fifty-one), David Andrew Spears (forty-seven), Charles E. Carskaddon, Jr (forty), Peter Siems (sixty-five), Troy Eugene 'Buddy' Burress (fifty), Charles Richard 'Dick' Humphreys (fifty-six) and Walter Gino Antonio (sixty)

Here are the final words of Aileen Wuornos before her execution by lethal injection on Wednesday, 9 October 2002, in Florida State Prison, Raiford: 'I'd just like to say I'm sailing with the rock, and I'll be back like Independence Day, with Jesus June 6. Like the movie, big mothership and all, I'll be back.'

It is quite clear from Lee's final words that she had already lost the plot; certainly forgetting that Independence Day falls on the Fourth of July (not 6 June), which is certainly confirmed in the plot of the 1996 blockbuster movie *Independence Day* starring Jeff Goldblum and Will Smith, and you can also take their word for it, I'm sure. However, considering the fix Lee now found herself in perhaps you may forgive her for this terminal slip-up, but I do like the 'I shall return' part. This brings back memories of that old WWII warhorse, the corncob pipe smoking General Douglas McArthur, and his famous speech on Wednesday, 11 March 1942 before he fled the Philippines to escape the Japs, with this twist. MacArthur did return to liberate the country while Aileen was reduced to ashes. God Bless her cotton socks.

For those even remotely acquainted with 'Doug', one will know that he carried a 1903 .45-calibre ACP Colt semi-automatic pistol. Lee Wuornos packed 'heat' as well. Her choice of weapon was a 'Hi-Standard' double and single action 9-chambered .22-calibre revolver. This was a sweet-shooting little pistol with its six right twist 4-inch barrel firing .22 cal copper-jacketed rimfire long or short 40 grain rounds, most probably of Blazer manufacture, available at any Wal-Mart store for about fifteen bucks per 500. So, this was Lee's firearm. She kept it in her shoulder bag or her purse. Really ideal only for target shooting and killing at close quarters, nevertheless, travelling at 12,222 feet per second those little slugs certainly did the job Lee intended them for – blasting holes in her victims at point-blank range.

Like scores of other writers over the years I too have written extensively about Aileen Wuornos. Indeed, my book *Monster* published by John Blake accompanied the 2003 movie *Monster* starring Charlize Theron playing Aileen, and Christina Ricci starring as her lesbian girlfriend, Selby Wall (her name being changed in the film for legal reasons). I have interviewed Lee on Death Row, so I like to think I know quite a bit about this serial killer, aka: Sandra Kretcsch, Susan Lynn Blahovec, Lee Blahovec, Cammie Marsh Green, Lori Kristine Grody to round off with her full name at the time of death being: Aileen Carol Wuornos Pralle, born Troy, Michigan, on Wednesday, 29 February 1956, as Aileen Carol Pitman.

De mortuis nil nisi bonum ([say] of the dead nothing but good) is a phrase I am going turn upside down in this grim, often heart-breaking account of Lee's life and crimes, pulling no punches whatsoever in doing so this time around. For more questions are now being raised for which there are answers.

Before I plunge the reader into this nitty-gritty world of blood, brains and gore, I need to say that I've always asked myself the following question. With Lee being a two-Star hooker with interstate flight plastered all over her face and with an established two-hundred 'clients' of whom a great number say that she was a good lass, why did she murder Mallory, Spears, Carskaddon, Siems, Burress, Humphries and Antonio? What was it that triggered Lee into shooting to death these seven men? What was her motive for killing these men and not others amongst her wide and varied customer base? Could it be, as dreadful as this may sound, a case of them getting their just deserts? Because as we delve deeper into Lee's seven-fold victimology we find terrifying echoes from her past – from as early as when she was the age of nine, maybe younger.

One of two siblings, Lee was born on the wrong side of the tracks in Troy, Michigan. 1956 was a leap year, and during the early hours of 29 February, at Clinton Hospital Detroit, she came struggling into this world, her parents being teenager Diana Wuornos and her estranged husband nineteen-year-old odd-job man, Leo Dale Pittman. Lee never knew her father and this was probably a good thing. He was jailed on charges of kidnapping, rape and child molestation. He fashioned a noose from a bed sheet and hanged himself while in prison. Lee was, by then, fifteen years old.

Having now disposed of Lee's father we can turn back the clock to her mother, who soon found the responsibilities of looking after three children unbearable. When Lee was just six months old, Diane upped sticks, left home and never returned, and if you think things couldn't have got worse, think again – enter Ford factory worker Laurie Wuornos and his wife, Britta, who subsequently adopted Lee, and her older brother Keith, to place both children into a house of sexual horrors.

The most remarkable thing about the home – an unprepossessing single floor, yellow wooden cladded place amidst a cluster of trees set back from the roadside – was its unremarkabilty. There are millions of almost identical homes scattered across the US of A, however, although innocent looking to passers-by, it was nevertheless a place of sick and sexually perverse secrets.

To begin with, the Wuornoses were not neighbourly folk. No yard sales or Sunday barbeques for them. There were insular people who minded their own business and demanded that everyone else minded theirs. There were never any casual pleasantries; no neighbour was ever invited in, let alone to put a foot on the stoop. The curtains were always drawn tight, the inference being that the outside world should be kept very much at arm's length.

The Wuornoses raised Lee and Keith as their own children, never letting on that they were, in fact, their grandparents. There may be some justification for this deception, but Lee and her adoptive and heavy-drinking father did not get on. Frequent clashes took place, the omnipresent third party, not being Britta but a wide, brown Western-tooled leather belt with a heavy brass buckle. Laurie kept it hanging on a peg behind his bedroom door. At his bidding, this belt was cleaned, almost repetitively, by Lee with saddle soap and conditioner.

There are accounts arguing that Laurie or 'Lauri' was a good, hard-working man, almost a Bible-thumping Christian with not a stain attached to his character. However, what transpires is that he often forced Lee to strip naked, forced her to bend over the kitchen table, so that the terrified seven and eight and nine-year-old child was being frequently beaten black and blue with the doubled-over cowhide belt. Sometimes she lay face down, spread-eagled, naked on her bed to receive her whippings and God only knows what else, while all the time her 'father' screamed that she was worthless and should never have been born. 'You ain't even worthy of the air you breathe,' he shouted, as the belt lashed down and down again.

When she was around eleven years of age, Lee learned the truth: that her parents were in fact her grandparents. She was already a rebellious youngster with a fearsome temper, all of which did nothing to improve things at home. Then, aged fourteen, she fell pregnant and was sent to an unmarried mothers' home to await the birth of her child. The baby was adopted in January 1971. That July, Britta Wuornos died of natural causes. On hearing the sad news, the formerly, longtime absent real mother, Diane, invited Lee and Keith to stay with her in 'The Lone Star State', but the children declined. Keith went his own way and little more of him is known, but Lee dropped out of school, left home, and took up hitchhiking and prostitution.

In March 1976, now aged twenty, she married multi-millionaire Lewis Gratz Fell, whose age was sixty-nine. This union, as might be expected, soon fell apart with the old codger being beaten up by her every time he tried to curb Lee's riotous lifestyle. He had been forced to obtain a restraining order and an annulment of the marriage. He claimed that she had squandered his money and beaten him with a walking cane. The divorce decree stated: 'Respondent has a violent and ungovernable temper and has threatened to do bodily harm to the Petitioner and from her past actions will injure Petitioner and his property...unless the court enjoins and restrains said Respondent from assaulting...or interfering with Petitioner or his property.' The marriage officially ended on 19 July 1976, with a divorce issued at the Volusia County courthouse in Florida. She pawned her expensive diamond engagement ring.

Lee next comes to our attention on Tuesday, 13 July 1976, in the sleepy village of Mancelona in Antrim County, Michigan. She was at the smoke-filled Bernie's Club, hustling pool, drunk and flaunting her slim figure. At around midnight, the barman and manager, Danny Moore, had seen enough of her so he asked her to leave. He walked over to close down the table and as he was gathering up the snooker balls, someone shouted 'Duck!' He turned just in time to see Lee aim a ball at his head. It missed him by a whisker, but had been hurled with such force that the missile became lodged in the wall.

The violent young woman was soon arrested and hauled off to jail. She was also charged on fugitive warrants. The Troy PD had requested that she be picked up for drinking alcohol in a car, unlawful use of a driver's licence, and for not having a Michigan state driver's licence. A friend who found $1,450 in her purse bailed her. Three days later, her brother, Keith, aged twenty-one, died of throat cancer.

On Wednesday, 4 August 1976, Aileen pleaded guilty to the assault and battery charge committed at Bernie's Club, paying a fine and costs of $105.00. Then she had a windfall. Keith's very brief army life insurance policy paid out and, as next-of-kin, she received $10,000. The money was immediately put down as a deposit on a shiny black Pontiac (which was soon repossessed because she failed to keep up the payments). She also squandered money on a mixed bag of antiques and a massive stereo system, although she had no home at the time. All of the money was frittered away within three months.

Aileen Wuornos was only twenty years old at this time and her life had been a car wreck from the get-go, and now, adrift in the world once again, she embarked on a series of failed relationships and small time forgery, theft, prostitution and a somewhat ridiculous robbery, committed while she was highly intoxicated, that put her in prison for a spell.

Aside from all of this, Lee more-or-less vanishes under our radar until 1986 when she arrived in Daytona Beach, Florida. She had hitchhiked south on Interstate 95, and thought she had found paradise. There was sunshine, job opportunities and living was cheap. You might say that Lee was in her element in Daytona Beach: sex, sea, prosperity and exhaust fumes – an All-American illusion served up on white, sandy beaches lined with bars and booze galore, and it was in one of these bars – a girlie gay bar – that she met twenty-four-year-old Tyria 'Ty' Jolene Moore.

Her life on the road had not treated Aileen Wuornos well. She was starting to lose her once pretty looks and was putting on weight. For her part the now thirty-year-old interstate hooker, with a growing criminal record, fell in love with the slim, taller Tyria and, for a while, life was great. Ty loved Lee and stayed close to her. She even quit her job as a motel maid for a while – allowing her more 'butch' dominant girlfriend to support her with earnings from prostitution. In due course, perhaps predictably, their ardour cooled and money began to run short. Yet, still Ty stayed with Lee, following her around like a puppy, from cheap hotel to cheap motel, with stints sleeping in old barns and outhouses in between – their dream to move onto Miami, settle down and try to live 'The All-American Dream'. But Lee's market value as a hooker, never spectacular, now fell even further: she was thirty-three-years-old, and her sell-by date as a hooker all but a distant memory. We do not find here some glamorous, leggy, streetwalker so often portrayed in the Hollywood movies, but before us we have a mostly unkempt, scruffy, loud-mouthed piece-of-work; a two-star prostitute as far down on her luck as she could go.

RICHARD MALLORY

People get murdered in Daytona, as in any city for the usual reasons – money, revenge, sex and business – but Daytona Beach seems to provoke a unique end-of-the-line dementia with an average homicide rate of around fifteen killings a year. Lee would account for seven of them.

This gritty beach town is also a good bet for a cheap, working man's vacation. Redneck tourists from all over the southeast knew this, and so did fifty-one-year-old Richard Mallory, out of Clearwater, Florida, who disappeared on Thursday, 30 November 1989.

On Friday 1 December, police were called to an abandoned car near John Anderson Drive in Ormond Beach. The cop walked around the car noting that it was a light beige, two-door, 1987 Cadillac Coup de Ville, with a brown interior and tinted windows. Deputy Bonnevier noticed bloodstains on the front seat backrest, behind the steering wheel, but there were no signs of the driver or any passengers. The car ignition keys were not in the switch, but numerous items were found a short distance from the vehicle. Partially buried in the sandy soil was a blue nylon wallet containing a Florida driving licence in the name of Richard Mallory, miscellaneous papers, and two long-expired credit cards. There were also two plastic tumbler-type glasses and a half-empty bottle of vodka, along with several other items, all of which suggested that the driver had not been alone. A further check by Officer Bonnevier confirmed that Mallory lived at a multi-family apartment complex called 'The Oaks' in Clearwater. He had spent ten years in prison for sexual violence, and was known to the Clearwater PD as a regular user of hookers, most of whom knew him by sight, and he was a frequent visitor to go-go bars and strip clubs. He liked the way women looked, they smelled and they way they walked. But, perhaps, with the discovery of his abandoned car, his days spent trawling for sex had come to a sticky end? And, indeed they had.

On Wednesday, 13 December, two young men out scavenging for scrap metal, found a corpse at a spot roughly five miles across the Halifax River from where the Cadillac had been found. Volusia County deputies soon arrived at the scene to find a body which was skeletonised from the collarbone to the top of the head. It lay under a piece of cardboard with only the fingers showing. It was fully dressed in jeans and a pullover, the belt slightly askew. The pockets of the jeans had been turned inside out. The man's dentures lay on the ground next to the body.

Charles James Lau, an investigator with the Volusia County Sheriff's Department, oversaw an immediate autopsy and recovered four bullets from the torso. The hands of the victim were removed and taken to the crime lab for latent print examination because, as Lau explained, 'When we have an unidentified body, you can't roll the fingerprints because of the decomposition.' The body was that of Richard Mallory.

Born on 18 October 1938, in Sumter County, Florida, Mallory had been a private man, not very communicative, a mystery even to those who should have known him best. He lived, however, an erratic lifestyle and ran a failing television and video repair shop called Mallory Electronics, in the strip shopping mall in Palm Harbor. Some say that he was a good-looking man with a full head of dark hair combed back from a high forehead. Standing at just under six foot tall, the neatly moustachioed Mallory surveyed the world through hazel eyes behind wide-rimmed spectacles. He cut a trim physique, tipping the scales at just less than 170 pounds, a self-serving ladies' man who thought of himself as fifty-one years young.

Be that as it may, Mr Mallory was in dire financial straits. He owed $4,000 in rent arrears and his finances were due to be audited by the Inland Revenue Service (IRS). Despite this, he owned two vans, one white and the other maroon – he owed money on them, too.

Piecing together Mallory's last drive in this world it has been established that after a handful of northbound rides Lee Wuornos had been dropped off outside Tampa on Interstate Highway 1-4, right at the junction where it passes under Highway I-17. Quite why Lee was so far west is unknown, however, it was raining heavily and she was lingering under the overpass In order to avoid the downpour until the weather improved. Mallory spotted her and slowed down, then reversed and offered her a lift. As they drove, they chatted amicably, and en route, stopped to buy a pack of beer. It was around 5.00 a.m. when, according to Lee, Mallory broached the subject of sex. At the location where his corpse was found, he pulled off the road and into nearby woods. Lee peeled off her clothes before he did, and they hugged and kissed for a while.

According to police, suddenly, and apparently without being provoked, she produced her revolver and began firing at Mallory. The first .22-calibre bullet struck his right arm and entered his body. Desperately, he tied to crawl out of the car when another bullet slammed into his torso, quickly followed by a third and a fourth. Mallory did not die immediately. The copper-coated, hollow-nose bullet, which struck him in the right side of his chest, had penetrated his left lung, passing through the organ before coming to rest in the chest cavity. During its passage, the bullet caused massive and fatal haemorrhage. He struggled to cling on to life for a further fifteen minutes as Aileen stood close and watched him expire. This is what the police will have us to believe, however, the truth is something quite different, as we shall learn later.

DAVID ANDREW SPEARS

By the middle of May 1990, the Volusia County Sheriff's Department had all but forgotten the murder of Richard Mallory. There was, seemingly, no reason to believe it was anything other than an isolated homicide, but then another man's body was found.

On Sunday, 20 May, a cream pickup truck was found abandoned near County Road 318 and I-75 in Marion County. A long, blonde hair was found on the steering wheel and a torn open condom packet was discovered on the floor of the cab, which was registered to one David Spears, a Universal Concrete construction worker, who lived in Winter Garden, near Orlando. All of the man's personal property, including tools, clothing and a 'one-of-a-kind' ceramic statue of a panther, which he had bought as a gift for his former wife, Dee, was missing. A closer inspection revealed that the driver's seat was pulled too close to the steering wheel for a man of David's height, indicating to investigators that someone else had driven the truck, but there was not a sign of David Spears to be found at the scene.

On Friday, 1 June, a man stumbled upon the body of a male lying in a clearing amidst pine trees and palmettos. Mathew Cocking had just walked past an illegal dumping site on West Fling Lane, a dirt road south of Chassahowitzka in Citrus County, and running adjacent to US 19/South Suncoast Bvld and S. Knightswood Point.

When law enforcement arrived, they found the badly decomposing body, naked except for a camouflage baseball cap which sat jauntily atop a ravaged head. On the ground near the body were a used Trojan brand condom, its torn black packet, and several empty cans of Busch and Budweiser beer. At first, because of the state of the body, the police were unable to determine the sex, age or likely cause of death, which was certainly not a natural death by any means. The corpse had been laid on its back, legs apart, arms outstretched, palms facing skyward.

Dr Janet Pillow carried out the autopsy on Monday 4 June. The man, who weighed approximately 195 pounds in life, had been reduced to 40 pounds by the time he was discovered. Six .22-calibre bullets were recovered from the corpse.

As ex-husbands go, it appears that forty-seven-year-old David Spears was perfect. Predictable, honest and hardworking, he was a man people counted on. Keen eyes, a rich head of dark hair, a shy, soft-spoken giant standing six-foot four-inches tall, bearded, greying and weather-lined from his outdoor lifestyle, he cared enough about his former wife, Dee, to give her a regular portion of his monthly pay cheque. Just before lunchtime on Friday, 18 May 1990, David called

Dee and told her to expect him to pop in to visit with her somewhere between 2 and 2.30 p.m. the next day. He was last seen leaving work at about 2.10 p.m. driving his cream pickup truck, never to been seen alive again.

From the evidence gathered by police, indeed from Aileen Wuornos herself, it has been established that he spotted Lee thumbing for a ride somewhere near the point where Route 27 intersects with I-4, about thirty-six miles from Spears's home in Winter Garden, and he offered her a ride. She told him that she needed to get to Homosassa Springs, and this was right out of his way. Nevertheless, he obliged, and nevertheless, at some place en route he stopped at a store and bought beer. They ended up pulling off the road on US 19, close to Homosassa Springs, and then with sex in mind he drove so deep into the woods that Spears was worried that his truck would get stuck. Shortly, thereafter, Lee pulled out her revolver and shot him dead. She dumped the body and stole her victim's wages, his granddaughter's graduation money and a quantity of cash, which was hidden in the truck for emergencies amounting to about $600.00.

David Spears is buried in the Winter Garden Cemetery, Winter Garden, Orange County, Florida.

CHARLES E. CARSKADDON, JR

On Wednesday, 6 June 1990, a man's naked body was found off State Route 52 and I-75 in Pascoe County. The corpse was covered with grass and foliage and a green electric blanket. Autopsy examination revealed that the man had been shot nine times with a .22-calibre handgun.

The following day, police attention was drawn to an

abandoned brown 1975 Cadillac near 1-75 and County Road 484 in Marion County. Although the licence plate had been removed, the vehicle's identification number (VIN) was still intact and this revealed the registered owner's name as forty-year-old Charles Carskaddon, a sometime road digger and rodeo rider.

Carskaddon's mother, Florence, told police that when her only son left her home in Prairie, Missouri, to travel to Tampa, Florida, to pick up his fiancée, Peggy, he was carrying a blue steel .45-calibre revolver with a pearl handle, a Mexican blanket, stun gun, flip-top lighter, watch and a tan suitcase. He was wearing a black T-shirt and grey, snakeskin cowboy boots. She told police. 'He'd removed the firing pin from the gun,' adding, 'because he was scared to use it.'

None of the aforementioned items were found in his abandoned Cadillac. Whether money was stolen we do not know.

Charles Carskaddon is buried at the Walnut Grove Cemetery, Boonville, Cooper County, Missouri.

PETER SIEMS

On Wednesday, 4 July 1990, an elderly couple called Jim and Rhonda Bailey, were sitting on their stoop enjoying a balmy evening. Their home was set back from a sharp bend along State Road 315, near Orange Springs, an unincorporated community in Florida, when a spectacular accident happened before their very eyes. They heard a screech of brakes then saw a four-door silver-grey Pontiac Sunbird career across the road, and it smashed through their steel gate and barbed wire fence, shattering the windscreen before coming to rest in the undergrowth. For a moment it appeared that the car might roll over, but it righted itself, with steam hissing from the radiator.

Jim and Rhonda then saw two dishevelled women clamber out of the wreck, noting that one was a short, heavy blonde (Aileen Wuornos) and the other, a tall brunette (Tyria Moore). The blonde, whose arms were bleeding from the cuts sustained in the crash, started throwing beers cans into the woods and swearing at her friend, who said very little. It was obvious that both women were very drunk.

Rising to their feet, the two bemused witnesses noted that the women grabbed a red-and-white beer cooler from the back seat and, still arguing, staggered off down the road. At the approach of other cars, they would dash into the woods and hide; only to reappear after the vehicles had passed and returned to the car.

When Rhonda rushed over to offer what little assistance she could, the blonde begged her not to call the police, saying that her father lived just up the road. Then the two women climbed back into the vehicle and, with some difficulty, managed to reverse it onto the road and drive off. Within minutes, a front tyre went flat and, with the Pontiac now disabled, Wuornos and Moore had no other option than to abandon it. They ripped off the rear licence plate and threw it, together with the car keys, into the woods and walked away.

A public-spirited motorist, thinking that the women might need help, pulled over and offered assistance. He noticed that the blonde was not only bleeding but also very drunk. When she asked him for a lift, he thought better of it and refused, whereupon Wuornos became very abusive. The man drove off, but contacted the Orange Springs Fire Department and told them about the injured woman.

Two emergency vehicles were despatched to the scene, but when they arrived, Wuornos denied that they had been in the car. 'I don't know anything about any accident,' she snapped. 'I want people to stop telling lies and leave us alone.'

At 9.44 p.m., Trooper Rickey responded to the emergency call, and found the car. (It was not until almost two months later that detectives learned exactly where it had first crashed, or heard the account given by Rhonda and Jim Bailey.) Marion County's Deputy Lawing was sent over to investigate the abandoned, smashed-up Pontiac. The VIN was checked, identifying the owner as Peter Siems, who was now reported as missing.

Born on Thursday, 21 May 1925, Peter was a sixty-five-year-old retired merchant seaman, living in Jupiter, Florida. He stood five-foot seven-inches tall, and weighed 160 pounds. He had grey hair and brown eyes. Early in the morning of Thursday, 7 June 1990, neighbours saw him outside his home in the 100 block of Beverley Road, placing luggage and a stack of Bibles into his silver-grey Pontiac. They assumed, correctly, that the balding, bespectacled man was off on another of his 'Word-spreading' trips as a member of the evangelical 'Christ Is the Answer' crusade. He was supposed to visit his mother in West Milford, New Jersey, possibly travel to Arkansas to visit his son, and then join members of his missionary group in Fort Payne, Alabama. Then he was reported as missing.

His suspicions further aroused as to obvious foul play, Deputy Lawing made a thorough examination of the car's interior. Latent bloody fingerprints were found and there were bloodstains on the seat fabric and on the door handles. He recovered Busch and Budweiser beer cans, as well as Marlborough cigarettes and two beverage cosies. Underneath the front passenger seat was a bottle of Windex window spray with an Eckerd Drugs price label attached to it. This ticket was easily traceable to a store in Gordon Street in Atlanta, Georgia.

By now, a police artist had drawn composites of the two women based on descriptions given by several witnesses of the incident with the Pontiac. Armed with these sketches and the bottle of Windex, investigators travelled to Atlanta to question the manager of Eckerd Drugs. Viewing the pictures, he recalled the two women entering his store on a Friday night. 'We are in a bad part of town in a predominantly black area and white people do not venture into this area after dark,' he said. The manager remembered that the two women purchased cosmetics and a black box of Trojan condoms, the same brand found near David Spears's body and inside his truck. A beverage cosy was also traceable to a Speedway store near to the entrance/exit ramps of 1-75 in Wildwood, Georgia, close to the state line between Tennessee – a 680-mile, 10-hour drive north from Siems's home in Jupiter, Florida.

Both Peter and his wife were both part-time missionaries. They neither drank nor smoked, and relatives stated that the couple had never travelled to Atlanta. John Wisnieski of the Jupiter PD had been working on the case since Siems was reported missing. He sent out a nationwide Teletype containing descriptions of the two women, and he also sent a synopsis of the case, together with the descriptions and sketches of the two women, to the *Florida Criminal Activity Bulletin*. Then he waited. He was not optimistic about finding

Siems alive: the man's body had not been found, his credit cards had not been used, and money had not been withdrawn from his bank account.

Peter's body has never been found.

TROY EUGENE 'BUDDY' BURRESS

Born in Savannah, Hardin County, Tennessee, on Sunday, 28 January 1940, to John Solomon and Clara Imogen Burress, the ever-smiling Troy had celebrated his fiftieth birthday in January 1990. With a natural gift for the gab, he was employed as a part-time salesman for the Gilchrist Sausage Company in Ocala, a resort town in Marion County, Florida, where he also lived. He also ran his own company, Troy's Pools, in Boca Raton, 263 miles south of his home.

On Monday, 30 July 1990, Troy set out on Gilchrist business, travelling the firm's Daytona route, which took him to several customers throughout central Florida. His last planned stop was to have been Salt Springs, in Marion County. This was Wuornos's 'Killing Country', and he never arrived.

When he failed to report to his office after work, Gilchrist manager, Mrs Jonnie Mae Thompson, started calling around and discovered that her employee had failed to show up for his last delivery. She immediately went out in search of him and, at 2 a.m. his wife Rose reported him as missing. The police recorded her description of a slightly built man, around five-foot six-inches in height and weighing about 155 pounds, with blue eyes and blond hair.

This time around there was a fast response and a quick, though tragic outcome. For at 4 a.m., Marion County deputies located the Gilchrist delivery van, distinctive with its black cab, white refrigerator and company logo, on the shoulder of State Road 19, twenty miles east of Ocala. The vehicle was locked and the keys were missing – as was Troy Burress.

Five days later, a family were out picnicking in the Ocala National Forest, when they chanced upon a body, in a clearing, just off Highway 19, and about eight miles from the abandoned delivery van. Florida's heat and humidity had hastened decomposition, precluding identification at the scene, however, this issue was soon resolved – Troy's wife recognised the wedding ring on his finger.

Troy had been killed by two shots from a .22-calibre handgun, one to the chest and one to the back. A clipboard with delivery details and receipts, which had been removed from the van, was found near the corpse, but the company's takings were missing.

Following Aileen's execution, Troy's sister, Leta Prater, said: 'She had death on her face. She looked rough but she always looked rough. I for one am glad she's gone.'

Troy Burress is buried at The Good Shepherd Memorial Gardens, Ocala.

CHARLES RICHARD 'DICK' HUMPHREYS

Born on Friday, 15 December 1933, Dick Humphreys, of Crystal River, a coastal city in Citrus County, Western Florida, never made it home from his last day of work at the Sumterville office of the Florida's Department of Health and Rehabilitation Services. An investigator specialising in protecting abused and injured children, the fifty-six-year-old was about to transfer to the department's office at Ocala. He was man of some experience who had formerly served as a police chief in Alabama.

Here we find a man who should have known better than pick up a hooker, but he did, for on Tuesday, 11 September 1990, he disappeared. The following evening, his body was found off County Road 484 near I-75 in Marion County. Dick had been shot seven times. Six .22-calibre bullets were recovered from his body but the seventh copper-jacketed round had passed through his wrist and was never found. His wallet and money were missing.

Humphreys's Oldsmobile Firenza car was found on Wednesday, 19 September, some seventy miles to the north. It had been backed into a space behind an abandoned Banner gas station at the intersection of I-10 and State Route 90, near Live Oak, in Suwannee County. The licence plate, keys and a bright yellow Highway Patrol Association sticker had been removed from the car.

During an initial examination of the vehicle, it was noted that almost everything which told the world it had belonged to Dick Humphreys was gone or had been trashed, just like his life. Even his ice-scrapers, his maps, his personal papers, business documents and warranties. His favourite pipe, in the newly-carved wooden tray up on the dashboard, was also missing. By way of a 'thank you', Wuornos left one can of Budweiser beer under the front passenger seat. Nevertheless, back at the police pound, investigators looked closer.

The interior revealed a cash register receipt for beer or wine from EMRO store number 8237 – a Speedway truck stop and convenience store located at State Route 44 and I-75 in Wildwood. This was vital evidence because the receipt was time-stamped 4.19 p.m. on 11 September 1990, and the same day that Dick left his Sumterville office. The female clerk who had been on duty at the time could not identify the man in the car but did recognise the composite police sketches of Wuornos and Moore. From their body language, the clerk formed the impression they were hookers. When they left the store, she believed they drove away together with the man and therefore did not call the police, as she was obliged to – this was because prostitutes are banned from truck stops as well as rest areas throughout Florida.

Most of Dick Humphreys's personal effects, including his pipe, which was returned to his wife, were found a month later in a wooded field off Boggy Marsh Road, Clermont, in southern Lake County near US 27.

Dick Humphreys is buried at the Florida National Cemetery, Bushnell, Sumter County.

WALTER GINO ANTONIO

Born on Thursday, 22 November 1928, sixty-two-year-old Walter, from Cocoa, Florida, was driving his maroon Pontiac Grand Prix car to Alabama, in search of a job. Recently engaged to be married he wore a gold-and-silver diamond ring, a gift from his fiancée. When his beloved didn't hear from him she reported him to police, as missing.

On Sunday, 18 November 1990, an off-duty cop, out hunting, stumbled upon a man's body, naked except for a pair of tube socks, near the intersection of US19 and US 27 in Dixie County. At autopsy, it was determined that Walter had been shot four times, three times in the torso and once in the head, with a .22-calibre handgun. On Saturday, 24 November the man's car was found in a wooded area near I-95 and US 1, in northern Brevard County. The licence plate and keys were missing and, like Humphreys's car, a bumper sticker had been removed. A piece of paper had been crudely pasted over the VIN, and the doors were locked. Empty Budweiser cans were found on the ground near the vehicle, which had been wiped clean of prints.

Detectives soon learned that the deceased had meticulously recorded every purchase he made of car fuel, retaining the gas station receipts on which he noted his mileage. From this methodical behaviour, they were able to deduce that, in the week since his disappearance, his car had been driven for over 1,000 miles.

Walter Antonio's fiancée gave the police a list of possessions that had been in his car, which included handcuffs, a reserve deputy badge, police Billy club, flashlight, a Timex wristwatch, a suitcase, a toolbox and a baseball cap. All of these items were missing. The man's personal identification and clothing were discovered in a wooded area in Taylor County, approximately thirty-eight miles north of the body's location. The rest was never found.

In just over a year, Lee Wuornos had scattered a trail of middle-aged male corpses across the highways of central Florida. But does she deserve the bad press and notoriety she has subsequently earned as being toe-tagged one of the most heinous female serial killers of all time? Maybe yes. Maybe no!

HER CAPTURE

Following a lengthy investigation, Aileen Wuornos was arrested just after midnight on Wednesday 9 January 1991. Her companion, Tyria Moore, was located on 10 January, living with her sister in Pittston, Pennsylvania. She was interviewed and eventually gave evidence for the prosecution at Lee's trial.

My book, *Monster* (John Blake Publishing, 2006), thoroughly details the life and crimes of Lee Wuornos. As stated earlier, this book formed the foundation of the movie by the same name, starring Charlize Theron.

WHY DID SHE KILL?

Florida derives its name after it was discovered on Palm Sunday 1513 by Spanish explorer, Ponce de Leon, who called it Pascua de Florida, 'Feast of the Flowers', and on the roads of 'The Sunshine State' there are highways and byways and dirt roads, crossroads, on and off ramps, where two lives can meet with destructive results. One life comes to an end, and the other takes a permanent detour. I call these places 'Murder Crossroads' and Lee Wuornos haunted these places like a deadly spider sitting at the centre of its web.

To all intents and purposes, on the face of it she was a non-threatening woman thumbing a lift. As she explained to me: 'What I'm saying...you want the truth. I want to tell as it was. I'm telling you that I was always going somewhere, and most times I hitched a ride. There are thousands of guys and women out there who'll say they gave me a ride, and we got on just fine, ya know. They gave me no hassle. I'm a good person inside, but when I get drunk, I just don't know. It's just when I'm drunk it's don't mess the fuck with me. Ya know. That's the truth. I've got nothing to lose. That's the truth.'

It is fair to say that Lee has changed her story, and her motives for killing, more times than one can count, which brings me back to the beginning of this chapter when I say one should never speak ill of the dead. However, considering her abused formative years into her very early teens therein we might find clues as to why, out of the hundreds of men she had sex with (most of them saying that she was a fair trade and didn't cause any problems at all) why did she choose to kill the men she undoubtedly did?

When I asked Lee Wuornos who had initiated the subject of sex during the rides, she claimed, 'I was always short of money, so I guess sometimes I brought up sex. Mallory wanted to fuck straight off. He was a mean motherfucker with a dirty mouth. He got drunk and it was a physical situation, so I popped him and watched the man die.' Of course, at that time, Lee hadn't a clue that she'd accepted a ride from a sexual predator with a confirmed history of ill-treating women, so I do find some truth in what she was telling me. To put it bluntly, this time around he appears to have bitten off more than he could chew.

Recalling David Spears, Lee claimed that he made himself out to be a nice, decent guy. 'That's shit,' she told me point-blank. 'He bought a few beers and wanted a free fuck...an' you wanna know about the third one [Carskaddon]. How do you think he got undressed? Wise up. He wanted sex. Ask yourself, what's all that about if he didn't want a cheap fuck? Cos the cops didn't say anything about the others... never found the johnnies.'

At this point in my short time with Lee, I could see that she was seething inside, then she added: 'Yeah, OK, man. Look you gotta understand that guys don't get nude with some broad if they don't want sex. The last one...I can't remember his name [Walter Antonio] was...Jesus Christ...

he was boasting that he was fucking engaged. He bought a six-pack. The dirty motherfucker. And, I do have one thing, though…their families must know that no matter how they loved the people that I killed, they were bad 'cause they were going to hurt me, some slapped me around like Humphreys did. One of 'em really treated me like I was dirt until I pulled out my pistol. Then he ran off naked. Then I shot the fucker. I suppose you think I really suck?'

Most killers are able to describe their crimes, and Lee Wuornos was more adept than some of those I have interviewed, telling and retelling her story with added layers of gloss to suit her own ends. But one aspect of her story remained constant. She said that each of her victims wanted sex, and either wanted a 'freebie' and then raped her against her will, or intended to. For my part, I can see this writ large over the shooting death of the drunken Richard Mallory. For this very reason she shot them dead, eliminating them with no more compassion that swatting a fly.

She explained, 'You've gotta understand. I ain't so bad. I've been with hundreds and hundreds of men. I just ain't killed them all, have I? I would make money but they wouldn't abuse me or nothin'. I'd just take my money out in the boonies, stick it in my wallet and go. Never hurt them, right? Then you get a few dirty old men who go radical on me. So you see what I'm saying? I kinda had to do what I had to do. What am I supposed to do? Just sit back. Get beaten about and fuckin' raped? It was all their fault and that's the God's honest truth.'

Because the body of Peter Siems has never been found, I asked Lee where she had dumped his corpse. 'Look. I don't remember their faces or their names, so don't shit me. How the fuck am I going to recall where he is? But I'm tellin' you that he's got to be seriously dead by now.'

Asked if her grandfather, Laurie Wuornos, had sexually abused her, Lee said, 'Ya know. I have said different things about this over the years, but the truth is, yeah. I was. He'd do stuff to me and give me pocket money to shut up. He'd finger me. I lost my virginity to his fuckin' finger when I was about seven. He'd beat the shit outa me, ya know. But he'd strip naked beforehand...that's fuckin' wrong...you understand? He made me what I am. He made me hate men like him. Dirty, cheap, no-good motherfuckers like him. Look at me... I'm shaking all over even thinking about it. For fuck's sake, let's leave it. OK Christopher? I'm sort of getting freaked out and I don't need this right now.'

Criminal history tells us that prostitutes most often become the victims of rape and homicide. The annals of criminal history are littered with such cases where a hooker has been smashed about and brutally killed, but then none of them carried a firearm to 'equalise' their assailant as Lee Wuornos did with such deadly effect. And, looking back through the case files, considering the dire circumstances they were in, perhaps a large number of these women would have wished they had.

Knowing the enormity of the murders committed by Lee, it is easy to follow the general line of thinking and dismiss her simply as another one in a long line of serial killers. While there have been many female mass murderers, there have been few female serial killers, and, like all of them she stands out because of her gender and her dismissal of the compassionate, life-giving qualities of her sex, not in response to a single act of murderous impulse but, time after time, in a series of bloody, shooting deaths. By making the aggressor suffer, she transformed herself from a victim to the victimiser, eagerly grabbing power for herself with both hands and with the aid of a handgun she made herself unique to criminology in a gross kind of way.

Without any doubt, Lee Wuornos had an antisocial personality disorder. Whether she was a psychopath is another question to be debated time and again. Although one-in-twenty males suffer from antisocial personality disorder, meaning that their actions are not inhibited by guilt or moral boundaries, very few kill, and even far less women kill men. Indeed, I am struggling to find another single female prostitute serial murderer, although I am quite sure at least one of my readers will accommodate me on the matter with this one thought in mind.

Even fewer in numbers are street girls who kill a client for money basically because of common sense business savvy. They often hand out business cards. They are keen to please their 'Johns' in return for hoped for repeat business. This is the way the 'oldest profession' works across the world. Prostitutes simply don't want to kill the Golden Goose, if you catch my drift and this *is* a matter of fact.

Most often alone on the highways, Lee found 'Murder Crossroads'. She encountered men making their way across Florida, perhaps the thought of sex being the last thing on their minds, that is, until they saw a blonde thumbing a ride. Seemingly respectable men with money, wives, lovers and money, who grasped the opportunity to buy a six-pack of beer in exchange for cheap sex in the confines of a car in an isolated place.

'I was really OK with these guys, Christopher. That's the God's honest truth. A few drinks, they thought I was cheap cos of my loud mouth, maybe. They started talking rough an' dirty like I'm shit, man. I've had that all my life…didn't need the shit…I'm a reasonable person. Some of them wanted to fuck my ass…couldn't get that with their wives an' stuff. They wanted to abuse and humiliate me. Ya know, despite what you think, I've got respect for myself. Always did have. Weird, right?'

Giving a ride to Aileen Wuornos; buying her a few drinks, pulling off the highway and talking her down proved to be a murderous cocktail, indeed.

Was Lee more deadly than the male? In this respect, I think not because it is an undeniable fact that countless beyond countless male serial killers have been murdering and butchering prostitutes for decades, so, please make of this as you will!

Alice Mary Crimmins

Method of Killing: Strangulation with a Ligature
Death is caused by a constricting force around the neck exerted by means of some pliable strip, such as a rope, necktie, etc., but unlike hanging is not dependent on the suspended weight of the victim's body. The ligature may well have been knotted, tied into a running noose, or simply had the ends crossed over; in any event, in cases of homicide, in most incients some agent other than the victim will need to have pulled the ligature tight in order for strangulation to occur.

Death is by asphyxia. Ligature marks usually consist of a furrow (or furrows) impressed horizontally around the neck; because the weight of the body has not been pulling against the noose, the mark will be lower that that characterising hanging, and less well defined. The nature of the ligature and the degree of pressure exerted will dictate the physical appearance of the marks – a wire noose will produce a thin deep mark, while the trauma made by a soft scarf may hardly be noticeable.

Victims

Alice 'Missy' Marie Crimmins (four) and Edmond 'Eddie' Michael Crimmins, Jr (five)

'The cemetery is high up in the Bronx, close to the Throgs Neck Bridge. The children lie deepest in the ground, lying above them is their father, Edmund.' (Author Sarah Weinman describing the graves of murdered Alice and Eddie Crimmins.)

Even today, Queens is still seen as the least glamorous of New York City's boroughs. Manhattan is Manhattan; the Bronx has a frisson of danger. Brooklyn has its own accent and ethnic culture, but Queens is just the place where the blue-collar workers live, pretending they are not in New York City at all.

In the 1950s and 60s, when the housing developments of northwest Queens really expanded, this stereotype was even more true. Many families migrated to the new garden developments in the borough to get away from what was happening in the urban streets they were raised in.

Regal Gardens, the development that Alice Crimmins lived in, was typical. It was dull, but it was safe. Each block had the same symmetrical arrangement of low redbrick buildings surrounded by grass and footpaths. They had a ground floor garden apartment at 150-22 72nd Drive, and the locality was populated by a heady mix of middle-class Irish, Italian and Jewish families.

For children, it seemed a safe haven: most passers-by

were neighbours, there was little traffic to worry about and everywhere was overlooked by someone's window. For the ambitious, the apartment buildings were only a stepping-stone to better things – a house of their own in a leafier part of Queens, or even on Long Island, which merges with Queens to the east. Those who could never achieve that might have felt that they were in a dead-end on a road to nowhere.

Alice Mary Crimmins was born Alice Mary Burke, named after her mother, a pinched-faced yet good Irish girl from County Limerick, on Thursday, 9 March 1939. Her more exuberant father, Michael, was also a religious man, but Alice and her older brother John, growing up in the forties and fifties in the Bronx, were part of a shifting society where their parents' values could easily be undermined. However, theirs was not the Bronx of today, home to a criminal underclass, but was a hard-working Catholic community where families consulted the local priest in times of trouble, and housewives scrubbed their humble rented homes free of urban grime and, perhaps by implication, any big city corruption.

Alice went to convent schools and was taught the old-fashioned virtues of modesty, chastity and obedience. She was also warned of the perils of vanity, and although they could not subdue her flaming red hair, her face, like her mother's house, had to be scrubbed clean, and free of any make-up.

Like many adolescents she felt disfigured by her acne, so perhaps this prohibition was extra hard for her. Certainly very attractive in adult life she was never ever to be seen without full make-up covering every blemish. The ritual of applying it took an hour every day, and the habit was to condemn her forever in the eyes of those who saw her on the morning of her children's disappearance, on Wednesday, 14 July 1965.

Although she was to revel in the trappings of femininity, Alice was not a sissy. Even as an adult with her fiery Irish blood and red hair she was proud of her toughness and never refused a challenge. Like many girls growing up in the shadow of an older brother, she wanted to do anything he could do. For his part, John was older by one year and ran in the high school athletics team. When he trained, Alice would pant around the track after him, convinced that she could keep up and even outdo him. Endearing in a young girl, this determination to keep up with the boys was to appear unseemly in a young mother. In the community she was raised in, the men went out drinking and the women stayed at home. She was to reverse the roles with a vengeance.

Alice's mother, brought to up find dignity in the woman's traditional role of obedience and stoicism, could never get on with her headstrong daughter. Alice, impulsive, emotional and burning with unexpressed ambitions, found her mother cold. She had more in common with her father whom she loved. However, their relationship deteriorated when Alice started going out with boys, for Michael Burke disapproved of all of her boyfriends, even chasing one poor Puerto Rican lad off by brandishing a kitchen knife. Nevertheless, there seemed to be one exception to this rule: Edmund 'Eddie' Crimmins, whose father worked for the same firm as Michael Burke, and the Crimmins were a good Catholic family. So by saying 'yes' to Eddie's proposal of marriage, Alice was also pleasing her otherwise belligerent father.

Eddie and Alice were married in the Bronx on Saturday, 8 November 1958. Crossing the East River, they settled in the borough of Queens and for a few years seemed contented enough. Little Eddie was born in October 1959, and Alice 'Missy' Marie in October 1960.

Alice's husband worked nights while she stayed in and watched television. But this was the 'Swinging Sixties'. It was the time of New York World's Fair at Shea Stadium, attended by the Beatles and Pope Paul VI – when an estimated 600,000 lined the streets despite the icy winds as the pontiff's motorcade drove eleven miles through Queens to Flushing Meadows. Elsewhere in the same city there were folk cashing in on the economic boom, living fast, colourful, dangerous lives: having fun. No doubt Alice loved her children, and no doubt when they were babies they consumed most of her considerable energy. But after Missy was born, Alice bought a diaphragm contaceptive device and this horrified Eddie, who still cherished traditional Catholic values. From then on the couple were pulling in different directions, and some time in 1963, Alice broke away.

At first, she got a job as a cocktail waitress at the Bourbon House in Syosset, Long Island and started to meet other men, who knew her only as 'Rusty'. They were big spenders; they drank spirits instead of beer; they made deals and took risks instead of grubbing for a weekly wage. They took her to expensive restaurants and they did not disapprove or judge her.

By February 1964, Eddie had had enough; he moved out. He did not keep away though, but tortured himself by creeping back in, crouching in the basement and listening via a makeshift bug he'd installed to his wife making love upstairs, and simultaneously making tape recordings of what he was hearing. She was defiant in the face of his criticism, pointing out that they were separated, weren't they? Everyone said that Eddie, Jr. and Missy were great kids. So, what was the problem?

In May 1965, Alice's father passed away. Alice's mother blamed the worry and shame of the broken marriage. 'You killed him!' she hissed at her daughter during the funeral. That night Alice went out, got drunk and forgot herself with strangers. A month later the slim, vivacious redhead went to a party on a yacht owned by millionaire highway contractor, fifty-two-year-old Tony Grace, who had ties with important Democratic politicians. She said that she found herself locked in the toilet and ended up in the Bahamas. The children were left with the nanny, Evelyn Atkins Linder, and there was no food in the kitchen. (Later, Linder sued Alice for $600.00 back pay. Alice claimed she owed her former maid a mere $150, and said the nanny had stolen money from her.)

On Tuesday, 22 June, Eddie started custody proceedings for sole custody. Without saying so outright he hinted that Alice was an immoral slut, and her own mother was on his side. Alice remained unrepentant and determined to fight. Her children had a mother who enjoyed life, who took them to the park in the sunshine, who kept them clean, who made them say their prayers each night, and who fed them well, she argued. What difference did it make what she did after dark? To Eddie it made all the difference in the world. Unfortunately for Alice, twelve other men would one day agree with him.

It was the morning of Wednesday, 14 July 1965. In the borough of Queens, in a housing development called Regal Gardens, 150 police officers were searching each of the identical redbrick blocks, questioning everyone they met.

They carried photographs of two smiling faces – the faces of Missy and Eddie Crimmins, aged four and five.

Meanwhile, back at the family apartment, the parents were being questioned. The father, Eddie Crimmins, an aircraft mechanic, was separated from his wife Alice and had not been there that morning when she had discovered the children missing from their beds and Alice was the focus of attention. 'If this is a game, you better stop now!' said Detective Michael Clifford to Alice and Eddie Crimmins.

In front of the officers was a very attractive twenty-six-year-old redhead, but that morning she was not every policeman's idea of what a distraught mother should like. With her almond eyes, sultry Bronx accent and hourglass figure, wearing skin-tight turquoise slacks, a flowery blouse and high-heeled white shoes, she had full make-up on and her hair was teased up high on her head. Today she might have resembled Lindsay Lohan or Emma Stone. She was a traffic-stopper then and would be today.

Jerry Piering, the lead detective, was shocked. There were also things about the apartment he was uncomfortable with. There was hardly any food in the place and a box full of empty spirit bottles. Most shocking of all, was Alice's little black book full of men's names (some of which were inconveniently eminent enough to include Mayor Robert Wagner and Senator Robert Kennedy) and addresses. Hinting towards prostitution, 'It's a hell of a way to bring up kids,' Piering commented to a colleague.

Another red flag that made Detective Piering uneasy was the hook-and-eye on the outside of the children's bedroom door. Alice had stated that she always locked the children in: 'Because Eddie, Jr. has a habit of getting up early in the morning and raiding the refrigerator.' She added that it had still been fastened in the morning. The chain on the front door was also in place, implying that the children could only have been taken out of their bedroom window, which was open. However, Piering noticed that the inside sill of the window was covered with an undisturbed film of dust, although he failed to mention this in his notes.

By now Piering suspected the parents of foul play. The couple had to attend court in eight days to contest the custody of their children. He looked at them grave-faced. 'This is a heck of a thing to do, having 150 cops searching for your kids if you know where they are.' They both denied it, so the search carried on.

Alice then gave Detective Piering a full account of the events leading up to the disappearance. On the way home from an afternoon in the park with the children, she had bought a pack of frozen veal, a tin of string beans and a bottle of soda from Sever's Deli. Later the contents of the dinner would be vitally important to the investigation. Unfortunately Piering only wrote down the time that Alice fed the children, not what she gave them. She went on to say that when they arrived back home she tidied up in readiness for an inspection by a coming visit by welfare workers to decide her fitness to keep her children. At 7 p.m. she phoned a boyfriend called Tony Grace. At 7.30 she ate with the children and afterwards took them for a drive. She told Piering that she was trying to get something on her husband; that she hoped to spot him in the street and trail him to his new address. She failed in her search and returned home about 9.15 p.m., when she put the children to bed.

Mindful of the inspection, she unscrewed the screen from

their window as it had a hole in it and would let the bugs in. Noticing the replacement was dirty, she propped it up again and threw the damaged screen outside.

At 10.30 she called Tony Grace again. Their brief conversation concerned the custody suit. After this she watched *The Defenders* on TV, interrupted only by a phone call from Joseph 'Joe' Rorech, another boyfriend. At midnight she woke little Eddie to take him to the toilet but Missy said she did not need to go. This sleepy encounter was the last she had with her children before they vanished.

Detective Jerry Piering, a devout Catholic father of six, suspected Alice almost from the get-go. Her glamorous appearance on the day she found her children missing seemed to him totally inappropriate and distasteful and he was disgusted by her apparent promiscuity.

Piering had only recently been promoted to detective when he took on the investigation of two missing children. So, for the crucial first two weeks this major murder hunt was run by a low-ranking detective – yet, perhaps it was not his fault that several mistakes were made.

'Did you lock the door of your apartment when you went out, Mrs Crimmins?' Piering inquired. 'No,' she replied, 'because I was right in the front of the house all the time. I slept until around 3 a.m. when my husband rang me. We exchanged a few bitter words. I was unable to sleep so I went outside for a while with our pregnant dog called 'Brandy' before going back, taking a bath and returning to bed.'

Alice continued by explaining that at 9 a.m. she went to wake the children and found them gone. She rang her estranged husband and asked him if he had the kiddies. He denied it and told her to look around the neighbourhood for them.

'I went and looked,' Alice claimed. 'I checked with people on the street and a number of neighbours where I thought they might have gone to play with their friends. When I saw that Eddie and Missy were nowhere to be found, I called my husband again and told him. He told me to go look some more and that he'd be right over.'

She then drove around the outskirts of their housing estate for several minutes and arrived at the parking lot where she saw Eddie draw up in his car. She told him that she still had not found the children and her husband then telephoned the police.

Piering left the interrogation of Eddie Crimmins to another officer. He was concentrating on Alice's story. Eddie's account revealed that he too was around that night and had the custody battle on his mind. In the afternoon he drove to Joe Rorech's house looking for Alice's battered car. Back at his place he watched television until 11 p.m., when he went out for a pizza. He then went drinking until 3 a.m., when he drove to Regal Gardens. Here, he sat looking up at Alice's bedroom, and then he went home to call her, and fell asleep watching a film. There was one flaw in his story: the film he claimed to have watched was on much earlier. However, the police saw no great significance in this at the time.

At precisely 1.45 p.m. on 14 July, police received the call they had been dreading. Missy's body was found by a local boy, nine-year-old Jay Silverman. She had on the clothes she wore to bed, and a pyjama top was tied around her neck. She had clearly been strangled. There were no immediate signs of a struggle or that she had been drugged or molested.

Piering's first thought was to study Alice's reaction and without explanation he drove her to the spot where Missy lay. The officers present watched her as she looked down at her daughter. She cringed, moaned and responded to their questions with a bleak 'That's Missy'. There were no tears (they only came later in the full glare of press flashbulbs). There were no attempts to embrace the little lifeless body, no farewells or protests.

In effect, Alice's numb response condemned her in the eyes of all the men present. The case had become a murder enquiry and the number-one suspect had already been identified.

Every officer on the case had been moved by little fair-haired Missy's lifeless body. They and all the good people of Queens were out for someone's blood. So, even as they waited for news of their son, his parents faced hours of gruelling interrogation.

At autopsy, the medical examiner (ME) found several abrasions on her body, but concluded that they had been present before her death. The ME also determined that little damage had been caused to the underlying muscles, although there was a little blood due to ruptured vessels. The cartilages of the trachea and larynx were mostly intact. Death was from asphyxiation – the means of killing was the use of a pyjama top.

In the meantime, the emerging details of Alice's phenomenal sex life deepened the police suspicion of her: for surely a woman of such appetites could never be a loving mother?

Missy was buried at the Saint Raymond Cemetery on Saturday, 17 July.

Two days after Missy's funeral, Vernon Warnecke was

walking with his son, Ralph, along 162nd Street in Kew Gardens Hills, a mile from the Crimmins's home, when they found the fast-decomposing corpse of blond-haired Eddie. The body was discovered concealed under a blue-and-white blanket. It was high summer and the work of flies and vermin meant that the parents would never be called upon to identify their little son. They were given just one day's grace to grieve before the questions started again. Indeed the child was so badly decomposed that he could only be identified by matching his fingerprints with those on his toy truck.

At first, the interrogation was replaced by an accusation as the police tried in vain to extract confessions from both parents. Alice felt the police's hostility keenly, and she was not satisfied with the way they were running the enquiry. She suggested to her husband that they bring in the FBI. Eddie was not keen, 'The police are handling it,' he said.

The results of the detailed autopsy had come through, and Piering tried another tack. He agreed to meet Alice in a place of her choice – a Bronx bar ironically called the 'Tender Trap'. She was nervous, but dressed as for a date, perhaps hoping to win the detective over, as did Lauren Staton, brilliantly played by Faye Dunaway when she tried to seduce Lt Columbo in the 31 October 1993 release of *It's All in the Game*.

Cop and prime suspect chatted for a while until Piering challenged his quarry with the scientific evidence of the autopsy, saying it proved that she could not have fed the children at 7.30 p.m. and seen them alive at midnight.

The autopsy report noted the contents of Missy's stomach as various vegetables, peach, macaroni and chewing gum. Dr Milton Helpern, the Chief Examiner for New York, would later testify at trial that the large amount of undigested food present suggested that Missy had died within two hours of eating. Alice had told police that she had fed the children at around 7.30 p.m. Piering said that he remembered leftover pasta in the fridge, and that the undigested macaroni meant that Alice could not have seen Missy at midnight. For her part, Alice claimed that she had fed them veal – that somebody else could have given Missy this other food later: all a very unconvincing story indeed.

So, perhaps she was hiding something else? Perhaps she had left them alone and gone out with a man? Alice was being tempted to construct an alibi. However, she stuck like glue to her first statement, and bluntly rejected the scientific evidence. Incensed, Piering resorted to shock tactics, suddenly bringing out Missy's clothes for Alice to identify. However, if this rookie detective had hoped to provoke a tearful confession, he was wrong-footed. Alice identified them, frostily, but gave nothing more away.

Two weeks into the case, a more senior detective, Cuban cigar-chewing John Kelly, was assigned to head the enquiry. He wanted the Crimminses to take a lie-detector test. Eddie agreed and passed. Alice was very reluctant and ten minutes into the test she ripped the wires off. She would never agree to retake it, or take a truth drug, claiming that despite her innocence, she was afraid of what she might say.

Any lingering suspicions of Eddie being the murderer were dismissed and all suspicion was now directed at Alice. Police bugged her apartment for six years and they never heard anything incriminating, apart from the sexual encounters, which continued unabated by the children's deaths. They also tapped her telephone, which Alice was aware of – often prefacing her conversations with the aside 'Drop dead, you guys!'

All of the many lovers in Alice's little black book were contacted, but police found only one, Joe Rorech, a slick, oily, down-at-the-heel entrepreneur, who was willing to make a statement against her.

The case was now growing cold and getting nowhere, which did not please the public. The prosecution failed to get an indictment in 1996, but as a result of the renewed publicity, the usual flood of cranky letters was received. One anonymous writer told of looking out on the night of the murders and seeing what could have been Alice and an accomplice disposing of Missy's body. The handwriting was that of a woman and the police set out to track down a likely candidate in Regal Gardens who had a window facing the right way. Painstaking detective work finally led them to Sophie Earomirski, whose testimony was to seal Alice's fate. The prosecution were ready at last and she was arrested twenty-two months after the crimes had taken place; collapsing in the police station, some say she was frail, some declared her drunk, nevertheless, the courteous Detective John Kelly helped her to her feet.

But, what of this winning witness, the plump, greying Sophie Earomirski? She would later make a good impression on the jury, although her medical history of brain damage throws doubt on her reliability. Nevertheless, spectators cheered her during the defence's attempts to discredit her as a witness. In fact, the defence had learned that she had once been found unconscious with her head in her gas oven. She replied, to loud laughter and applause, that she was only checking the dinner. She was a strong witness, and left with her hands clenched like a victorious boxer.

When the trial of Alice Crimmins opened on Monday, 13 May 1968, there were crowds of spectators attracted by the whiff of a sex scandal. Women particularly were fascinated to see this ordinary wife and mother who had perhaps broken all the rules, and perhaps even sunk to the ultimate evil. These women, like vultures, came every day, with their sandwiches and newspapers and flasks of tea or coffee, and, like the all-male jury, they passed judgment.

This trial was only for Missy's killing, though of course little Eddie's murder was on everyone's mind. The prosecution first established, with Detective Piering's film of dust evidence, that the two kiddies could not have been abducted through the bedroom window because the dust was undisturbed. Dr Milton Helpern, with all his authority as chief examiner, then explained that Missy must have been killed within two hours of eating – certainly around about 9.30 p.m., throwing doubt on Alice's claim that the little girl was still alive at midnight when she took little Eddie to the toilet.

However, the fact is that your body is not just your home. Rather it is also home to a host of bacteria that live on your skin, in your stomach and everywhere else you can imagine. Some of these bacteria are rather inert as far as we are concerned, while others can be malicious or helpful – even serving important roles in our body. The bacteria in the gut falls into this category and is, therefore, responsible in part for digestion – meaning that a body may be able to digest food after death has occurred.

The prosecutor, DA Anthony 'Tony' Lombardino, then called a string of Alice's lovers. A showman, a bruiser, brash and loud, he was not averse to getting personal with a witness in order to shock any jury. These twelve working men, with plain wives and a enduring a daily struggle to make ends meet, were presented with a portrait of promiscuity and undeserved luxury. Then it was Joe Rorech's turn. He was only meant to have testified that when he called Alice Crimmins that night at 2 a.m., there was no answer. However, as the case was looking thin, Lombardino leaned hard on Rorech, with startling results. In court, the DA led him back to a night with Alice in September 1966.

A hush fell as Rorech's voice sank lower and everyone strained to hear. He said that they had been drowning their sorrows together and talking of the children, and Alice had sobbed out: 'Joseph, please forgive me. I killed her.'

The courtroom erupted. Alice flew to her feet, and above the rising tumult she screamed, 'Joseph! How could you do this? This is not true! Oh, my God!' A recess was called, and the reporters raced to the phones.

Thereafter, it was only left for Sophie Earomirski to drive the final nail into Alice's coffin. The accused's reaction was instant and dramatic. 'You liar! You liar!' she screamed. 'I heard you!' retorted Sophie as the judge gavelled for order. The defence tried to fight back for Alice, with witnesses who said she was a good mother, or that there was not enough light in the road for Sophie to have seen much at all. Then Alice took the stand. In doing this, she really put the noose around her own neck. When defendants stand, the prosecution has a free rein to question them about any aspect of their private life which may, or may not, have a bearing on their morals. Alice had the opportunity to deny Joe Rorech and Sophie Earomirski's testimony, but the price was high and Lombardino let rip.

Naked men shooed from her apartment by her irate

husband, sex in cars with her children's hairdresser, nude swimming in Rorech's pool when she should have been grieving for her children: Alice was torn apart at the seams and forced to admit to all these things and more. Angry at the line of questioning, she did so defiantly, and appeared to everyone to be a brazen hussy, a woman of loose morals and having no conscience at all.

In the summing up, the defence tried to make Joe and Sophie appear unsavoury and pathetic. Lombardino defended his witnesses and damned Alice in a comparison with a rotten egg: 'Just beautiful on the outside…but when you break the egg open…probably the worst stench you can find anyplace in this world.'

Mindful of an appeal, the judge reminded the jury that they were trying a homicide, not Alice's morals, but that was difficult advice to follow after so much lurid testimony. Nevertheless, the jury did not reach a verdict until the following afternoon. Alice had spent a sleepless night and passed the morning in a nearby restaurant. On Friday, 9 August 1968, she was wearing a red dress, and her face showed ghostly pale against it. The verdict was first-degree manslaughter. She collapsed and was carried to hospital in a dead faint. Was she numb with shock or just plain drunk, yet again? As usual, there were just two interpretations of her behaviour, as she was sentenced to a term of not less than five years, and no more than twenty years – of tears.

Watching the sentencing, and as she protested her innocence, was Herbert Lyon, a well-known attorney. He was convinced of her innocence and prepared to take on her appeal free-of-charge. And, he quickly secured a retrial, too. On Wednesday, 4 September 1968, Alice was released on bail pending appeal, then, on Monday, 22 December 1969, she was granted a new trial. During this time she enjoyed two years of liberty, although she was constantly under surveillance, and police tip-offs to employers made it hard for her to keep down a job. But, even this limited freedom could not last, and the second time Alice was arrested, it was for little Eddie's murder as well as Missy's manslaughter – now the proverbial s★★★ truly hit the proverbial fan.

On Friday, 13 July 1970 – exactly five years after the two murders were committed – she was taken to the local police station to be booked for Eddie's murder and Alice's manslaughter. Her second trial started on Monday 15 March 1971, and was this time a relatively quiet affair. Alice did not take the stand; nevertheless, she faced an all-male jury again, though it proved hard to find jurors who had not been prejudiced by the newspaper stories they had read over the years.

This time, the prosecution aimed to prove that Alice had killed Missy. Joe Rorech's testimony now went beyond Alice confessing to killing Missy, to her agreeing to Eddie's death. Again, Alice was outraged: 'You miserable lying worm!' she screamed, and as he left the stand, called out, 'What did you buy Joseph?'

Sophie Earomirski gave her evidence with the same amount of gusto as in the earlier trial. The defence questioned her about her fall and whether there had been any medical repercussions. She explained that she fell because a mouse ran up her arm. 'A mouse?' asked Lyon sarcastically, but Sophie's sarcasm equalled his: 'Yes, a mouse,' she replied. 'You know, an itty-bitty thing with a tail on it.' Again she won over the spectators with her refusal to be cowed and left with her prizefighter's salute.

This time there were new witnesses to back up Earomirski's account. Among these was another neighbour who had seen the group she described, and the milkman who said that Alice's dog had not barked when he delivered at 2.15 that morning. Alice's response was to make a tearful plea to the public: 'Now, I don't know where these people are coming from. But I'm asking for help from my side.' The result was dramatic. A Mr Marvin Weinstein came forward to say that he had been visiting a Mr King, in Regal Gardens that night, and left around 2 a.m. along with his wife, son and sleeping baby daughter and dog. Alice's joy at this was short-lived, however, as the prosecution found King and he denied that Weinstein had visited him that night. Not to be outdone, the defence called someone who claimed that King was a liar. What the jury made of all this testimony and counter-testimony we cannot know and never will.

In his summing up, Lyon made a passionate five-hour plea to the jury and sought to portray Sophie Earomirski as a neurotic, Rorech as a bitter, jilted failure, and the police as fabricators. For their part, the prosecution focused on Alice's reluctance to take the stand: 'She doesn't have the courage to stand up there and tell the world she killed her daughter...' Indignant screams from Alice and protests from Lyon were to no avail. The jury deliberated overnight and, on Friday, 23 April, Alice was found guilty on both counts. The appeal for a retrial had brought her out of the frying pan and into the fire. The sentence for manslaughter still stood, and on Monday, 3 May 1971, she also received a life sentence for murder.

The mind is apt to take a pleasure in adapting circumstances to one another, and even straining them a little, if needs be, to force them to form parts of one connected whole; and the more ingenious the mind of the individual, the more likely is it, in considering such matters, to overreach and mislead itself, to supply some little link that is wanting, to take for granted some fact consistent with its previous theories and necessary to render them complete.

(Sir Edward Hall Alderson. British lawyer and judge (1787–1857) on circumstantial evidence.)

'Maternal Filicide' is the deliberate act of a parent killing their own child, and Alice Crimmins was convicted of murdering both her son and daughter – heinous crimes indeed. She was convicted solely on the accumulation of circumstantial evidence and it is this cumulative effect, the 'arithmetic of circumstantial evidence', which causes so many juries to say that even though the evidence before them is entirely indirect they are 'satisfied beyond any reasonable doubt', of the safety of convicting.

Much is written about and said of this 'chain of evidence', and herein lies the danger of circumstantial evidence. The strength of a chain is the strength of its weakest link, and the mind, in racing to the conclusion which it wants to draw is apt to strengthen the weakest links with fancied evidence of its own, and even to supply deficiencies as quoted by Sir Edward Hall Alderson above. Therefore, it is vitally important to eliminate from one's chain all links which are of ambiguous value; that is to say which are equally consistent with the defendant's innocence as his, or her, guilt.

But whatever be the strength or weakness of circumstantial evidence, there is no question that it has to be used, and it is

CHRISTOPHER BERRY-DEE

in fact far commoner in criminal cases than is realised. Crime is not always committed in the midst of watching multitudes, and generally speaking, the greater the crime the less likely is it that there will be those who saw it done. The danger of the abuse of this type of evidence, however, is never absent, for whereas direct evidence is the evidence of observation, or forensic evidence linking the crime directly to the offender, circumstantial evidence is, as related to the crime itself, a matter of inference, therefore a matter of opinion, and opinions must be very firm when the life of a fellow man or woman hangs upon it.

Who can say for sure whether Alice was the killer? She certainly did herself no favours in her dealings with the police, but no good motive has ever been found. But do we need to find a motive when examining the Crimmins's case? For no good motive has ever been found.

Motive may be described as the mental mainspring of the crime, and it is not to be confused with the intention with which the crime was done. As pointed out by Judge Christmas Humphreys, a man's motive may be good but his intention bad, for example: A loaf is stolen. The *intention* was to steal and the act therefore criminal, although the *motive*, to save a starving child, was good. Generally speaking, however, the two are so entwined that it is difficult to separate them. Although it may be of great assistance to a jury to establish a motive, proof of motive is never necessary in the proof of a crime. Absence of any discoverable motive is of little consequence in deciding whether or not the defendant committed the crime, for the most brilliant jury is helpless in deciding the mental processes which actuate the criminal, which is obviously the case with Alice Crimmins.

The prosecution suggested that Alice strangled Missy in a fit of temper, then called Tony Grace to help her get rid of little Eddie. But Grace married Alice while she was in prison. A man might sleep with a woman who killed her own children, but would he marry her?

Still the doubts about Alice remain. She would never take a truth test, and certain things about her bereavement stick in the gullet. She did not weep for her daughter and she did not help in the search for her missing son. At her second trial, she appealed to the general public to come to her aid, but she made no such appeal when her children disappeared.

Looking back through Alice Cummins's history, we can see from whence she came and the position she found herself in prior to her killing her children. In a nutshell, she had tasted the good life and removed a dull and boring husband from hers. She had fallen in love with a millionaire in Tony Grace; travelled on his yacht to the Bahamas, enjoyed good food and the accompanying champagne lifestyle. Her children, as shocking this is to consider, had become an impediment to her. She certainly had time to prepare for the crime and the opportunity to kill her children in their beds when, by her own testimony, no one else had been in her apartment on that fateful night. There were only two means of access and egress to the apartment: the alleged open bedroom window and the front door — the latter she said no one else came through as she was in the room next to the front door and would have heard a noise. This only leaves us with the bedroom window, but police found that the dust on the sill had never been disturbed.

There is also the matter of being in possession of the fruits of the crime to be considered. In her case the 'fruits of the crime' are writ large – that of her embarking on a new life with all of the glamour and glitz that she always craved. And, we might also take stock of tampering with or fabricating evidence. We know that only Alice could have strangled her children in their bedroom. If it had been an intruder he would have done so and left the bodies in situ, for why would he risk leaving the property with the bodies and dumping them in different locations at the great risk of being seen by witnesses? Added to which, by her own account she had put the chain on the children's bedroom door when she said goodnight to them and she said that the door was still in place when she went into the room in the morning.

Then there are acts indicative of guilty consciousness, all evidenced by her bland, non-caring demeanour, on the morning her children first disappeared. Made up to the nines, her delays in reporting the missing kids to her husband, her total lack of grief or empathy when she saw Missy lying stone dead on a vacant lot later the same day, all have to be taken into consideration. We see this callous, cold lack of concern in so many psychopathic killers because unlike you and me they have no conscience. They can commit the most dreadful of crimes then, without exhibiting any remorse carry on with their lives as if nothing had happened at all. Chilling, is it not?

Scientific testimony in the Crimmins's case was, to be generous, thin on the ground, but we can certainly place some weight on Dr Milton Helpern's autopsy findings: that Alice lied about the time she gave her children their last meal, indeed, she even lied about what she had fed them, as an examination of the stomach contents proved.

Much has been argued – back at the time of the trials and

even today – as to whether or not Alice Crimmins had an accomplice to filicide during the night of 13/14 July 1965. I think not. I say this because Alice was perfectly capable of lifting and carrying her four-year-old daughter and her five-year-old son as she had done many times before. She lived in a ground floor garden apartment, the front door opening straight onto the street, where, outside, was her parked car. She alibied herself by claiming that she had gone out for a drive with her dog in the hope of spotting her estranged husband someplace, when in fact she was using this ploy as a smokescreen for the dumping of the two little bodies. Where, however, the police seriously slipped up was on the discovery of little Eddie's decomposing body. It was found covered by a blanket but none of the detectives had the intelligence to track that blanket back to the children's bedroom, from where it quite possibly had come.

As for all of the other wild and woolly theories surrounding the reasons why Missy and little Eddie were murdered, I suggest this is simply a matter of ill-educated folk, many of whom were either sensation seekers or conspiratorists, trying to blow smoke into our yard.

Anthony Lombardino became an Assistant US Attorney. He resigned after a financial scandal. Jerry Piering was promoted to second-grade detective. In 1976 Alice joined a work-release scheme, and worked as a secretary. According to outraged newspaper reports, she in fact spent every other weekend basking on Tony Grace's yacht bearing the name *Alice*, and in July 1977 she married him. In September 1977 she was granted parole. Other reports suggest that she has since lived in various parts of Florida. Other times it is rumoured that after Tony passed away she went back to Queens and then to nearby Nassau County or someplace along the Metro-North's New Haven line.

At the time of writing, if she is still alive Alice Crimmins will be seventy-nine years old. Everybody speculates as to what became of her but nobody knows. So, look around you. The somewhat glamorous pensioner standing at the bus stop you have just passed could be her.

In that cemetery high up in the Bronx, close to the Throgs Neck Bridge, Missy and little Eddie lie the deepest in the ground. Lying above them is their father, Edmund. God rest their souls.

Some of the Most Evil Women Long Dead or Still Alive Today

So far, this book has focused in-depth upon the likes of nurses' aides, Cathy May Wood and Gwendolyn Graham, who burked five elderly patients in their beds. We looked at Joanna Dennehy who stabbed three men to death in cold blood, before moving on to Suzanne Basso, who committed one of the most atrocious one-off homicides in US criminal history. Many killers commit murder for financial gain, and this is why I have included Patricia Wright in this book. Thus far we arrived at Alice Crimmins and, as far as I can determine, and despite the fact that conspiracy theories abound that she may have not killed her two children, I say that she did. That she probably had an affair with then Senator Robert Kennedy is neither here nor there...that there was some kind of political cover-up seems ludicrous to me. Indeed, the killing of her children would only draw attention to the numerous men in positions of power she slept with, which seems a commonsense proposition to this writer whichever way one wishes to cut the cake.

But now is the time to move on and take a look at other women who have committed the most sickening of murders, again asking the question: 'are women more deadly than the male?'

CAROL MARY BUNDY

Bundy – no relation to the monster Ted Bundy – is a serial killer who, with Douglas Daniel Clark, aka 'The Sunset Slayer', killed prostitutes in Los Angeles from 1 June to August 1980. Their known victims are: Gina Marano (fifteen); Cynthia Chandler (sixteen), Karen Jones, Exxie Wilson; Marnette Comer (seventeen) and John Murray.

Doug (Clark) gave me a rare filmed death-row interview way back in 1995, which became one of my twelve-part programmes in the TV series *The Serial Killers*.

Again, in fear of being accused of self-promoting another of my books, I dedicated a chapter to Clark and Bundy in my international bestseller *Talking with Serial Killers*, also published by John Blake. It is my professional opinion that although Doug was involved in most of these murders, therefore giving him no mitigation at all, just like Joanna Dennehy with Gary Stretch, Rose with Fred West, Hindley with Brady, he would never have killed anyone unless Carol Bundy had been the principal offender and the controlling and manipulating influence. And, we do know that it was Carol Bundy, acting alone, who enticed her former lover, wannabe country and western singer, John Murray, into having perverted sex in his Chevrolet camper van and then blasting his brains to bits. Carol Bundy made a plea bargain and in return for her testimony received only a 52-years-to-life prison sentence. She effectively placed all of the blame onto Doug Clark, which resonates with the behaviour of Cathy May Wood who likewise made a plea bargain and gave evidence against her co-accused, all of which, to my mind, makes her more deadly than the male.

Carol Bundy died of heart failure on 9 December 2003, aged sixty-one. At the time of writing Doug Clark is sixty-nine years old and he regularly corresponds with me. My uncut filmed interview with him can be found as: *Douglas Clark Interview – Sunset Slayer Case* on YouTube, and as you will see, he is bloody wild.

MELANIE 'MEL' LYN MCGUIRE

Mel McGuire is another highly manipulative homicidal personality whom I have had extensive past dealings with. Dubbed by the media 'The Ice Queen', this mother of two, one-time high-class, once extremely attractive woman, killed her husband, William, at their brand new upscale New Jersey home during the night of 29/30 April 2004. Thereafter, she power-sawed the corpse into pieces, placed the body parts into bin liners, stuffed them into two suitcases and dumped them off a bridge into the swirling waters of the Chesapeake Bay. Her story, which was a complete exclusive for me, features in my book *Dead Men Talking*. For outright brazen manipulation by a femme fatale one could do no better and she enjoys corresponding if the subject is about good food, intelligent reading material and French perfume – if you are a guy she has a favourite cologne called Chanel Égoïste, so spray it liberally on your well-presented stationery if you want a quick reply.

Melanie is now serving a natural life sentence in the New Jersey Department of Corrections, her motive being one of getting rid of an obnoxious rival and connection so that she could better her life – a bit like Alice Crimmins if you will!

WANDA JEAN ALLEN

Wanda murdered her girlfriend, Gloria J. Leathers, outside of all places The Village Police Station in Oklahoma County. She was convicted in 1989.

Allen had met Ms Leathers while serving two years of a four-year prison term for a manslaughter conviction relating to the death of a previous girlfriend. Police reports indicate that Allen and Leathers fought often, and Leathers was on her way into the police station to file a complaint against Allen, who was the first woman to be executed in Oklahoma's history on Thursday, 11 January 2001, her motive being pathological jealousy.

BETTY LOU DUNEVANT BEETS

If there ever was a 'Black Widow, a female more deadly than the male', this mother of six children takes the biscuit. Born on Friday, 12 March 1937, she earned the distinction of becoming the fourth woman to be executed in the United States since the Supreme Court in 1976 allowed the death penalty to resume after a ten-year moratorium. Aged sixty-two, she was the second woman to be executed in The Lone Star State since the Civil War of 1861. She gave no final statement, as she lay strapped to the death chamber gurney on 24 February 2000. The former cashier and waitress made no eye contact with the victim's family, but smiled at her own relatives.

> The cause of death of Mr Beets was the gunshot defect in the skull and locating of not one, but two bullets, one in the region of the skull and the other in the region of the bones of the trunk. In my opinion, death was due to one, if not two, gunshot wounds…one in the head and one in the trunk, somewhere.
>
> (Dr Charles S. Petty. Chief Medical Examiner and Director of the Dallas County Forensic Science Laboratory.)

Beets was convicted of the Saturday, 6 August 1983 shooting death of her recently married fifth husband, forty-six-year-old Jimmy Don Beets, using a .38-calibre handgun, at the couple's home near Gun Barrel City, Henderson County, in east Texas.

I simply love the names of many of these US places and towns with the impertinence of calling themselves a city: Gun Barrel City (pop 5672), Tombstone (pop 1,300) Rattlesnake Creek, Cody, Bumble Bee Just Never Quite Made It (pop 0), and Rosebud (pop 1, 377), Deadwood (pop 1.270), Durango (pop 18,500) and Shit Creek where Betty Lou Beets would soon find herself.

Prosecutors said that the diminutive, brown haired woman – she was a mere five-foot two-inches tall and weighed 118 pounds – murdered her husband, a Dallas Fire Department captain, to collect circa $100,000 on a J.C. Penny life insurance policy along with pension benefits amounting to $1,200 every month. Two years later, following an anonymous tip-off (later learned to be from her stepson Robert), Jimmy's body was found buried in a wishing well which was used as a flower garden. The corpse had been there two years after Jimmy had been reported missing.

A lady called Lil Smith, owner of the Redwood Beach Marina, located between the communities of Kemp and Seven Points and Gun Barrel City on Cedar Creek Lake (any references as to the location being Lake Athens are incorrect) later testified that at around 10 p.m. on 6 August 1983, several of her customers noticed an empty boat drifting on the Cedar Creek Reservoir. Two men went and got the empty boat and brought it to the shore. Inside was a fishing licence with the name 'Jimmy Beets', along with a bottle of nitroglycerine tablets and a life jacket. The Coast Guard and Wildlife were notified and 'personnel came to the marina'.

And, here is yet another thing I don't get about our friends across the pond. Why call out The US Coast Guard *and* The US Fish and Wildlife Service to the *edge* of a lake for fuck's sake? Along with Fire and Rescue and around two hundred local cops and state troopers, the marina's small car park must have been jam packed full.

Nevertheless, Lil Smith then looked in the telephone book to see if anyone by the name of Jimmy Don Beets was listed. Smith soon tracked down Betty Lou, who went to the marina and identified the boat and fishing licence as belonging to her husband. Because of the high winds, it was decided that a search for Beets's body would not commence until the next morning. Despite extensive searches lasting three weeks, the body was not found – and it still hasn't!

Police also found the skeletal remains of Beets's fourth husband, Doyle Wayne Barker, under a storage shed at the property. Barker, who had disappeared in 1981, had been shot, execution-style, in the back of the head. Both bodies had been stuffed into blue sleeping bags. She was also convicted of shooting and wounding her second husband, William 'Billy' York Lane.

Despite her claims in mitigation that she had been sexually abused and suffered from domestic violence through all of her five marriages, all of which has never been substantiated, Betty Lou did have some criminal history. She had been previously convicted of public lewdness, which occurred when she worked in Charlie's Angels Bar, in Dallas. She alleged that she had been 'auditioned' one night, without specifying what type of audition it was for: 'Well, it's a topless place but I wasn't topless,' she told the cops who were looking at the crusty old bird in front of them and thinking 'topless, no chance!' She had also been convicted of another misdemeanor offence that resulted when she shot another former husband, Bill Lane, in the side of the stomach.

Betty Lou Beets's body is buried in the Captain Joe Byrd Cemetery, better known as the Peckerwood Hill Cemetery, Huntsville, Texas – the final resting place of over one hundred executed inmates – and Jimmy Don Beets is buried at the Roselawn Memorial Gardens, Seagoville, Dallas County.

DEBRA DENISE BROWN

Ms Brown is an African-American who along with Alton Coleman was tried and convicted for her crimes. This 'Mid-West Monster' was sentenced to death but this was commuted to life without parole, while the only good thing to emerge from the proceedings was that Coleman was executed by lethal injection on Friday, 26 April 2002, at the Southern Ohio Correctional Facility, Lucasville, Indiana. Giving no problems to officials, and wearing a non-denominational shawl, he recited the better part of the 23rd Psalm 'The Lord is my Shepherd', took eight short breaths and was gone.

The Hon. Fred Foreman, former state's attorney, commented on the murder of nine-year-old Vernita Wheat, whose decomposing body was found wedged in an abandoned warehouse's bathroom door on 18 June 1984, in Gary, Indiana, saying: 'I've been to several murder scenes. I have prosecuted several homicides. I don't think there's one I've forgotten. Each time a child is involved, it has a traumatic effect on so many people. You just don't forget them. What possesses someone to commit such terrible offenses against a young child?'

Responsible for a cross-country binge of up to eight murders, seven rapes, three kidnappings fourteen brutal robberies and leaving diners without paying their bills in Ohio, Michigan and Illinois, their trail of repugnant and perverted acts of sadistic violence far exceeds that of Myra Hindley and Ian Brady. It ended only when they were arrested following the abduction of two little girls in Indiana. Their victims are: Vernita Wheat (nine), Tamika Turks (seven), Donna Williams (twenty-five), Virginia Temple and her daughter, Rachelle (nine), Marlene Walters (forty-four) and a seventy-seven-year-old man, whose name is still unknown.

On Saturday, 18 June 1983, seven-year-old Tamika Turks and her nine-year-old niece, Annie, were walking from a candy store to their home when Brown and Coleman confronted them. The two persuaded the children to walk into nearby woods to play a game. Once there, they removed Tamika's shirt and tore it into small strips, which they used to bind and gag their terrified victims.

Tamika began to cry. Infuriated by this, Brown held the child's nose and mouth closed, while Coleman stomped on her chest before strangling her to death.

After being carried a short distance, Annie was forced to perform oral sex on both Brown and Coleman. Then the man raped her. The two perverted fiends finally choked the child until she became unconscious. They tied a leather belt around her neck and left her for dead. Mercifully, when she awoke, they were gone.

Police discovered Tamika dead in bushes close by. She had been strangled with an elastic strip of bed sheet. (The same fabric was later found in the apartment shared by the killers.) Annie had received cuts so deep that her intestines were protruding from her vagina.

This was the not the first of such crimes committed by this evil pair; evidence of a remarkably similar murder, in Ohio, was also admitted at the trial.

'I killed the bitch and I don't give a damn. I had fun out of it.' (A note Brown sent to the trial judge concerning the murder of Tamika Turks.)

Of some interest to the reader will be the mitigation Brown put forward which allowed commutation of her death sentence.

Her father had severe mental problems. She was one of no less than eleven children and she had experienced a drug overdose, which required hospitalisation in 1980. She was a regular drug user. She claimed that she was beaten and abused by Coleman throughout their relationship and forced into prostitution. She has limited intelligence and scores 75 on the Wechsler Intelligence IQ Test. Be that as it may, and in considering the disgusting note she passed to the judge, one might still consider this woman to certainly be as deadly as any male.

Born on Sunday, 11 November 1962, Inmate # W025932 Debra Brown is presently serving a life term at the Dayton Correctional Institution, Montgomery County, Ohio.

VIRGINIA SUSAN CAUDILL

Born on Saturday, 10 September 1960, the ugly and overweight Virginia Caudill was sentenced to death on Friday, 24 March 2000 in Fayette County, Kentucky, for capital murder, robbery, burglary, arson and tampering with physical evidence.

In the early hours of Sunday, 15 March 1998, the loathsome woman and her accomplice, moustachioed and balding Jonathan Wayne Goforth, entered the Lexington home of seventy-three-year-old African-American Lonetta White, where they beat her to death and burgled her house. They then placed their victim's body in the trunk of her car and drove her to a desolate area in Fayette County, where they set the vehicle, and the deceased, on fire.

The following is an except from the Victim Impact Statements that were submitted to the Court in March 2000:

'These two people left my mother in such a distorted, dismembered, and ashened state that she was identifiable inly by her dental record. My life has been ripped apart at the seams – left broken down and unstable. My life is unmanageable; it's just a chaotic mess.' (Steve White, Lonetta White's son.)

'When you sleep all you hear is "bloody scrambled eggs". It is so horrible. It was tragic and it is very hard to handle. The death is one thing in life we will never get over. It was so very horrible and brutal. I cannot get that crushed brain description out of my mind.' (Darlene Ward, Lonetta White's niece.)

Quite frankly, the lives of these two items of human scum are not worth the page this account is printed upon, however, it does give us an insight as to why some women became so conscienceless and cold-blooded.

Mrs Lonetta White was the mother of Caudill's estranged boyfriend, Steve White, and had been living at White's home until he kicked her out on 13 March following an argument concerning Caudill's drug abuse. After leaving, Caudill went to a nearby crack den where users gathered to buy, sell, and ingest controlled substances, especially crack. Here, she met Goforth, a casual acquaintance whom she'd not seen for over a decade.

Later, at trial, Caudill said that on the afternoon of 14 March, Goforth gave her a ride to Mrs White's place and she asked the old lady for twenty or thirty dollars so that she could rent a room for the night, which was a lie – she wanted the money for cocaine. Then, at about 3 a.m. on 15 March, Caudill and Goforth, high as kites, returned to Mrs White's home.

Anxious to place all of the blame onto Goforth, Caudill

said that she went to the front door and told Mrs White that she now needed more money to rent a room, while Goforth remained out of sight near the garage. When the old dear turned away to get the extra money, Goforth burst through the door and attacked her without warning, with Lonetta pleading, 'Please help me, Virginia.' Goforth then took Lonetta to a bedroom and bound her hands together and killed her. The couple ransacked the premises, taking valuables, money, jewellery, a white fur coat and firearms, then loaded up his pickup before wrapping the body in a carpet. The two of them then carried the dead Mrs White to the garage and loaded it into the trunk of the deceased's car, and proceeded to drive to a field where Goforth doused the car with gasoline and set it on fire.

For his part, and anxious to shift the blame onto Caudill, Goforth insisted that it was Caudill who induced Mrs White to admit them into her home on the pretence they were having problems with the pickup truck and needed to use the telephone. According to Goforth, once inside Caudill demanded money and, when Mrs White refused, she hit the victim twice over the head with a clock, then produced a roofer's hammer that she 'had secretly taken from my truck' and struck the elderly lady again in the back of the head. At autopsy it was established that there had been fifteen blows in all, ranging from lacerations to blows that forced fragments of skull to be driven into the brain.

If Goforth actually believed any of his own account we cannot know, but going further he explained that he'd asked Caudill why she'd hit Mrs White, before Caudill hit her again and again. While this was going on, he allegedly went into the living room, sat on the sofa, and pondered what he should do next – clearly trying to stop Caudill and saving Mrs White's life being the furthest thing from his tiny mind.

The two killers then fled Fayette County. They spent several days at a cabin near Herrington Lake in Mercer County and then moved to Ocala, Florida, then on to Gulfport, Mississippi, where they parted company because they were now being screened on the popular TV show, *America's Most Wanted*. Virginia Caudill then went to New Orleans, Louisiana, where she was subsequently arrested on Wednesday, 11 November 1998.

Goforth was taken into custody in Gulfport on Tuesday, 8 December 1998, at first saying that he had never heard of a person called Virginia Caudill, knew nothing about any murder, then in the same breath saying 'I never killed anyone, but Virginia told me that she and a black man had done kilt the old lady' – an assertion that he admitted at trial was a fabrication. I mean you could not make this up if one tried!

On Friday, 24 March 2000, a jury found both Caudill and Goforth guilty of murder, first-degree robbery, first-degree burglary, second-degree arson, and tampering with physical evidence. They both received the death sentence.

At the time of writing inmate #144124-W Virginia Caudill is housed at the Kentucky Correctional Institution for Women (KCIW), Pee Wee Valley. She has exhausted the appeal process although no date has yet been set for her execution by lethal injection.

Born Monday, 21 November 1960, Jonathan Wayne Goforth #127520 is still on Death Row, Kentucky State Penitentiary (KSP), Eddyville.

TALKING WITH FEMALE SERIAL KILLERS

PAULA R. COOPER

Ms Cooper was just fifteen years old when she devised a scheme with three juvenile friends: Denise Thomas (fourteen), Karen Coder (sixteen) and April Beverly (fifteen) to obtain ready money to buy drink and drugs. After skipping school, they had smoked marijuana and drank alcohol then they went to the Indiana home of a septuagenarian Bible teacher, Ruth Pelke, and asked her to write down information about her classes. One of the girls hit the elderly lady over the head with a vase, knocking her to the floor. In a frenzied attack, Cooper slashed her arms and legs, before stabbing her in the chest and stomach thirty-three times with a twelve-inch butcher's knife. Callously indifferent to the woman's agonised death, the girls searched the house for money and took a derisory ten dollars before driving off in the victim's old 1976 Plymouth car.

On 11 July 1986, at Lake County Superior Court, Judge James Kimbrough sentenced Cooper to death. The other girls received sentences ranging between twenty-six to sixty years. In mitigation, the defence argued that Cooper was only fifteen years old at the time of the murder. Her lawyers claimed that Paula was a victim of physical child abuse; that she had been forced to watch the rape of her mother and violent assaults by her father. It was also alleged that her mother had once tried to kill her. She had attended ten different schools by the time of the murder. However, she had a prior criminal history as a chronic runaway and for burglary. Her attorney told her to plead 'guilty' and throw herself on the mercy of the court – as in throw in the towel!

Lake County prosecutor, James McNew, would have none of it. He described Cooper as a 'social misfit' and asked for the death penalty. Nevertheless, so heinous was the nature of this homicide, that the judge would not relent and, in 1987, Paula Cooper became the youngest person ever to inhabit Indiana's grim Death Row. Her death sentence outraged human activists in the US and Europe and drew a plea for clemency from Pope John Paul II. In 1988, a priest delivered a petition to Indianapolis with more than two million signatures protesting Cooper's sentence.

Also in 1988, the US Supreme Court, in *Thompson v. Oklahoma*, ruled in an unrelated case that those under the age of sixteen at the time of an offence couldn't be executed. The court ruled such sentences were cruel and unusual punishment and thus unconstitutional. Therefore, Indiana lawmakers later passed a law raising the minimum age limit from ten years to sixteen, and, in 1988, the state's High Court set aside Cooper's death sentence and ordered her to serve sixty years in prison, effective from Thursday, 13 July 1989, less time served.

Inmate #864800 Cooper's sentence was further reduced due to her good behaviour in prison, where she earned a bachelor's degree, then on Monday, 17 June 2013, after spending twenty-eight years behind bars she was released on parole back into society where she remained until Tuesday, 26 May 2015, when Indianapolis Police found the forty-five-year-old woman dead from a self-inflicted gunshot wound to the head and lying under a tree outside a residence on the city's north-west side.

According to her friend, Ormeshia Linton, just before 8 p.m., Paula had decided to go shopping for a new outfit. 'She wanted to go to 'Rainbow' (a chain that sells youthful clothes and accessories) to get it,' Linton told police, adding,

'I said, Rainbow's closed, baby. The furthest we're gonna get is Walmart, so that's where we went.'

Linton was herself no stranger to the prison system. She had been sentenced to jail facing thirty years on drugs charges when she met Cooper in the Rockville Correctional Facility. Linton explained that despite Cooper's notoriety, she had a reputation for kindness to other prisoners. She used to put together small packs of noodles and other food items for women who didn't have any money to spend in the commissary. Linton had been released on parole in 2010.

Before the two women ended up at Walmart that Monday night, Ormeshia had received a telephone call from Paula. 'I knew something was wrong with her,' she told police. 'I invited her to come by during her lunch break at work, but I guess she got lost because she didn't know her way around Indianapolis. She relied on GPS for everything.'

When Cooper finally arrived, the two sat down at a table. Paula began to sob uncontrollably like a small child. To Ormeshia she seemed 'defeated, all washed out and depleted'. 'I can't do it no more,' cried Cooper, 'It's on the inside.'

According to Ormeshia Linton, Paula was a very private person and she figured that there was trouble with her fiancé, so she invited her to come and stay with her for a few days, offering the use of the spare room in her house.

Later, at Walmart, Paula seemed to be in better spirits. She bought a new outfit: grey khaki pants; a grey, black and white top, and black Dr Scholl's sandals. She even bought new underwear – satin panties lined with black lace.

Back at the house, Paula asked for some writing paper and envelopes, and then she spent time out on the patio, smoking cigarettes and writing.

It was not until early the next morning, 26 May, when Ormeshia awoke to find Paula gone, the tags on her new clothes on the bed, that the pieces would start to fall into place. Ormeshia's husband went down into the kitchen and started calling his wife's name 'Meshia, Meshia, before handing her three envelopes. Later the police phoned to say that they had found Paula Cooper, shot dead.

This, for me, is a difficult case to call. I think that one might agree that for the better part of Paula's early years she suffered from a dysfunctional childhood. Most certainly she had been moved from school to school, probably because of her disruptive behaviour and an early introduction into drinking alcohol and marijuana. She was also a 'chronic runaway' from school and home, she was rebellious and, as the prosecutor rightly opined, she had become a social misfit.

And, it is here I have to say, so what? There are millions of young teenagers across the world suffering the same problems, but they don't turn to committing such a terrible murder on a vulnerable, old lady, do they? In this respect, Paula Cooper was certainly as deadly as any male.

There is also no doubt that Paula tried to better herself while in prison despite a somewhat problematic time shortly after she was incarcerated. She attacked other inmates and a prison guard, to spend three years in solitary confinement, or 'lock', twenty-three-hours-a-day in a cell the size of a small bathroom. Yet again, with the death sentence hanging over her head, in any event it would have taken a lengthy period for this incorrigible teenager to settle down to the strict custodial regime in the first instance.

At this point, however, I am reminded of a letter the late

Lord Chief Justice of England, The Lord Lane, wrote to me way back in 1992:

> The prospect of a young person spending the rest of their life in prison is appalling. It is a pity that there seems to be no humane alternative. There is good in the worst of us. Oddly enough, prison sometimes serves that fact to be proved.

I also have to reflect on the compassionate and very Christian attitude adopted by Bill Pelke, the grandson of Cooper's victim, Ruth. One of his quotes is below:

> The death penalty has absolutely nothing to do with healing. [It] just continues the cycle of violence and creates more murder victims' family members. We become what we hate. We become killers.

Bill authored a book entitled *Journey of Hope...From Violence to Healing*, which details the murder of his grandmother Ruth Elizabeth Pelke, a Bible teacher. Pelke originally supported the sentence of death for Cooper, but went through a spiritual transformation in 1986 after praying for love and compassion for Paula Cooper and her family. He met Paula several times in prison and forgave her entirely.

If Bill Pelke can forgive Paula Cooper then so must I. However, if one might think that she was young when she committed a brutal murder, let's now look at one home-grown in Great Britain, because Mary Bell was just eleven years old when she strangled to death two little boys.

Mary Flora Bell

Method of Killing: Manual Strangulation
Sometimes described as 'throttling', manual strangulation is caused by compression of the throat by the hands and fingers of an assailant. There are three ways in which the natural functions of the body are impeded by strangulation – the obstruction of respiration, obstruction of the blood supply to the brain, and pressure on the carotid nerve plexuses. Although the victim may put up a struggle – and the physical signs of that struggle may be observed on the body – throttling renders victims helpless very quickly as anoxia overcomes them and they fall into unconsciousness.

With this being said, I have personally interviewed a number of notorious male serial killers who all say that 'strangling someone ain't like on TV.' By way of example, both the heavily-built Arthur John

Shawcross, aka, 'The Monster of the Rivers', and the slightly-built Michael Bruce Ross, aka 'The Roadside Strangler', both explained to me that the victims often writhed around for quiet a considerable period before they died. In Ross's case, he had to stop several times to massage his cramped fingers and hands before death supervened. Shawcross, who was a very strong man, said that on several occasions it took up to ten minutes of 'hard work'.

Victims

Martin Brown (four) and Brian Howe (three)

A serial killer is defined by the FBI as an offender who commits three or more murders with a cooling off period between the 'events'. If this is not shocking enough, imagine an English girl who becomes an emerging serial murderer – at the age of eleven!

MARTIN BROWN

Our journey into the mind and twisted crimes of the youngest British female killer starts on Saturday, 25 May 1968, when three young lads were looking for scrap wood to make a pigeon coop, while others will say they were collecting fire wood. Their home was Scotswood, a working-class area of Newcastle, and their search took them to St Margaret's Road – a mixture of council-owned places and derelict terraced houses – which runs from Whitfield Road through a dogleg to Whitehouse Road. The kids were heading for No. 85, an old condemned redbrick terraced property. They ventured upstairs and in the back bedroom found the body of a young, grey-faced child lying stiff and ice cold among the rubbish scattered over the floor.

The youngest lad scarpered, and the two older boys, Walter and John, ran downstairs to fetch two men who were repairing electricity equipment just outside the front door. As one of the men tried to resuscitate the child in vain, his workmate went off to call an ambulance. Walter, feeling sick and faint, took deep breaths out of the front window.

As Walter stood in the window, he saw two girls arrive. He recognised the younger one immediately. He knew her to be eleven years old. She was extremely pretty, with dark hair and bright blue eyes. Her name was Mary Flora Bell, and she was a streetwise and tough kid. She lived at 70 Whitehouse Road. The other girl was called Norma Joyce Bell. They were in no way related, just next-door neighbours from the aforementioned nearby Whitehouse Road. Walter then watched the girls climb through the window of the house next door. It seemed that the two girls knew the complicated way of getting into the derelict place, out of a tumbledown outhouse at the back of it, over the wall into the garden of number 85 and then into the place through the broken back door. On this day, the two girls would become a nuisance, hovering around, getting in the way, and all the time displaying an offensive curiosity.

Martin Brown was four years old. He lived with his parents George and June and baby sister, Linda, at 140 St Margaret's Road. On his last day, he got up by himself, got washed and dressed, and ate a breakfast of milk and Sugarpops at around 9 a.m. Then he grabbed his anorak, shouted 'Tarra' to his parents and went out to play. That was the last time his mother heard his voice. The next time she saw her son he was deathly silent.

The call made by the workman was received at 3.35 p.m. and the police were informed just five minutes later. They arrived very quickly, but could find no obvious cause of death. There were some empty bottles lying around, but later analysis found no trace of toxins in the body. A brief inspection of the property found a hole in the roof with broken tiles below it, but these tiles were not in any way related to the child's death – Martin had been found lying on the opposite side of the room.

At post mortem, the deceased was found to be well fed and healthy. He had no broken bones and only one slight bruise on a knee. However, this examination threw up one irregularity: a small haemorrhage in the brain. The famous pathologist Dr Bernard Knight was puzzled. In the absence of ligature marks around the neck, he would have assumed manual strangulation as the cause of death, but there were no visible pressure marks on the neck, so what else seemed possible?

I would suggest that today one would never dream of allowing a four-year-old child to wander off unsupervised for hours on end, but in the late sixties, the streets, car parks, wasteland and shops of Scotswood were homes and playground to all the local children, and they drifted around all day in straggling groups. In those days, parents did not feel the need to watch over their offspring all the time, and Martin, who was a confident child, came and went in a free and easy fashion. In fact, his movements that fateful day show how far he roamed.

He had spent some time talking to the workmen, who had given the child a biscuit. He popped in on his Aunt Rita down the road where his grandmother gave him egg on toast, and then he called in on his father for money for a lollipop. At about 3.15 p.m., he was in a queue for sweets at Dixon's, a wooden shack-type sweet shop. Here he saw his Aunt Rita again. The shopkeeper had told him off for having dirty hands and he went back home with his aunt to wash them and have a slice of bread and margarine. This, according to police, must have been about 3.20 p.m. At 3.30 he was found in the derelict house over the road.

We might now consider several incidents that took place around the time of Martin's murder, which with the great gift of hindsight, were extremely significant, but at the time went unremarked. On 26 May, the day following Martin's death, Norma's parents caught Mary Bell with her hands around the neck of their younger daughter, Susan. Mr Bell knocked her hands away and gave her a 'clip on the shoulder'. Norma's parents forbade Susan to ever play with Mary Bell again.

The second incident came from an entirely different quarter. The local authority day nursery at Woodland's Crescent was broken into over the weekend. Among the chaos, several scribbled notes written in red ballpoint pen were left, which were obviously the work of two children. The notes referred to Martin's death, insulted the police, and bragged of murder. However, the officer who found these notes merely assumed that they were just a childish prank, if an extremely tasteless one. Below are the notes – they are written verbatim:

1. I murder so THAT I may come back fuch of we murder watch out Danny and Faggot.
2. WE did murder Martain brown Fuckof you Bastard.
3. You are mice y Becurse we murdered Martain Go

Brown you Bete Look out there are Murders about
by FANNYAND auld Faggot you Srcews.

'Srcews' was clearly meant to be 'Screws' meaning police.
'Micey' was a local word for 'Stupid'.

The third incident took place on Friday, 31 May. The
nursery was broken into again. This time the intruders, Mary
Bell and Norma Bell, were caught red-handed. Indeed, the
two girls had already been in trouble that week. Four days after
the death, Mary Bell called on George Brown and his wife and
asked to see Martin. Mrs Brown, gentle in her grief, tearfully
replied: 'No pet. Martin is dead.' Mary was unperturbed by
this and grinned. 'Oh, I know he's fuckin' dead. I wanted
to see him in his coffin.' Mrs Brown was shocked and hurt.
She shut the door on Mary Bell, who we can judge already
by now as a child with a very juvenile, dangerous, antisocial
personality – current medical understanding is that for the
most part this condition can be managed but not cured.

A fourth incident occurred when a twelve-year-old boy
dismissed a scene he had witnessed at the nursery sandpit as
just another example of Mary Bell's showing off. She was
playing with Norma, and jumped on top of her screaming
'I'm a murderer.' She pulled Norma's hair, kicked her in the
eye and pointed in the direction of the murder house. 'That's
where I killed Brown,' she shouted. The boy laughed but just
ignored her, although he may well have been too scared of
this horrible girl to tell anyone at the time.

On 7 June, the inquest left the cause of death open and
a group of neighbours staged a protest in Newcastle Civic
centre against the dangerous housing conditions in Scotswood.
However, the disturbing events of the coming month were to

hush such protests and totally eclipse the problems of housing. Eight weeks after the inquest, and just over nine weeks after Martin Brown's death, another child went missing.

Born in Gateshead, Tyne and Wear, on Sunday 26 May 1957, perhaps Mary Bell's evil can be traced to the bizarre childhood behaviour of her mother Betty – one of four children – and Mary turned out to be the only rotten apple in the basket. When Betty was three her father became an invalid and her mother became the breadwinner. Whether it was this stress in the family or some mental issues with no obvious cause, Betty's behaviour began to change. She became obsessively interested in religion and she refused to eat with the rest of her family.

When Betty left school, she could never hold down a job for long and, at the age of fifteen, after a row with a boyfriend, she took an overdose of drugs. Soon after, the family moved to Gateshead, but the change of scene did nothing to help her. However, it was there, at the age of seventeen that she gave birth to Mary.

Betty married her boyfriend, William 'Billy' Bell on Saturday, 18 March 1958 and he moved into the family flat in Redheughbridge Road (the A189 today), Gateshead. The grandmother looked after little Mary while the child's parents were at work.

When she was twelve months old, Mary suffered the first in a series of near-fatal accidents which were never fully explained, although one incident involved swallowing some of her grandmother's pills. Fortunately she was found and rushed to hospital where her stomach was pumped out. Nevertheless, not long after this, Betty had another child, a boy. Gateshead Council then gave the grandmother a spacious new house with a garden, 27 Huxley Crescent – which still stands today. However, when she returned from work one afternoon the grandmother was greeted by the sight of her possessions piled up in the street outside and a locked front door. She returned to Glasgow, and Betty and Billy and the two little children had the house to themselves.

Betty Bell now began to go off for long periods on her own, leaving her children with various friends and relations. More often than not, Mary would stay with her 'Aunt Cath', and when she was two years old, Cath wrote to Betty offering adopt her. Betty arrived the day after and took Mary away.

It was becoming obvious that the realities of caring for the little girl were too much for Betty, and a fortnight later she took her back to Cathy and left her there again. The pattern of rejection and reacceptance was now established, but took on a more bizarre turn in November 1959 when Betty arrived at Cath's house in a state of terrible distress. She explained that Mary had had a horrific accident involving a lorry. 'They had to cut her clothes off her, she is that bad,' she said through her tears. However, the next day Betty explained that in fact she had just left Mary with some friends of the family, a couple who had also repeatedly offered to adopt her.

When Mary was three, Cath called in to visit Betty and brought the children some sweets. Coming back from making a cup of tea, she found the children eating them from the floor with Betty's Purple Hearts mixed in among them. Known as 'Drinamyl', the triangular-shaped tablets were prescribed to housewives who suffered from tiredness and anxiety. They were also used as a dietary aid. Cath promptly made the kids sick with salted water and then got Billy to rush them to hospital.

It is now 1961, and yet again Mary, now almost four, was rushed into hospital after eating her mother's iron pills. Thereafter, a quarrel erupted between Betty and the rest of the family and she did not see them for over a year – the family fortunes were now on the slide when they upped sticks yet again and moved to number 147 Westmoreland Road, one of the roughest parts of Newcastle. This was an environment a far cry from the trim three-bedroomed council house in Huxley Crescent where the roads were quiet and safe and there were green fields close by. Here, in this squalid place, the local kids only had the streets to play in, and here, at the age of six, a fourteen-year-old lad stabbed Mary in the back with a broken bottle. It was yet another trip to hospital for the little girl, but here the family stayed until 1966 when they moved once again, this time to 70 Whitehouse Road.

Soon afterwards, another family named Bell moved into number 68, and Mary and her neighbour's daughter Norma became close friends. Theirs was a close-knit community and where the wasteland, although very dangerous by today's standards, served as an adventure playground, and the swarms of children drifted from house to house and from the sweetshop to sweetshop, returning home only for meals and sleep. Mary was now in her element.

BRIAN HOWE

Brian, aged three, was barely out of babyhood when he was murdered by Mary Bell. But he was a little boy you could easily talk to. He lived with his father, his teenage sister, Patricia, aka Pat, and his brother. His black-and-white dog Lassie was his constant companion.

It was late afternoon of Wednesday, 31 July 1966, when Pat stood on a railway bridge scanning the 'Tin Lizzie' – a wasteland of old tin drums, rusty tanks, builders' rubble and huge concrete blocks. She was desperately searching for her little stepbrother, Brian. With her on the bridge were Mary and Norma Bell. The threesome kept looking for him until 7 p.m., when the police were called in.

At 7.30, Mary's father called her in for tea. At 11.10 p.m. Brian's dead body was found between two concrete blocks on the waste ground. His body was strewn with long grass and purple flowers, his left arm stretched out and his hand was black with dirt. His lips were blue and there was froth on them. There were marks on his neck, scratches on his nose and puncture wounds on his legs. On the ground nearby was a pair of scissors. One blade was broken off and the other bent back.

By the time Chief Inspector James Dobson of the CID had been woken from his sleep and driven at high speed to Scotswood, it was 1.10 a.m., and the uniformed officers had already set up lights and cordoned off the area. As he parked up and walked down the hill he was struck by the place's proximity to St Margaret's Road. The unsolved case of little Martin came into his mind and he suddenly feared a connection.

During that night, Brian's body was examined more closely. The marks of compression on his nose and throat indicated that he had been strangled and his nose pinched. But Dr Bernard Tomlinson, the pathologist, concluded that although the boy had been manually strangled, remarkably little pressure had been exerted by his killer. He pointed out that an adult would usually use much more force than was required, and this, together with the shallow wounds on the legs which hardly punctured the skin, indicated a child's touch.

DI Dobson and his murder squad knew then that they were looking for a child: a child who was highly dangerous. They were worried and felt a great sense of urgency. One hundred CID officers were called in, and they were told that they would be working day and night until the case was solved.

During that first night, a questionnaire was drawn up and copies made. It would be used to collect statements from all the children in the neighbourhood. The interviews started at 8 a.m. the next day, when police visited approximately one thousand Scotswood homes and gave out questionnaires to 1,200 children. As expected, when the responses of the kids or their parents were studied, there were many inconsistencies. The police repeatedly visited those whose statements were most inconsistent – among those were the completed questionnaires from Mary Bell and Norma Bell.

Both girls said that they had not seen Brian after lunchtime, but they also both changed their accounts of their afternoon's activities several times. In addition, their attitude was noticeably different from that of the other children. Detective Constable Kerr visited Norma, then Mary on Thursday, 1 August. Although Norma's family seemed a close and happy one, the officer felt that Norma herself was being evasive and peculiar. 'She was continually smiling, as if at a huge joke,' he remarked.

The next day, another detective, Detective Sergeant Docherty, went back to see Mary again. When he talked to her, it seemed that she had remembered something about her afternoon. Mary said that she had seen a boy she knew playing with scissors which were broken or bent, that he was covered in grass and little purple flowers, and that she had seen him hit Brian on the face for no reason at all. This was of great concern to the police. They had not released any information about the scissors that had been found near the body, and so they were keen to question the boy.

Police soon located the lad Mary had referred to. He was eight years old and not very quick-thinking for his age. Chief Inspector Dobson talked to the boy himself, the first of the children he had interviewed. He was questioned for two days, and his statements checked and double-checked. He had a solid alibi, backed up by reliable witnesses, and although he had played with Brian in the morning, he had not even been in Scotswood that afternoon. So, the boy was eliminated from the inquiries, but the fact that Mary Bell had known about the scissors had focused attention on her and Norma.

At 8.10 p.m., on 4 August, Dobson met Norma Bell. A slow-witted girl, she was nervous and tearful and wanted to talk without her father being present. This time she described going out with Mary and her dog to the concrete blocks on the Tin Lizzie waste ground. Her statement began, 'We walked in among the blocks and I tripped over something. I looked down and saw it was Brian Howe's head…Mary said, "Keep your nose dry, he's dead".' Norma went on to say that Mary had demonstrated how she had strangled the child and how she had cut his belly with a razor blade then hidden under one of the blocks before covering his body with purple flowers.

Norma was taken to the Tin Lizzie and asked to lie down to imitate the way that she had seen Brian lying that day. She did so, and sure enough she lay in exactly the position that he had been found. That night, Norma was taken to stay at the nearby Fernwood Remand Home. Then Dobson and two constables went to call on Mary. It was now 12.30 a.m. and she was asleep in bed. After some argument, her father, Billy Bell, agreed to wake her up and fetch her sister to travel with Mary to the police station.

Despite being woken in the middle of the night, Mary was alert during the questioning and had all her wits about her. She denied having been anywhere near the blocks that afternoon, fidgeted and was generally uncooperative. Already the inquiry was a game to her, and in this grave situation her behaviour was clearly influenced by television dramas and films. At one point the phone rang and she said, 'Is this place bugged?' Then she jumped up to leave and, on being told she could not, said, 'I'll phone for some solicitors, they'll get me out. This is being brainwashed.' At 3.30 a.m., they sent Mary home, having learned nothing.

By now, other serious matters were coming to the attention of police, things which strengthened the case against Mary and Norma. During the inquiry they recalled that on Saturday, 11 May 1968, just sixteen days before Martin Brown was murdered, a young boy [I shall call him 'John G'] was found near the Delaval Arms public house in Scotswood. He was bleeding and had been sick, and although he recovered, his injuries were serious enough for the police and ambulance to be called. The two girls who found him were Mary Bell, who was then almost eleven years old and Norma Bell. Between 11.30 a.m. and 11.55 a.m., on 12 May 1968, Norma gave this statement to Sergeant 462 Thompson at her home:

I am 13 years of age and live with my mother and father at 68 Whitehouse Road, Newcastle-upon-Tyne. I attend Whickham View Benwell Lower School.

About 1.30 p.m. on Saturday, 11 May 1968, I was playing in the street with my friend Mary Bell and we met John G. We took him to the shop at the bottom of Delaval Road for some sweets. We then took him back to the top of the steps at Delaval Road/ Whitehouse Road and told him to go home.

Mary and I then went and got some wood from the old houses in Coanwood Road and brought that home to our mothers.

We then went to play on the car park beside the Delaval Arms.

While we were playing there Mary told me that she could hear some shouts from the direction of the old sheds beside the Delaval Arms.

We went over the grass and through the wire fence and found John G behind the sheds. He was bleeding from the head.

We jumped down and picked him up but could not lift him onto the grass. We climbed back onto the grass and pulled him up by his hands.

We shouted to a man who was passing on Scotswood Road but he would not help. Then we saw another man on Scotswood Road and shouted for him and he carried John to the Delaval Arms where an ambulance and the Police were sent for.

I have never seen John playing there before and I have never taken him down there.

Previously between 10.40 and 11.00 a.m., on 12 May 1968, Mary Bell had given her statement to Sergeant 462 Thompson at her home. It was almost identical to that given by Norma Bell, then later that day Mary and Norma struck again.

At 9.30 p.m., Mrs Watson of 48 Woodlands Crescent, made a complaint to the police, alleging that around 4.30 and 5.30 p.m. her daughter, Pauline, aged seven, and two friends, Cindy Hepple, aged six, and Susan Cornish, aged six, had been playing in the nursery sandpit and had been assaulted by one of two older girls.

In a statement taken by Police Sergeant A. Lindreen and WPC Charlton, Pauline said:

> The smaller of the two girls [Mary Bell] told me to get out of the sandpit. I said 'no!' She put her hands around my neck and squeezed hard. The bigger girl was behind the hut playing. The girl took her hands off my neck and she did the same to Susan. Me, Cindy and Susan all ran home. The girl who squeezed my neck had short hair. I don't know this girl and I have not seen her before.

The following day, the fifth, Norma was questioned again. Again she had more to add to her story. This time she admitted actually watching Mary strangle Brian. Then she described how Mary had pressed his belly with a razor blade and she drew a picture to illustrate where the wounds were made. Dobson re-examined Brian's body, and there were now five faint marks visible on the flesh, which could have represented the letter 'N' or 'M'. They must have been done soon after death, because they were not visible until decomposition set in. Over the days that followed, Norma was questioned again and again but always stuck to her story. As Dobson was to say later, 'Either she was a masterful liar, or she was telling the truth.'

On Wednesday, 7 August, Brian Howe was buried. This was a very sad occasion, and it was not only his family who cried. Mary Bell was outside the Howes' house when the coffin was brought out. DI Dobson watched her laughing and rubbing her hands and suddenly realised how dangerous she was. He decided to take her to the police station. When they went to get her at 4.30 p.m., her mother was still away and her father was out, so a hospital sister witnessed her statement.

Mary's version of events was now similar to Norma's, but in her version the strangler was Norma. Her story was also more dramatic and Norma became a swaggering villain who made menacing statements such as: 'This is the first but it'll not be the last.' This statement was even more detailed, describing how Norma banged Brian's head on some wood and how she demonstrated the sharpness of the razor blade by cutting the top of her dress. This studied but totally unnecessary embroidering was to be Mary's downfall.

During the interview, Dobson had the other little boy, Martin Brown, on his mind too. He decided to tell Mary that he suspected her and Norma of having written the notes found in the nursery. She admitted it at once and he left it at that for the time being. At 8 p.m. Dobson told Mary and Norma he was arresting them for the murder of Brian Howe. Mary replied, 'That's all right with me.' Later she was formally charged. Mary said nothing more and Norma cried, 'I never!'

The two girls spent the first night of their detention in

Newcastle West End Police Station. For the officers assigned to watch over them it was a disturbing experience. They knew what the girls had been charged with, and yet they seemed so very young. DI Dobson had bought them fish and chips for tea and Mary spent a sleepless night, worried that she might wet the bed and that she only had broken shoes for her court appearance the next day.

Norma was remanded to Carlisle and Mary to Croydon. In the train ride down south, Mary revealed her greatest worry: 'I hope me Mum won't have to pay a fine.' And she seemed unaware of the terrible trouble she was in. On Monday, 26 August, Norma was granted bail to spend the three-and-a-half months before the trial under the observation of medical experts at Prudhoe Monkton Mental Hospital near Newcastle. Mary was remanded to Seaham, where she was examined by four psychiatrists.

THE TRIAL AND THE AFTERMATH

The trial of Mary Bell started in Newcastle's Moot Hall on Thursday, 5 December 1968, and every care was taken to soften the forbidding atmosphere of the courtroom. During proceedings, Mary commented: 'When it's all over I'll go and stay with my gran in Scotland.'

The girls just sat in front of their parents, who could reach out to them of they were distressed, and the clerk who typed their testimony was seated beside them, so that it did not matter if the children could only speak in a whisper.

The judge, Sir Ralph Cusack was careful never to intimidate the girls, and he never got impatient with them. Nevertheless, the strain showed. Norma was restless and found it difficult to concentrate on what was being said or asked of her, often sitting daydreaming with her mouth open. When she did listen, she was often in tears, or looking around anxiously for sympathy or approval.

In contrast, Mary Bell was alert throughout, listened attentively to everything, even the technical evidence. She maintained an intelligent look of concentration – although no emotion, other than anger, could be read on her face. Her nerves revealed themselves in her fingers, which she spread wide in a nervous tic or stuffed into her mouth. Some witnesses thought that she boiled with an inner rage.

The sympathy of the court went to Norma and her family, who sat calmly behind her and occasionally reached out to give her support. Perhaps unfairly, Mary's mother received no such compassion. Her tatty blonde wig and heavy make-up, as well as her dramatic exits and wild outbursts could only alienate the authorities, and even Mary's father seemed to ignore her, sitting hunched and silent throughout.

This was a short trial. The verdict was given on Saturday, 7 December, a typically bleak Newcastle winter's day. Norma was acquitted and Mary was found guilty of double manslaughter on the grounds of diminished responsibility. The judge showed compassion for Mary when he sentenced her. She did not have to stand, and he made it clear that there was no question of imprisonment in the case of such a young child. However, he was unable to make a hospital order, because there was no facility prepared to admit her. In the absence of this, the judge sentenced her to detention for life. There could be no time limit set on this detention because his first duty was to protect others, and she had been proved to be not only a very dangerous person but also a liar – despite her tender years she was a homicidal psychopath and an emerging serial killer.

It fell to the then Home Secretary, James Callaghan, to decide what to do with her. So Mary Bell began her sentence at a girl's remand home, Cumberlow Lodge, in London, and then in February 1969 she was sent to an approved school in Lancashire. After two years there she was transferred to an open prison. Aged twenty [some say she was seventeen] she escaped from Moor Court Prison with another girl called Annette Priest. During their brief three days of freedom, they met some young men and Mary later claimed that she lost her virginity.

Of course, Mary Bell is not alone. There are always a small number of severely disturbed children who could be labelled as psychopaths because they are violent, asocial, unloved and incapable of love. As early as 1907, the Austrian psychoanalyst August Aichorn developed the idea of 'Milieu Therapy', which involved the affectionate care of asocial children in a closed home or village. At one point, Mary Bell was sent to Red Bank Approved School in Newton-le-Willows, Lancashire; this was a school that tried to provide the kind of care that Aichorn had envisaged. She was placed in a special unit that had the necessary security, but it was not ideal. To begin with all the other inmates were boys, and she could not receive psychiatric treatment there.

In June 1970, always proving that a leopard never changes its spots, Mary Bell alleged that a member of staff had sexually assaulted her. The man was cleared of the charge later that year, and it was proved that Mary had made up the incident.

However, nobody could deny that great thought and effort had gone into deciding on the best care for this double killer.

Some might argue that it was outrageous that a child who had, after all, committed vile crimes should have so much thought and attention lavished on her when others have so little. As one of Mary's aunts said, without rancour, 'Mary's probably getting better schooling than ours ever will.'

Mary Bell was released from Askham Grange Prison in 1980. Granted anonymity for life she had a daughter in 1984, and is now reported to be a grandmother. Bestselling author, Gitta Sereny cooperated with Bell in a book called *Cries Unheard: The Story of Mary Bell*. Published in May 1998 – it is claimed that Mary received £50,000 for her exclusive input – it received mixed reviews – like all authors do!

Norma Bell was placed under psychiatric supervision, but returned to school and as normal a life as possible after a short holiday with one of her brothers. Her present status is unknown. For her part, Mary Bell is still alive and she could be living next door to you!

It goes without saying that the case of Mary Bell has been in the headlines way back since her arrest for double murder in 1968. Indeed, her story is remarkable because she is, at the time of writing, the youngest 'emerging female serial killer' in UK and US criminal history. All the signs are that had she not been apprehended after the killing of Brian Howe she would have killed again.

Psychiatrists at Mary's trial all concurred because her murders were not provoked by fear, jealousy or hatred, but were 'motiveless'. However, there can be no such thing as a motiveless crime because all crimes are carried out for some reason or other. I will go further by adding that everything we do in our daily lives is done because there is a reason for doing it. We go shopping for food because we need to satisfy hunger. We get our cars serviced and repaired because we need them for travel, ad infinitum, if you catch my drift.

Like all of the other killers referred to in this book, Mary Bell had/has all the hallmarks of a psychopathic/sociopathic personality disorder. She was aggressive and craved excitement, totally unable – like you and me – to feel gentler emotions like love, compassion and she felt no remorse. .

The killing of the two little boys seemed no worse to her than the cruelty she had shown in throttling birds and small animals – all admitted to in her interviews with psychiatrists before her trial. And we often see this sort of behaviour – this pleasure in the torture and killing of small animals – writ large throughout the early histories of those people who later graduate to serial homicide.

Mary was obviously highly manipulative and dangerous at around the age of ten and eleven, but what, to me, is interesting about her case was that she had subconsciously shown signs of wanting help long beforehand. Often her attacks had taken place in full view of adults. She had always openly pinched and kicked other children at school; she had throttled pigeons, and had tried to strangle a tiny baby in front of her relatives. When she attacked the little girls in the sandpit she was merely told off by the police and nothing more was done.

When Mary killed Martin Brown, it was in a deserted house, it is true. It is also true that she left boasting notes in the nursery. When asked in court why, she blamed Norma, proceeding to shift the blame for the two killings onto Norma, who was obviously too dimwitted to stop following Mary around like a doting puppy. In so many words, Mary Bell was a manipulator who enjoyed the 'contest' between herself and the police throughout – again, exhibiting all the hallmarks of an even more mature psychopathic personality.

It is also true that at the same time she made two 'confessions' to the female police officers guarding her during this period between arrest and trial. The first came when a cat appeared at the window of her room. One officer allowed her to let it in, but then had to prise her fingers from around its neck. When reprimanded she replied, 'Oh, she doesn't feel that, and anyway, I like hurting little things that can't fight back.'

The second 'confession' came about when she expressed a wish to be a policewoman herself but received the retort, 'You've had that.' Mary's response was, 'Then I'd like to be a nurse. Because then I can stick needles into people…I like hurting people.'

And, have we not seen that all of the killers mentioned in this book are without a conscience? Moreover, I have not yet met any serial killer, male or female, who is an exception to this rule, for they are all sadistic monsters whichever way one cuts the cake.

In conclusion: much has been written in mitigation for young Mary Bell's behaviour and, thus, the reason behind her evil crimes, as being her upbringing. It has also been submitted by the more liberal-minded that where she lived was in some way responsible for her antisocial behaviour in extremis. Yes, one would be correct in noting that the decline of heavy industry, coal mines and shipyards meant that Newcastle in 1969 had one of the highest unemployment rates in Britain. Alongside this went the highest levels of crime in the country (32,882 recorded offences in a population of around 250,000 people) and the highest incidence of alcoholism.

It is also right to report that in an area such as Scotswood, the statistics were worse, with every other man being out of a job. Behind the solid Victorian exteriors of the houses, many homes were almost bare of furniture and families had to struggle to find enough coal for the fire (this is why Mary and Norma went scavenging for wood and sticks) and enough coins for the electricity meter. Most families were up to their eyes in debt, with the 'tally man' always hammering on their doors demanding weekly repayments on the loans. But, again, so what? If the 250,000 residents of Newcastle were all in more-or-less the same boat, with the residents of Scotswood in an even more financially unstable craft, why was it that Mary Bell emerged as the only homicidal juvenile amongst them?

But, you see, Scotswood was not without amenities such as the Woodlands Crescent Nursery, equipped with a playground and sandpit, and staff to look after the children of the many working mothers eking out an income in the neighbourhood. And, Scotswood streets were – despite the hardship – warm, vibrant communities where children could flourish in the freedom of roaming at will and amongst people that they knew well – after all, everyone knew one another. In so many ways, it was a safer place for kids to run around and play in than a similar area would be today, when we dare not let our kids out of our sight for more than a few moments at a time, because communities are now so different.

As for Mary Bell's motive for committing murder, it is a simple one to get to grips with. She killed two little boys because she had previously gotten a kick out of torturing and killing small, helpless animals. She got a kick out of manipulating and controlling them, she got a kick out of the very idea of trawling for a helpless victim – as many serial killers do – and she gained a real sadistic buzz from watching them die, boastfully gloating afterwards with no signs of remorse at all. She was so cocksure, that she enjoyed playing mind games with the police.

At the time of writing, Mary Bell will be sixty years old. Just maybe, age might have changed her for the better. Perhaps it would be a good thing if she went public and sincerely apologised for the heinous offences she committed so many years ago, but I doubt that she will.

Eva Dugan

Using poison, fifty-two-year-old former nurse Eva Dugan was a convicted murderess, indeed a serial killer, who was spectacularly hanged at 5.02 a.m. on Friday, 21 February 1930, in Arizona's State Prison. It was the beginning of the end for the scaffold in that state for, when she plunged through the trapdoor and hit the end of the rope with a bouncing jolt, her head was ripped off and rolled towards the feet of the thunderstruck witnesses. And, as an aside, the same thing happened to Hussein's henchman, Military Commander, Chief of the Iraqi Intelligence Service Al Hass al-Majid al Tiriti, aka, 'Chemical Ali'. He was hanged on 25 January 2010, his head being ripped off to bounce in front of witnesses who were not thunderstruck but thrilled to bits!

Notwithstanding the fact that providing the procedure is followed correctly, such a horrific thing shouldn't happen, what followed Dugan's demise was an immediate widespread demand that a more 'humane' means of execution should be used. For instance there was the option of the then recently invented gas chamber – which incidentally is not 'humane' by any means – and some thought it ought to be substituted for what appeared to have been the unreliable gallows, used by more likely than not, an ill-trained hangman. Death by lethal gas became effective in Arizona on 28 October 1933.

But the facts of the case are chillingly simple. Dugan had gone to work as a housekeeper for sixty-year-old Tucson chicken rancher Andrew J. Mathis in January 1927. She was apparently fired after only two weeks in his employment. Shortly thereafter, Mathis disappeared, along with his Dodge Coupe and some personal possessions. Neighbours reported having been offered some of Mathis's belongings for sale by Eva, but when police tried to locate her, they found that she, too, had vanished. At the time of Mr Mathis's disappearance, a neighbour commented: 'Seemed funny that he'd light out to California without telling anybody.' And Sheriff Jim McDonald said to a local newspaper reporter: 'It was funny that he [A.J. Mathis] disappeared like that. Still, old men do queer things.'

The task of solving the mystery fell to Pinal County Sheriff Jim McDonald, and during a background check on his prime suspect, he discovered that Dugan had been married no less than five times, and that all of her husbands had disappeared under suspicious circumstances. But this time, it was a case of what goes around, comes around.

Sheriff McDonald was a legend, the stuff of American movie heroes of those days. A tall, lean man who wore a white sombrero, he visited the Mathis ranch and found nothing suspicious, apart from discovering that an ear trumpet (Mathis was hard of hearing) and a cash box were missing.

Neighbours explained that Eve Dugan had been calling and trying to sell off her alleged common-law husband's property, claiming at once that he'd upped sticks and gone to California. McDonald then visited the missing man's bank in Tucson. Calculating that he would have needed money to travel, it transpired that Mathis's bank account had not been touched – no withdrawals or deposits had been made. Something was afoot and the sheriff detected a big problem in the circumstances.

With a head start on the law, Dugan tried to shake off any pursuers, and botched the job. Her first mistake was writing to friends, the first being a postcard from Douglas, Arizona. She turned east and stopped off in Texas, Oklahoma and then Kansas City – where she sold the Dodge car for $600.00, then proceeded to White Plains, New York (where she had a daughter), and took up work as a hospital nurse, and was where local police finally caught up with her. Under questioning, Dugan tried to bluff her way out, telling the law: 'The old man is in California. Someday he'll wander home and make a fool of that sheriff.'

McDonald now faced a problem. State laws meant that he could not get her extradited back to Arizona on a murder charge so he opted for a lesser grand larceny charge of stealing Mathis's car – an extraditable offence and one that would ensure that he could keep her under observation until he'd completed his enquiries into the missing rancher, A.J. Mathis. She was taken back to Arizona in chains on 4 March 1927.

About nine months later, in a million-to-one happenstance, a Mr J.F. Nash, who was camping on Mathis's ranch, discovered the man's shallow grave. A dust storm had hit the place overnight and when Mr Nash awoke and went outside he saw a white skull grinning at him. Another account of events is that he discovered the body as he was driving a tent peg into the soil. I prefer the former rather than the latter, since the tourist was driving a camper van at the time, not needing to erect a tent. Nevertheless, the skeleton he discovered was encrusted in lime and had a gag rammed between its jaws. The man's remains were identified through his false dentures.

It took three years of appeals before Dugan learned of her execution date, during which time she charged newspaper reporters $1.00 for interviews, and allegedly saved up for her own coffin by selling embroidered silk handkerchiefs made in her cell. However, one of her last letters was to a friend, asking to send money to pay the balance she owed the undertaker, stating: 'Have to die Friday STOP Wire warden $50 STOP Will be buried in Florence STOP Eva FULL STOP.' It has been claimed that she had also recently bought a plot of land in a local cemetery, however, this was never the case. She is buried in plot # 14960330 in the Arizona State Prison Cemetery, Florence.

On the eve of her execution, she said to a reporter from *The Arizona Republic* newspaper, 'I am going to my Maker with a clear Conscience.'

Ever the optimist to the end, Dugan was sure that she would be spared the hangman's halter, indeed, as she left the women's cell block for the death house at Arizona State Prison, she said, 'The Attorney General is probably on his way here right now.' He wasn't. Flanked by two guards including an old-timer known as 'Daddy Allen', she seemed composed as she mounted the steps towards the noose. 'Don't hold my arms so tight. The people will think I'm afraid,' she said.

Unnerved by the sight of seventy-five witnesses, she

swayed slightly on the scaffold. She closed her eyes and shook her head when Warden Lo Wright asked her if she had any last words. Then she plunged to her doom in a beaded silk jazz dress she had made while awaiting her execution, to earn the distinction of being the first and the last woman to be hanged in Arizona.

Three More Despicable Killers

LAFONDA FAY FOSTER AND TINA HICKEY POWELL

The pair's victims were Carlos Kearns (seventy-three), Virginia Kearns (forty-five), Trudy Harrell (fifty-nine), Jimmy Roger Keene (forty-seven) and Theodore Sweet (fifty-two).

This murderous duo were no strangers to crime, both of them being both former inmates at the Kentucky Correctional Institution for Women. Their offences included dealing narcotics, robbery, forgery and fraud all topped up by carrying a concealed deadly weapon before they graduated to mass murder.

Twenty-two-year-old drug addict and prostitute LaFonda Fay Foster and her accomplice, twenty-seven-year-old Tina 'Marie' Hickey Powell were convicted of killing five acquaintances after a four-day binge on alcohol and cocaine. Trouble started brewing on Wednesday, 23 April 1986, when the two women ran short of cash to buy more drugs. They went to a friend's house and, armed with a gun, persuaded her and her mother, the housekeeper and two of the husband's friends, to go out with them to cash a cheque.

After a couple of hours driving around Lexington, Powell and Foster ordered the five passengers out of the car at gunpoint and forced them to lie flat in the grass. They shot two of the victims there, one of whom died after being dragged 'for a considerable distance' under the vehicle.

Then after stopping at a bar and buying more bullets, the killers drove to a loading dock behind a paint store. There they stabbed and shot another victim and drove over the body with the car. A few hours later, they took the two remaining victims to a deserted field, shot them in their heads, stabbed them repeatedly, cut their throats and, again ran over them with the car, which they then set on fire with one of the bodies inside it.

At the trial, the women admitted their guilt. Because Powell claimed that Foster had coerced her into committing the murders, the jury recommended she be sentenced to life imprisonment. At the time of the murders, Powell, in her late twenties, the mother of four children and then lesbian lover of Foster, claimed she recalled nothing of the murders because she had been on a drinking/drug binge for weeks. Her IQ was measured at 78, which borders on retardation. She is presently housed at the Kentucky Correctional Institution for Women (KCIW) Pee Wee Valley, Shelby County.

Foster, described in the press back then as a 'thirty-eight-year-old beauty' was sentenced to death by Judge James Keller of Fayette County Circuit Court, with an execution date slated for 22 April 1988. However, on Friday, 24 April 1987, her sentence was commuted to life imprisonment. She is presently incarcerated at the Western Kentucky Correctional Complex (WKCC), Fredonia.

Aside from the notoriety of being the most horrific case of mass murder in Kentucky state history it gained even more infamy in the 1997 independently produced thriller/killer movie, *100 Proof*, written and directed by Jeremy Horton which echoed the events of the Powell/Foster murders.

BRITTANY MARLOWE HOLBERG

Born on Monday, 1 January 1973, with a prior conviction for drug use, the once attractively proportioned, five-foot five-inches tall, 125-lb, brown-haired, green-eyed Brittany Holberg, was released from prison after completing a 'Substance Abuse Felony Programme', on Sunday, 1 September 1996. She had been raised in Potter County.

Her next crime would be that of murder, and no one had to wait too long for that to happen, either.

On Wednesday, 13 November 1996, aged just twenty-three, Holberg robbed and murdered eighty-year-old A.B. Towery Sr. in his southwest Amarillo home, and the crime has to feature in this book because it is simply monstrous. The weapons used were: a cast-iron skillet (heavy frying pan), a paring knife, a steam iron, a butcher's knife, a grapefruit fork and a carving knife. Holberg also rammed a metal candlestick more than five inches down her victim's throat. And, if this isn't going into a default overkill situation I cannot find a better example. Yet, was there some mitigation to be found for Brittany somewhere and perhaps – although I am loathe to suggest it – there is. For it seems that far from being portrayed as a helpless, elderly old man, 'A.B.' was quite the opposite.

Pretty Brittany worked as a topless dancer, and also as a prostitute, in which capacity she was hired by Towery, who lost his temper with her after finding a crack pipe in her possession. Indeed, he so lost the plot that he first hit her over the head with a cast-iron skillet while her back was turned, and then he threatened her with a knife. That was her defence. But was it the truth?

According to the prosecution, A.B. Towery was walking back to his apartment after buying groceries on that fateful 13 November afternoon, when Brittany asked to use his telephone. As soon as she had entered the apartment, a struggle ensued in which Towery sustained fifty-eight stab wounds and multiple blunt force injuries. The state's attorney also claimed that Brittany Holberg – who was severely addicted to drugs – was 'high on crack cocaine' when the attack occurred. Thereafter, she showered, changed into some of the now dead man's clean clothes, picked up some of his prescription medications and fled the scene with $1,400 in cash. Later that evening, she purchased more crack cocaine. Towery's son, Rocky, discovered his father's supine body at 7.45 a.m. the following morning with the candlestick base lodged in his throat, a knife stuck in his abdomen, and his dad's empty wallet lying on top of his body.

Brittany Holberg appealed her conviction on several legal technicalities; mainly claiming that she had not stolen any of the victim's property, which, when combined with committing homicide in Texas, constitutes a Capital Crime – and thus is punishable by death. Her argument was that there was no proof that she had ever touched the man's wallet, and to be fair to her, no DNA or blood evidence was found on the wallet to prove that she had rifled it. The second plank of her appeal was that she had not taken away 'seven to ten' bottles of medication, which, again, constituted theft. After all was said and done, did the police *not* find empty bottles of med in the apartment when they went through it?

Under Texas law, a person commits robbery if, in the course of committing theft and with intent to obtain or maintain control of the property, the person intentionally, knowingly, or recklessly causes bodily injury to another. Theft, on the other hand, occurs when a person unlawfully appropriates property with intent to deprive the owner of property. Thus, while the offence of theft has an acquisitive component, commission of the offence of robbery requires only that the person should be in the course of committing a theft.

With this being established – that is that Brittany Holberg had murdered A.B. Towery in the furtherance of robbery – on Wednesday, 2 April 2014, the Court of Criminal Appeals for Texas, upheld her death sentence conviction. The real truth of the matter sits somewhere in between the two.

Even today – although her prison mugshot does little for her because living on 'The Row' literally drains one's life away, as it did with Aileen Wuornos – having met her in the flesh as I have also done Lee and Darlie Routier (the latter having stabbed to death her two young sons), inmate # 999258 Brittany Holberg is still the most attractive woman on death row in the United States of America. She is housed at the Mountain View Unit, 2305 Ransom Road, Gatesville, TX 76528. Here, she shares her own 'Green Mile' with prisoners: # 999406 Linda Carty; # 9992200 Darlie Routier; # 999144 Erica Sheppard; # 999572 Kimberly Cargill, and # 999537 Melissa Elizabeth Lucio.

At the time of writing no dates for any of these women has been set for execution, and, when it comes down to that fateful day, what purpose will it serve, anyway?

And, if you think that women cannot get more evil and possessed by wickedness, then please think again.

KELLY 'GINNY' O'DONNELL

'He [the victim] was slimy. He once pulled out his penis and rubbed it on me.' (Kelly O'Donnell during her police interrogation.)

'I was higher than you can imagine. I did not mean to do that. I was not like that. I remember hitting him with the hammer, but I don't know how many times. Maybe five.' (A tearful William Gribble at the sentencing hearing part of his trial.)

We have become so familiar with the gruesome couples who kill multiple times over the years, notwithstanding Myra Hindley and Ian Brady, Rosemary and Fred West, and the countless more from 'The Legion of the Damned', but Kelly O'Donnell stands out as being altogether a very nasty woman indeed.

It all began on the morning of Friday, 13 November 1992, when Philadelphia police received a 911 report that someone had found some body parts on North Delaware Avenue. The officers who were despatched to the scene found a human torso with its head missing, the severed arms of a white male and a head which was minus a left eyeball. During a search of the area, police found papers strewn around, and among these was a letter addressed to Agnes McClinchey, of 3123 Richmond Street.

The remains were later identified, as 'belonging to' a Mr Eleftherios Eleftheriou, and the story of how they came to be there is a disturbing tale of violence and animal savagery, equal in its grisly nature to any plot from the imagination of horror writer Stephen King. What make it all the more shocking is that the macabre butcher was a woman!

Born on Thursday, 12 January 1967, Kelly O'Donnell, at that time had a thirty-year-old boyfriend called William Russell Gribble. She also had a drug problem, and so did he. Indeed, just eighteen months previously they'd had a daughter. Because they were both addicted to drugs they never removed the baby from the hospital and it was now in foster care. Nevertheless, early in November 1992, the couple went to live at 3123 Richmond Street, Philadelphia. This was the home of Gribble's mother Agnes McClinchey who had given them permission to stay there while she was away visiting an acquaintance. Also residing at the address at the time was James Mathews, an elderly friend of the homeowner.

Shortly after 10 p.m., on Wednesday, 11 November, McDonnell went to a pizza shop managed by one Eleftherios Eleftheriou, known more conveniently as 'Terry'. As well as running the pizza place, the enterprising and versatile Terry did some drug dealing and a little money-lending on the side. O'Donnell took with her a leather jacket, which she offered as collateral against a loan which she sought from this man.

According to a witness, an employee of the pizza shop, Terry took a large wad of notes from his pocket and gave

$10.00 to Kelly. Then the two arranged to meet later that night for sex. At around 1 a.m., Terry closed the business and drove to the rendezvous.

O'Donnell took him back to the rooms on Richmond Street, arriving there at about 1.30 a.m. What happened next is drawn from O'Donnell's confession and her evidence given at her trial.

Allegedly, Terry was looking out of the window when the young woman hit him over the head with a hammer. He fell to the ground and she continued to rain hammer blows down on his head.

The reason which she gave for this murderous attack, was, she claimed, that the man was a 'pervert' who had previously sexually assaulted her. Whatever the motive may have been, she now had a body lying on the floor needing to be disposed of, and an undertaker was, pretty obviously, not an option on this occasion. She enlisted the help of Gribble to drag the body down into the basement. There, in the anaemic half-light, in grim surroundings reminiscent of an Alfred Hitchcock scenario, they dismembered the Greek pizza man – sort of slicing him up!

Disposal of the component parts of Terry was effected by the simple, if irreverent expedient of placing them in black plastic trash bags. Not long afterwards, the two of them dumped one of the bags containing Terry's head on North Delaware Avenue, where it was soon discovered, and where it was bound to be found for North Delaware Avenue is a busy area running parallel to the Delaware Expressway. If you want to have a body part discovered very quickly, may I recommend this location to you!

The following day, elderly Agnes McClinchey returned

home. The place was not quite as she remembered it however, for she found blood on the front door and over the carpets. O'Donnell told the bewildered old dear that she and Gribble had been involved in a murder, adding that she had heard a report that the victim's head had been found on Delaware Avenue.

Later that day, Ms McClinchey overheard O'Donnell telling Gribble to burn Terry's car, which he did and, when he returned, she said to him, 'Thank God you didn't get caught.'

At 7.30 p.m. that evening, police responded to a report of a car on fire on D Street. When the blaze was eventually extinguished, they searched the burned-out vehicle and, not entirely to their delight, found the well-cooked missing bits of the pizza man's dismembered corpse.

An hour or so later, a now well-agitated Agnes called the police and they met her at a nearby gas station where she told them what she knew. Following their discussion with the distraught woman, law officers went to her apartment at 1.30 a.m. on the morning of 14 November, and there they arrested O'Donnell and Gribble.

There then began a search of the premises and basement. In the latter area police found a kitchen knife, a chisel and a claw hammer, each of which revealed traces of human tissue and blood.

Finally, they stumbled across the two missing pieces of the jigsaw puzzle that was Terry. Stuffed inside a pipe they found a black-and-white pencil case, inside which was an eyeball and a penis. O'Donnell later told police that she intended to send both to her abusive father, while admitting that she got a 'bit carried away,' adding with a wry smile: 'I used a plastic case because it wouldn't leak.'

Now that they could relax in the knowledge that nobody was going to turn up with more bits and pieces belonging to the murdered man, the cops got down to the business of interrogating the two suspects. While the arrests had been made pretty quickly, establishing the truth behind the killing proved, at first, to be as untidy as the distribution of the victim's body parts had been. Both O'Donnell and Gribble made statements in which each accepted personal responsibility for the murder while attempting to exculpate the other. Indeed, it got to the point where the police found themselves interviewing two suspects, who both admitted the killing while denying the murder at the same time. In the end, the frustrated police gave up and threw the book at them. O'Donnell and Gribble were both charged with murder, conspiracy, arson, possessing instruments of a crime, robbery, theft by unlawful taking, unauthorised use of a motor vehicle, forgery, abuse of a corpse and credit card fraud – all offences connected to the demise of Mr Eleftheriou.

The two suspected butchers were tried together and they both waived their right to trial by jury, electing instead to appear before a bench judge. The medical evidence given at the hearing makes for very disturbing reading.

An assistant medical examiner testified that there were numerous abrasions on the victim's head and these were consistent with blows from a hammer. This witness also testified that one person, acting alone, could not have killed and dismembered the victim's body in a manner consistent with the physical evidence. The most horrifying aspect of the murder was revealed during the witness's testimony when he stated that the red abrasions in the areas where the murdered man's head and right arm had been severed indicated that, at the time these parts were removed the man's heart had still been beating. Whether or not Terry could feel the pain at any time is not known. The medical examiner then went on to say that a single person on their own would not have been able to remove both the head and right arm of the muscular man in the estimated fifteen minutes that it took before Eleftheriou bled to death.

In contrast, yellow abrasions in those areas where the remaining body parts had been severed indicated that Terry's heart had stopped beating by the time they were cut off.

OC-0215 Kelly O'Donnell was found guilty of first degree murder and for this she was sentenced to death – later overturned – as was Gribble's, in favour of a natural life sentence. She is incarcerated at the Pennsylvania Correctional Institute, Muncy, Pennsylvania, while # CC76649 William Russell Gribble is presently housed at Somerset State Correctional Institution.

Conclusions – Mad, Bad or Sad?

As William Congreve (1670–1729) describes in his 1697 poem The Mourning Bride: 'Heaven has no rage like hatred turned, Nor hell a fury like a woman scorned.'

During my lengthy travels into the minds of women who commit the most dreadful of crimes, it occurs to me that their motives are generally non-sexual. By this I mean that, unlike their male counterparts, most of these killers gain no sexual satisfaction by way of release, from the act of premeditated homicide. In contrast, many male serial killers do achieve sexual release during such acts. And men most certainly do not become sexual serial predators overnight. In most examples they graduate through stalking their victims, moving onwards to rape, serial rape, murder, then serial killing until they are caught. They become trapped in this ever-escalating spiral of violence in a way that women do not.

As best I can, I have also taken out of account examples of women who commit manslaughter, or as they say across 'The

Pond', Second-Degree Murder, even justifiable homicide at best. This, as I have mentioned earlier in this book, may well have been the case with Aileen Wuornos, who shot to death the clients who 'turned on her' and put her in fear of her own wellbeing. And, I would like to qualify this further.

In a recent TV series I contributed to – being the ten-part docu-drama series *Voice of a Serial Killer*, screened by CBS Reality in the UK, the presenter, the admirable Professor David Wilson, went to great pains to point out – as I have done over many years – that Lee Wuornos suffered from a dreadful childhood, and this, I am sure, contributed to her later fatal shooting of men who took advantage of her and treated her like dirt – people who wanted to slap her around, while enjoying cheap sex into the bargain.

Appearing along with Professor Wilson is Professor of Forensic Psychiatry Michael Brooks OBE, who made quite a remarkable statement along the lines of: 'Aileen Wuornos chose to carry a gun and turn to prostitution', inferring that these were her life choices and that she chose whether or not to use the firearm. Maybe, maybe not.

I am paraphrasing Michael Brooks, but the point I am making, once again, is that Lee went with some 200 'clients' and never did it occur to her to shoot them when they treated her properly. It is also true that prostitution is the oldest profession in the world and why women turn to this means of earning money is not for any of us to judge. Live and let live, I say – or live and let die – as was the case with Lee Wuornos!

Of course, I will not beat about the bush here. Thousands of Floridians (indeed millions of US citizens) carry licensed or un-licensed firearms and Lee was no exception to the latter. She simply carried a gun for her own personal protection.

CHRISTOPHER BERRY-DEE

Therefore, sexual predators, of the twisted ilk of Peter Sutcliffe, Steve Wright, and the disgusting killer of homosexual men, Colin Ireland, might consider themselves very lucky to be enjoying a 'life' today if some of their vulnerable victims had carried a gun for protection, too!

Discounting the likes of lesbian lovers, Cathy Wood and Gwen Graham, who suffocated five elderly patients at the Grand Rapids nursing home as part of some bizarre love pact, another duo, Tracey Wiggington (twenty-four) and Lisa Ptaschinski (twenty-four), dubbed 'The Vampire Killers', spring to mind. When these women turned to murder, they seized on a man – any man.

In what might be called a 'motiveless murder', in 1989, Wiggington, the seventeen-stone 'Vampire', who was deeply committed to all her causes, that included occultism and devil worship, picked up and brutally stabbed a complete stranger in the form of Edward Baldock, who was drinking heavily in a Brisbane bar. It was a sad and undignified death for a blameless family man. His killers did not know him, and bore him no grudge, but they were utterly callous towards him.

Police claimed that horror videos were an influence on Wiggington and there is no doubt that she enjoyed watching these in graphic slow motion. The night before the murder. Wiggington's girlfriend, Donna Staib, said Tracey had seen a video with a slow motion sequence of a man being shot through the forehead and showed his head exploding. She said that Wiggington had watched this particular sequence at least half-a-dozen times.

At her trial, defence psychiatrists Quinn and Clarke pointed out that Wiggington had suffered a childhood that had included abandonment, cruelty and sexual abuse. They

281

diagnosed her as having a multiple personality disorder, which would account for her emotional instability. In short, they diagnosed her as mentally ill.

The Queensland Mental Health Tribunal, comprising Supreme Court Judge Mr Justice Ryan, Dr Norman Connell and Dr Gordon Urquhart, also interviewed Wiggington. After they had considered reports from other doctors, they decided that Tracey did not qualify as legally insane. They concluded that she was aware of her behaviour, she was responsible for her acts, she knew the difference between right and wrong and she understood the consequences of her actions throughout.

> The abhorrent and cruel nature of events to which you have been party on this night is obvious from the evidence heard during this trial and needs no elaboration. You knew what was likely to happen and you took no pity on Mr Baldock as another human being.
> (Mr Justice MacKenzie, sentencing Ptaschinski to life imprisonment.)

In late January 1991, Tracey Avril Wiggington, then aged twenty-four, a student of Wardell Street, Enoggera, Brisbane, pleaded guilty to murder. She was given a life sentence, to be served in Brisbane's Women's Jail on Boggo Road, where she became the librarian and learned about computers. For her part in the murder, twenty-four-year-old Ptaschinski received a life term of imprisonment. On 11 January 2012, Wiggington was released on life licence. The current status of Ptaschinski is unknown, but one suspects she is now a free woman too, while the next woman we look at is, today, very close to execution.

'That ain't blood on my shoes, that's blood. An' look here in this napkin. It's part of Colleen's skull. I just felt mean that day.' (Christa Gail Pike to fellow student Stephanie Wilson. Friday, 14 January 1995.)

In this case I am asking the reader to get up really close and very personal. Please imagine, if you will, being parents of an adorable nineteen-year-old daughter, who has been taken to some dark, godforsaken place where, pleading for her life over a period of several hours, she has been verbally abused, kicked, kneed, punched, beaten, mercilessly hacked at over one hundred times with a meat cleaver, slashed with a box-cutting knife – all the while begging for mercy and screaming out for you, Mum and Dad, to come and save her before her head, her skull and her brains are smashed to a pulp with several lumps of asphalt – with one of her killers taking part of your child's skull away and using it to eat her cereals with for breakfast the following morning?

Meet Christa Gail Pike.

Born on Monday, 10 March 1975, Christa Gail Pike became the youngest woman on Death Row at the age of twenty-one, and the crime that earned her this distinction was one of the most savage and evil single killings in the state of Tennessee. It is a story of the murder of Pike's nineteen-year-old love rival. It is a disturbing account of uncontrolled violence with sadistic and satanic undertones.

Looking back through this woman's earlier years, it is acknowledged that she had had a poor upbringing with little or no parental guidance: when she was only fourteen, her parents had allowed her to have a sexual relationship with her live-in boyfriend. Moreover, with her redneck parents' permission, she had dropped out of high school but had later decided to enroll in the Knoxville Jobs Corps Programme in order to ensure that she received her diploma.

While she was attending the classes Christa met up with two other youngsters, and close friendships developed. Black American, Tadaryl Darnell Shipp, was sixteen and came from Memphis. He and Christa began dating. The other friend was Shadolla Renee Peterson, aged eighteen. The two girls became inseparable.

At the same time, a nineteen-year-old girl called Colleen Slemmer appeared on the scene. It soon became apparent that she and Pike didn't get on well. The cause of the animosity stemmed from her suspicions about Colleen's interest in Tadaryl Shipp. Pike became openly hostile towards the slightly younger, fresh-faced girl, calling her names and starting malicious rumours about her. After the two had eventually had a fight, Christa made up her mind to really teach her rival a lesson. She and Shadolla Peterson conspired to get Colleen alone at a deserted spot on the University of Tennessee Agricultural Campus and give her a beating. The outcome of the plan was so terrible that it caused widespread panic among the 26,000 students in the city of Knoxville.

The murder took place on the freezing cold night of Thursday, 13 January 1995. Shortly after 9 p.m., Christa Pike, Shadolla Peterson and Tadaryl Shipp left the Jobs Corps Centre. As they were leaving, Pike persuaded Colleen to join them on the pretext that they would go to smoke marijuana as a peace offering.

After some debate it was decided that they would all go to

an abandoned coal-fired steam mill on the campus. According to one description of this place, it was so secluded that a person could scream at the top of their lungs and not be heard. With its massive rusting structure and tall, brick chimney pointing an accusing finger to the sky, this was to become a terrible place to die. The place was, and still is, near a bike trail and a thick clump of bushes and, littered around the area, was a mess of old building materials, including lumps of asphalt and big pieces of plastic.

When the quartet arrived at the mill, Colleen began talking with Shipp. Christa saw this and flew into a rage. Screaming obscenities, she dragged the girl away from Tadaryl Shipp and the attack on her rival began. Colleen was taken completely by surprise. Her first reaction was to try to get away from the onslaught and she set off, running down the muddy trackway. However, in the darkness, she slipped and fell, allowing Shipp to catch up with her. The young man hauled her back before her tormentors who recommenced their ignominious treatment.

Pike now forced the terrified girl to take off her sweater and bra, so that Colleen would not run away again, then she and Shadolla Peterson began to hit their humiliated victim with their knees and fists. Shipp turned away, but Colleen clung to him in the hope that he would somehow stop what was being done to her. The youth was having none of that, however, and pushed her away from him, slapping her when she wouldn't let go of his arm. All the while, Pike was punching and kicking Colleen, who eventually fell to the ground clutching her stomach.

Pike then pulled out a miniature meat cleaver and slashed her victim's forehead. In great pain, Colleen covered her face with her hands and begged Pike to stop and try to resolve the issue without any more violence. Her plea was to no avail. Pike slashed Colleen's pants open with the cleaver, taunting with remarks about having sex with Tadaryl Shipp as she did. The distraught girl staggered to her feet and made a dash for freedom but again she slipped and fell. The cowardly Shipp picked her up bodily and carried her back to the bushes where the merciless and depraved attack continued.

It was then that a box-cutter (like a Stanley knife) was produced and, for some thirty minutes or so, Colleen Slemmer was stabbed and slashed hundreds of times with the knife and the meat cleaver. Then, Pike and Shipp, working together in an act of appalling savagery, carved a pentagram into Colleen's chest and across her breasts.

Throughout this attack – of terrifying proportions – Colleen remained alive and Pike maintained her barrage of taunts. The young girl's life ended when the three attackers pounded the teenager's skull with chunks of asphalt.

If one were to imagine that the story of the dreadful murder of Colleen had ended here we would be sorely mistaken.

Following their brutal and monstrous act, Pike, Peterson and Shipp went to a service station, where, in the washrooms they rinsed off the blood and changed their clothes. At around 10.15 p.m. the trio returned to the Jobs Corps Center and, sometime later, Pike went to the room of fellow student, Kim Iloilo, where she brandished a piece of Colleen Slemmer's skull and gave a graphic and detailed account of the atrocity that she and the other two had carried out. She told Iloilo that Colleen had begged them to stop cutting and beating her, but Pike didn't stop because her victim continued to talk. The triumphant killer told her friend that she had thrown a large piece of asphalt at Colleen's head and, when it broke into smaller pieces, she had thrown those at her as well. She went on to tell the now horrified Kim Iloilo that a meat cleaver had been used to cut Colleen's back and the box-cutter had been used to slit her throat. Finally, she told the bewildered listener that a pentagram had been carved onto the teenager's chest and another one on her forehead while she was clinging on to life. All the time that Pike was narrating the tale, she was dancing in a circle around the dorm room.

The next morning, during breakfast at the Jobs Corps Center, Iloilo saw Pike and asked her what she had done with the piece of Colleen's skull. Pike replied that she still had it and then said, 'And, yes, I'm eating breakfast with it.'

Later in the day, according to court records, the garrulous Pike made a similar statement to another student, Stephanie Wilson. She pointed to brown spots on her shoes and said, 'That ain't mud on my shoes, that's blood.' She then pulled a napkin from her pocket and showed Wilson a piece of bone which, she asserted, was part of Colleen Slemmer's skull. Pike went on to say that the victim's blood and brains had been pouring out at the time that she looted the skull fragment as a grisly trophy of the macabre orgy.

At the time Christa Pike was gleefully relating details of how she had overcome her love rival, horrified and sickened officers from the University of Tennessee Police and the Knoxville PD were taping off the area around the butchered remains of Colleen Slemmer. A Tennessee Grounds Department worker had found her corpse, naked from the waist up, at 8.05 a.m. At first the man who had discovered the body, believed he had found the remains of a dead animal. It was only upon closer inspection that he saw the woman's clothes and her nude breasts and realised it was the body of a human female. He called the police who found her bra and sweater in nearby bushes.

The savagery of the killing and its location led to some panic in the university and 2,000 flyers advising students not to walk alone at night, nor to take shortcuts along isolated tracks or pathways, were posted around the campus.

Whether or not detectives from the Knoxville Police Department had been reading too many Dennis Wheatley novels is unknown, but they soon came to the conclusion – as wrong as wrong can be – that the murder was the work of people with Satanist connections. 'Old Nick' gets a bad rap most of the time but the pentagrams carved on Colleen's chest and her forehead were the source of this and the idea was not entirely without foundation. At least at that time it wasn't: evidence shortly came to light which demonstrated that both Pike and Shipp had shown 'some interest' in Satanic worship, although it is doubtful if this was to any profound extent.

On Saturday, two days after the killing, Pike and Shipp were arrested, following calls from the aforementioned informants who had listened to Pike's boasting. The two of them confessed to the crime then implicated Shadolla Peterson, whose arrest swiftly followed.

In a search of Pike's room, police found a copy of *The Satanic Bible* and a silver Satan figurine. A rummage through Tadaryl Shipp's cluttered digs revealed other evidence of Satanic worship. Most damning of all, however, was the evidence found in Christa's leather jacket: it was the piece of Colleen's Slemmer's skull.

Christa Pike's statement, made to Detective Randy York, contains details of the murderous events which make for chilling reading as they highlight the overpowering level of evil displayed by Pike and her two accomplices. At one point, she had begun to cut Colleen across the throat when the victim sat up and begged for her life. Pike's response was to cut her throat several more times.

The Knox County medical Examiner, Dr Sandra Elkins, performed the autopsy of Colleen Slemmer's body and she testified that she had attempted to catalogue the slash and stabs on the decedent's torso by assigning a letter of the alphabet to each one. There were so many that, eventually, Dr Elkins decided to catalogue only the most serious and major wounds. She explained that to catalogue every wound she would have been required to 'go through the alphabet again and again and stay in the morgue for three days.'

In order to determine cause of death, it was necessary to remove the head of Colleen and have the skull prepared by a Dr Murray Marks, a forensic anthropologist at the University of Tennessee. Dr Elkins explained that she removed the top of the victim's skull in order to remove the brain. Embedded inside the brain as a result of the blunt force were portions of the victim's skull. Dr Marks reconstructed the skull, fitting those loose portions into the left side. However, those pieces had not completely filled one area. The missing piece had been found in Pike's leather jacket.

However, perhaps the most chilling fact of all, according to Dr Elkins, was the certain knowledge that Colleen was conscious throughout the time she was being cut, slashed, punched and kicked. Blood in the sinus cavity and the appearance of some of the wounds bore testimony to that. The young victim would have slipped into unconsciousness only after the large lump of asphalt had hit her skull.

Although Christa Pike was sentenced to death, Tadaryl Shipp, because of his age, was sentenced to life imprisonment, somewhat astoundingly with the possibility of parole. Shadolla Peterson, however – and you may need to sit down with a stiff drink for this one – escaped with six months probation.

It is seldom understood just how much a tragedy of this magnitude can blight the lives of the victim's family and loved ones. Colleen's mother lost her home as the result of her having to spend an enormous amount of money travelling to and attending innumerable court hearings involving the three murderous conspirators. She has pursued every option to ensure that her daughter's killers receive the fullest punishment for their terrible crime and not be released on parole. Yet, many of these proceedings seem calculated to ride roughshod over the sensibilities of the bereaved and be downright harrowing in their lack of sensitivity. Nevertheless, there are a few examples that can compare to the treatment of Colleen Slemmer's parents at the behest of Christa Pike's legal team. Colleen's skull fragment, which was introduced as evidence at the original trial, is still, at the time of writing, being retained until Pike has exhausted the appeal system. Until that time, the murdered girl's parents cannot bury the piece of skull with the rest of her body to finally lay their daughter at rest – much in the very same way as if this had happened to you!

The only motive for this murder is not one associated with Satanic worship – it is one of the commonest amongst all who commit the ultimate crime: that of getting rid of a rival or an obnoxious connection. One might have thought that with a death sentence hanging over her head, Christa Pike might have modified her behaviour for the better, but this has not proved to be so.

On Friday, 24 August 2001 – along with the alleged assistance of twenty-two-year-old fellow inmate # 00288309 Natasha Wallen Cornett – she attacked and attempted to strangle Patricia Jones with a shoestring, nearly strangling her to death. This was a lesbian love killing between female inmates: the rival being Jones. Cornett is a story unto herself but she has been sentenced to life without parole for the 'Lillelid Murders' committed during 1997.

In March 2012, Pike made escape plans with prison officer Justin Heflin and a Donald Kohut, a prison visitor from New Jersey who had fallen in love with her. The plan failed.

Inmate # 00772533 Tadaryl Shipp is serving out his prison term sharing a dormitory with fifty other prisoners at the Northwest Correctional Complex, Tiptonville.

At the time of writing, inmate # 00261368 Christa Gail Pike's last chance saloon of avoiding execution has come and gone, although no date has yet been slated for her death by lethal injection execution. She is currently incarcerated at the Tennessee Prison for Women (TPFW), 3881 Stewarts Lane, Nashville, TN 37218.

Born on Thursday, 20 September 1975, Bucks County, Pennsylvania, Colleen is buried at the Lady of Grace Cemetery, in her home county. Her grave ID is # 149548954. May God rest her soul, for had she not fallen foul of Christa Pike, at the time of writing she would be forty-five today.

It is true, however, that when some women fall in love with each other the very idea of separation becomes utterly unbearable to them, as was the case with Cathy Wood, who was terrified of losing Gwen Graham to another much younger and prettier woman. While Wood decided to make sure that this never happened she confessed in part to the killings, at once blaming Graham for everything.

Turning the clock back, in 1980s Indiana, a lesbian wife concocted a way to rid herself of her husband. She persuaded her mud-wrestling female lover to shoot her spouse and dump his body in a pigsty – a convenient form of body disposal, as the man was a pig farmer. She also asked her male cousin for help in this enterprise. All three accomplices were locked up for decades and eating pork sausages in the prison canteens was likely to have been the furthest thought from their tiny minds when they committed the crime.

This is an interesting case insofar as flouncy, feminine Loretta Stonebraker and, six-foot tall 'Big Helen' Williams had been intimates many years previously, before they met again by chance, in Parke County, Indiana. A slow-witted, baby-faced giant – famed for her courage and her ability to fight men – Helen was crazy about Loretta, and do we not see a similar parallel between the heavily built Wood and more petite Graham, once again, and perhaps again with Aileen Wuornos and Tyria Moore?

Then one might look to the case of the New Zealand teenaged lesbian couple, Juliet Hulme and Pauline Parker, who battered Pauline's mother to death because she had threatened to part them, as yet another example, or the dictum proven to be equally true for Christine and Lea Papin, two orphaned sisters who had an incestuous, lesbian relationship. They were found guilty of brutally butchering their employer, Madame Lancelin and her daughter in Le Mans, France, in 1933. Christine and Lea turned on their victims with tremendous ferocity, gouging out their eyes with bare hands before hacking both of them to death with a knife and a hammer. Later, when the women were separated while awaiting trial, Christine became so violent she had to be put in a straitjacket, went on hunger strike, and howled like a dog all night for her 'Darling Lea'.

Christine, whose death sentence was commuted to life imprisonment with hard labour, showed severe signs of madness. She was transferred to a psychiatric hospital in 1937 where, four years afterwards, she died of a broken heart. Lea was released after ten years, and lived out her life in obscurity.

Another motive seemingly popular amongst female serial killers is one of financial gain. Fortunately, today in the UK this form of crime is an extremely rare occurrence while in the US it happens frequently, and has done throughout decades past. We have touched on a few 'Black Widow' examples in this book, but it would be remiss of me not to recall Simone Weber, the sixty-year-old French housewife accused of poisoning her husband and slicing up her lover.

This sickening case bears all the stamp of an Alfred Hitchcock horror movie: a rotting torso inside a missing man's suitcase found floating in the River Marne, a carefully cleaned circular electric saw; a false marriage certificate and a dramatic exhumation carried in in the dead of night, were just some of the macabre ingredients. Pursued with unremitting single-mindedness by gendarmes, Simone Weber was finally revealed as a murderess of extraordinary guile and duplicity.

When police finally arrested Weber they found in her various apartments one of her victim's identity cards and the keys to his car. The number plates on the missing man's blue Renault had been changed. A simultaneous search of her place at the Rue de Cronstadt in Nancy proved equally fruitful: police found a .22 LR Boere-Kufstein rifle, a used cartridge and silencer, a Marksman airgun and ammunition. At 158 Avenue de Strasbourg, another apartment which also belonged to Weber and her sister, Madeleine, an even larger cache was discovered: a .22 LR Army-Marocchi rifle equipped with a silencer and blocked by a used cartridge in the barrel, two smaller handguns, a used cartridge on a bedroom floor and three sticks of dynamite.

On Thursday, 17 January 1991, Simone Weber, dubbed by the media the 'She-Devil of Nancy' went on trial for the murder of her of her cheating lover, fifty-five-year-old Monsieur Bernard Hettier. She was accused of sedating him on 22 June 1985 then shooting him, prior to chopping off his head and limbs and disposing of a part of the body in a brown suitcase, which she threw into the river, where it was found on Sunday, 15 September 1985 by Marcel Rabeau and a friend who were fishing.

The now not-so-merry widow was also accused of the premeditated murder of eighty-year-old former army officer Monsieur Marcel Fixard, whom she fraudulently married then killed by using digitalis to induce a massive heart attack.

Liliane Glock, one of Weber's defence lawyers remarked: 'I am beginning to wonder if this is, in fact, a nineteenth-century trial, and exorcism or a police thriller!'

Hundreds of spectators besieged the Nancy Assize Court, eager to hear the grim and gory tale unfold. They were not to be disappointed – from the outset the once stunningly beautiful but now plump, sixty-year-old housewife, punctuated the proceedings by hurling abuse at lawyers and witnesses, and even shouting at the 'lynch mob' sitting quietly in the public gallery.

On Thursday, 28 February 1991, the wicked and totally unscrupulous Simone Weber was sentenced to twenty years for the poisoning of Marcel Fixard. She was acquitted of the killing of Bernard Hettier. Her sister, Madeleine, was given an eighteen-month prison term for complicity and for destroying Hettier's passport.

In July 2002, a film called *La Diabolique de Nancy* was released, immortalising Weber's wicked deeds on the silver screen for decades to come, which again brings me to the question asked at the start of this book: is the female of our species more deadly than the male? This is a poser that would require the study of thousands upon thousands of case histories. Sadly, I am not allocated the word count to do it here, but let me assure you that when a woman flies off of the handle God help anyone who gets under her skin or in her way. If she cuts up your shirts and suits, or splashes paint remover over your Porsche, or exposes you as the unscrupulous rat that you are across the social media, count your blessings and not the words inscribed on your tombstone. Something which you may be doing if you repeat your foolish behaviour again!

Criminal history is littered with references to 'Black Widow' serial killers – with the obvious inference being that this type of murderess behaves in much the same way as Latrodectus, the 'Widow Spider' genus where the female devours her mate through the act of sexual cannibalism; all of which is a somewhat arcane description. Although it may be said that 'Black Widow' killers certainly devour something of their prey – for example the contents of their wallets, bank accounts and often profit via double-indemnity life insurance policies, as did Simone Weber and countless others before her and since.

Also well documented throughout the annals of murder most foul are hundreds of examples of women who team up with a male to commit sexually motivated serial murder. We see this with Myra Hindley and Rose and Fred West, with the man being the more dominant of the pair. Turning things upside down, we find that Joanna Dennehy teamed up with Gary Stretch to kill men simply because she had an almost insatiable vampirish taste for blood and enjoyed killing for kicks.

The English-born John Martin Scripps, who was later hanged in Singapore, was a lone male serial killer who killed for financial gain, but his was a very rare scenario. With tongue-in-cheek, I mean we do not find very many 'Black Widowers' do we? In fact I witnessed this man's execution the day after my birthday on Friday, 19 April, 1996, anchoring the international news coverage with APTV. I then went to his cremation before fully documenting his case in my international bestseller, *Talking with Serial Killers*. When I left 'Singas' the police gave me a birthday present – an enamel mug depicting a man hanging from gallows which I thanked them for as being 'most kind'.

So, while there are few men who kill for money, nevertheless, there are hundreds of examples where a man and a woman, acting as a killing team, will trawl and kill their victim for financial gain, or out of sheer jealousy, or because of a sick love pact – as did Ruth Snyder and lover Judd Gray way back in 1927. Both, of course, were 'fried' after being strapped into Ossining 'Sing Sing' Prison's 'Old Sparky' on Saturday, 1 December 1928. Not forgetting Bonnie Parker and Clyde Barrow, aka, 'Bonnie and Clyde', whose passionate love for each other drove them into a frenzy of murders for financial gain. Their shocking crimes ensured that even today, eighty-six years later, they still retain an almost cult-like, mythical status when, in fact, they were nothing more than low-life common criminals who had a souped-up V8 car in which to outrun pursuing cops, and firearms that could outmatch the law's weaponry. Thank the Lord AK-47s weren't available to them back in the 30s, although they did carry a Thompson submachine gun – the 'Tommy Gun'.

What is particularly shocking is that female serial killers can start to emerge even *before* they reach their teens as we have noted with that horrible little girl, Mary Bell. We in the UK have, indeed, earned the notorious distinction of home-growing the youngest emerging female serial killer of all time. Well done, Great Britain. Indeed, I think our friends across the pond, or anywhere else would be hard-pressed to equal it!

Unlike their male counterparts, women certainly come into a league of their own when they commit murder out of sheer spite. Can one imagine anyone, or *anything* more despicable than twenty-one-year-old Christa Gail Pike, or come to think of it, any of the other extremely dangerous women on Death Rows in the U.S. today? Pike's motive was one of ridding herself of a self-perceived 'obnoxious rival', as did another killer I spent much time communicating with: petite Melanie 'Mel' Lyn McGuire, aka 'The Ice Queen' out of 'The Garden State' New Jersey.

'There is no fury like a wife searching for a new lover.' (Cyril Connolly [Palinurus] *The Unquiet Grave*, 1944.)

This could well apply to Mel who wanted rid of her husband, Bill, as she'd fallen for another, perhaps more successful man, so she drugged Bill, then, in the same way as Simone Weber, took a power saw to his body, quartered him, stuffed the gory artifacts into a couple of suitcases which she then chucked over a bridge into the swirling waters of the Chesapeake Bay. There is a chapter dedicated to Mel in my book *Dead Men Talking*: also published by John Blake, it includes some of her letters to me, which give an in-depth insight as to how ice cold many of these deadly, often quite skin-deep beautiful, femme fatales, can be.

Missing from the ranks of male serial killers are the 'Baby Farmers': women who foster babies and very young children, collect the support money for years but kill these little ones almost directly after taking custody, as was the case of Amelia Dyer who emerged during the late-Victorian era Britain.

In 1996, I travelled to India on a criminology-related project and managed to wheedle my way onto Mumbai's death row, where I saw Renuke Kiran Shinde and Seema Mohan Gavit in their respective cells. Perhaps, at this point I can state that when the likes of Joanna Dennehy complain about prison living conditions, as do so many others of her morally bigoted breed, she doesn't know she is born when considering the grim conditions Shinde and Gavit were, and still are, living under. As for an Internet connection or TV – fat chance of that! The Sodexo privately run HMP Bronzefield is akin to a five-star correctional facility compared with the lodgings now occupied by Shinde and Gavit.

Unless things have changed for the better since, both women sleep on a straw-covered floor. A mattress? No chance. Chained by their ankles to a strong point in the wall, they are forbidden from reading anything, holding a conversation with each other, and communication with their guards is limited to simple requests. And that's it, except the place is infested with lice and rats, and 'The Row' stinks to high heaven with the sweet smell of cheap disinfectant, urine, stale food and faeces permeating every brick.

As far as I can determine, these two female monsters from the western state of Maharashtra deserve what they are about to get since quite recently all appeals have failed. They are soon to be executed by hanging, with shooting reserved for military offenders as a form of 'mortal perks'. As mentioned earlier, over a period of years, these women kidnapped at least thirteen little kids from the slums and forced them into pickpocketing. To make things even worse, they broke some of the children's arms and legs, scalded them with boiling water or burned them with acid and ripped an eye or two out to make the children appear more pitiful and harmless to passers-by. When five of the kids had effectively passed their 'sell-by dates' they were murdered in the most heinous ways, their broken bodies dumped like trash while the women were enjoying it, too. If that isn't more deadly than the male, I don't know what is.

Ripping out an eye or two reminds one of an 'an eye for an eye, tooth for a tooth'; the controversial theory of 'retributivism' that embraces the concept that the best response to a crime is a punishment proportional to the offences committed, because evil people like Shinde and Gavit deserve it because they knew precisely what they were doing was murderous, moreover, they knew that if they were caught they could well be executed. Therefore, they brought about their own death sentences and, as far as India's judicial system is concerned, that is the end of the matter.

What I can tell you is that the furthest concern of the minds of India's judicial system is 'utilitarianism': that punishment should be forward-looking, all justified by the purported ability to achieve future social benefits, take for instance a reduction in crime, which appears to me – and I know that I will be boiled alive by some of my more liberal readers for even suggesting it – as being poppycock. The problem being, that those who support correctional utilitarianism, have not seen the sickening post mortem crime photographs of the butchered and starved children; one wonders if there might be a change of heart if one of those kiddies were their own?

The late His Honor Judge Thomas M. Stark notable influential Suffolk County, NY, presiding justice, who tried mass murderer Ronald 'Butch' DeFeo of Amityville Horror infamy, spoke to me in an interview in 1994. Here is an extract:

> As a society we have to make quite liberal rules that govern our behavior for the common good. There are those who choose to break the rules; those, who by their own volition, step outside of the norms we generalise as social cohesion in the knowledge that the consequences could be severe. It is they who make their own life choices – not me. If the death sentence is applicable then so be it. It is their call, not mine.
>
> Chris, you ask me if the threat of a death sentence acts as a deterrent for committing murder in the first-degree. In all of my years on the bench my answer has to be, no!

So, with my hand on my heart, I also state that I have not yet met, or had any dealings with a serial killer, spree killer, a mass murderer, or a one-off offender from any country being deterred from committing homicide because the threat of a life, or a death sentence, may result. All of which rather throws the utilitarianism theory out of a rose-tinted window. Indeed, not one of the female killers featured in this book gave a damn as to the consequences afforded to themselves while in the act of committing their awful crimes which places them on a par with men – both the male and female being as equally deadly when it comes down to committing murder most foul.

As all of my loyal readers will know, I do so enjoy leaving a book on a high note; in this instance recalling the 1987 psychological thriller, *Fatal Attraction*, starring Michael Douglas and the knife-wielding bunny boiler, Glen Close. But like many men, most especially Hollywood stars who live galactically far beyond Planet Earth, Doug never learned his lesson from this previous troublesome encounter because he later hooked up with Sharon Stone in the 1992 neo-noir thriller, *Basic Instinct* and who can blame him?

If, however, you are determined to ignore the countless warnings throughout this book and need to hook up with a lady with a colourful history, I strongly recommend the web site 'Meet a Beautiful Inmate.com', with this proviso. Most of these gals do not post their criminal CVs, so if you are seeking a partner who is very dangerous and you truly want to get fleeced, I'd shop around a bit if I were you. A little research into their Department of Corrections status will eventually find you the woman of your dreams.

So, guys, before you sleep tonight, have a fumble – as in

feel around for an icepick under the bed because *you* could be next. God forbid you wake up dead in the morning!

Yes! Women can be as lethal as any male.